More praise for *Dreamers, Discoverers, and Dynamos*

"*Dreamers, Discoverers, and Dynamos* brings together much of the best of current scientific research on the developing mind, along with much original advice. The result is a satisfying blend of information and guidance that will greatly assist parents in allowing their child's creativity to come forth. It is a book that is sound, well researched, and fun to read."
　　　　—ROBERT ORNSTEIN
　　　　　　Author of *The Right Mind: Making Sense of Hemispheres*

"An exciting and important book for all parents who want their child to develop his or her potential as an intelligent, creative, and happy individual. It is full of proven, practical ideas you can use immediately to bring out the very best in your child."
　　　　—BRIAN TRACY
　　　　　　Internationally renowned business consultant and author of *The Psychology of Achievement*

"This book is a 'must read' for my parents and teachers, as it is the first to create a positive mindset for those specific individuals who have the greatest impact on how the child views himself. Dr. Palladino's work reflects her broad and up-to-date knowledge, in addition to insight into the emotional roller coaster which parents are feeling."
　　　　—JUDI PANTON, M.A.
　　　　　　Director, Del Mar Pines School

"A very practical, conceptually sound book that provides keen insight, understanding, and hands-on wisdom to a very difficult childhood problem area. Excellent reading for practicing professionals and parents searching for answers."
　　　　—JOSEPH M. CERVANTES, Ph.D., FAClinP
　　　　　　Associate Professor, California University, Fullerton

"*Dreamers, Discoverers, and Dynamos* is a well-organized and user-friendly resource for those of us who either live with or must deal with people who have 'dazzling intelligence, an active imagination, a free-spirited approach to life, and the ability to drive everyone around them crazy.' That includes our children, our family, and most especially ourselves. . . . It's a must read!"
　　　　—MIKE MCCARTHY
　　　　　　Publisher/editor, *San Diego Writers' Monthly*

Please turn

"*Dreamers, Discoverers, and Dynamos* is one of the most exciting new books in the field. It is an excellent blend of the latest research findings with very useful and practical tips—written in a very readable, entertaining style. Dr. Palladino combines well-thought-out and scientifically sound principles with common sense, humor, and advice. It is a *must* for every parent, teacher, and child therapist."
> —LILLIE WEISS, Ph.D.
> Psychologist and author of *Dream Analysis in Psychotherapy*

Selected as one of the top three parenting books of the year. "The book is convincing, reassuring, and accessible. Perhaps it will help parents of nonconforming kids resist the pressure to make their kids 'just fit in.' "
> —*Amazon.com*

"Dr. Palladino, a highly qualified psychologist, has written a book that is well designed to help parents of children with or without ADD. It is insightful, original, and easy to read, yet well founded in current scientific knowledge."
> —LEE MEYERSON, Ph.D.
> Arizona Regents Professor of Psychology

"*Dreamers, Discoverers, and Dynamos* is a warmly written book. It provides for our better understanding of ADHD, and for clear direction and practical suggestions to help children who are growing up and living with the Edison trait. It is an inspiring and motivating guide. I recommend it to parents and educators, and medical and mental health professionals as well."
> —JOEL OXMAN, Ph.D.
> Child Psychologist

"If children cannot explore through imagination, then there would not have been a Thomas Edison, an Albert Einstein, or a Bill Gates. *Dreamers, Discoverers, and Dynamos* should be in the hands of all educators, psychotherapists, and parents."
> —NANCY T. SAGER
> Principal, Santa Fe Montessori Schools

"An excellent resource for both parents and professionals. This book addresses the ADHD phenomena in creative, positive terms and provides parents with practical suggestions. It is a caring, sensitive, and very readable book, yet it also includes accurate, current scientific knowledge. I have recommended *Dreamers, Discoverers, and Dynamos* to many of my clients and it has always been well received. I strongly urge all parents, teachers, and professionals who love and work with children to read this book."
> —LINDA C. CATERINO, Ph.D., ABPP
> Child Psychologist, Adjunct Professor, Arizona State University
> and co-author of the Caterino Attention Deficit Scale (CADS)

"Students from age three to adult will benefit from the concepts and methods of *Dreamers, Discoverers, and Dynamos*. Dr. Palladino's ideas are sensible, caring, and refreshing. The Edison trait is a new and much needed approach whose time has come. It offers insight and advice so parents can help their children learn more, get better grades, and feel happier with themselves as people."
> —FIBI FORUTANPOUR
> Teacher with twenty-five years' experience

DREAMERS,

DISCOVERERS,

& DYNAMOS

*how to help the child who is bright,
bored, and having problems in school*

LUCY JO PALLADINO, PH.D.

(formerly titled *The Edison Trait*)

BALLANTINE BOOKS • New York

To Arthur, Julia, and Jeni

A Ballantine Book
Published by The Ballantine Publishing Group

Copyright © 1997, 1999 by Lucy Jo Palladino, Ph.D.

All rights reserved under International and Pan-American Copyright Conventions. Published in the United States by The Ballantine Publishing Group, a division of Random House, Inc., New York, and simultaneously in Canada by Random House of Canada Limited, Toronto. Originally published by Times Books, a division of Random House, Inc., in 1997 as *The Edison Trait*.

Ballantine and colophon are registered trademarks of Random House, Inc.

Grateful acknowledgment is made to the following for permission to reprint previously published material:

Alfred A. Knopf, Inc., and Colucci & Umans on behalf of the National Committee of Gibran: Excerpt from "On Children" from *The Prophet* by Kahlil Gibran. Copyright © 1923 by Kahlil Gibran. Copyright renewed 1951 by Administrators C T A of Kahlil Gibran Estate and Mary G. Gibran. Rights throughout Canada and the British Commonwealth are controlled by Colucci & Umans on behalf of the National Committee of Gibran. Reprinted by permission.

www.randomhouse.com/BB/

Library of Congress Catalog Card Number: 98-96660

ISBN: 0-345-40573-0

This edition published by arrangement with Times Books, a division of Random House, Inc.

Cover design by Cathy Colbert

Manufactured in the United States of America

First Ballantine Books Edition: January 1999

10 9 8 7 6 5

Acknowledgments

Dreamers, Discoverers, and Dynamos was born of the courage, determination, and inspiration of my clients. I am grateful for their trust. We have traveled many roads of discovery and change together.

I thank my husband, Arthur, for believing in me as an author. I thank him for taking on numerous chores so I could write this book. And I thank him for his ever-present generosity of spirit.

I thank my daughters, Jeni and Julia, for their faith and joy, clerical help, and fresh flowers in my contemplation bowl.

I am grateful to my primary editor, Betsy Rapoport, for her vision, expertise, honesty, and responsiveness. I am also grateful to Ginny Faber for her foresight and support.

I acknowledge my agents, Laurie Fox and Linda Chester, for their confidence, direction, and skill.

My decision to propose this book began with the kindness and coaching of author and teacher Gayle Lynds. At a critical juncture, Jonathan Kirsch, author and attorney, guided my way. Divine Providence stepped in on numerous occasions, thank God.

I am grateful to the Southern California Writers Conference for their support and for honoring me with their annual award for Best Nonfiction for *Dreamers, Discoverers, and Dynamos*. I thank Jay

Braun, Ph.D., for reminding me to keep my outlook balanced, Nancy Sager for her helpful suggestions, and Emilie Winthrop for her warm enthusiasm. I acknowledge the contributions of Nedra Lasley, Ph.D., and Judi Panton, M.A.

I thank my parents, John and Lucy Palladino, and my sister, Maria Gill. I appreciate the support of Fay Cormano, Wini Daniel, M.S.W., Fibi Forutanpour, Melvin Goldzband, M.D., Jean Jenkins, Nancy Kerr, Ph.D., Lee Meyerson, Ph.D., Joel Oxman, Ph.D., Joy Parker, Katherine Saideman, Ellen Salk, Lillie Weiss, Ph.D., and the staff and parents at the Santa Fe Montessori Schools and Del Mar Pines School.

If Thomas Edison were alive today, he would find kindred spirits in writers like Thom Hartmann and Dave deBronkart. It is the inventive mind of Thom Hartmann that came up with the metaphor of hunters in a farmers' world. In his seminal work, *ADD: A Different Perception,* Hartmann sees the Edison trait as a quality found in illustrious hunters like Thomas Edison, Benjamin Franklin, and Ernest Hemingway. Using electronic media, Dave deBronkart advocated the use of the term on CompuServe message threads that first appeared on the EDFORUM in August 1992. I respectfully acknowledge the contributions of these pioneer thinkers.

While writing this manuscript, I had as my touchstone a friend who read and discussed each chapter with me. That friend, Alan Karol Reeter, is an astute and accomplished Edisonian thinker—an engineer, pilot, award-winning writer and producer, and founder and president of Medfilms, Inc. His ideas and opinions were invaluable to me. I thank him for his sound advice and for encouraging me to trust my own wings.

Contents

Introduction

Kate is nine years old. She is bright, pleasant, and imaginative. At home, she spends hours in her room daydreaming. At school, her mind wanders. Her teachers say she underachieves. She misses directions, loses her place, and forgets to hand in her papers.

Kate's parents help her with her homework every night. These sessions often erupt in anger and frustration. Kate's parents have tried to learn about different methods to teach her. However, it often seems to them that the more they do, the less Kate does. They bought top-of-the-line educational software for Kate, but she spends her time at the computer playing games or fooling around with graphics. Last summer, Kate's parents enrolled her at an expensive learning center, which solved some problems but created others. Kate's complaints about going triggered hostile arguments between her and her parents. In fact, the family seemed to be fighting all the time.

The irony is that Kate is an exceptionally astute, sensitive, and artistic child who comes up with ideas and remarks most children her age would not think of. When Kate's mom does not feel provoked by her daughter's immutable style, she calls her child a "jungle orchid." With sadness and resignation in his voice, Kate's dad describes her as "a wooden raft adrift on the open sea."

Brian is twelve. He has a knack for persuading others to see things his way. He refuses to take no for an answer. Sometimes this works in his favor. But many times his indomitable personal style works against him. He battles so fiercely that he alienates those around him. He domineers and gets blindly competitive. As his dad says, "It's Brian's way or no way at all."

Brian's teachers regard him as a quick and resourceful thinker, but a poor planner and an obstinate pupil. His grades are erratic. He is a regular in detention.

Brian starts way more things than he finishes. His family and friends love his spontaneity and spirit, but feel frustrated by his lack of consideration and accountability. Brian promises more than he delivers, and refuses to take responsibility when he doesn't follow through. If he does not show up on time, it is because he "couldn't." If he leaves a mess of someone else's things, he had "no choice."

Brian's parents are frustrated beyond tolerance. Their home life is a series of standoffs and shouting matches. They have tried a full range of strategies from quiet patience to strict punishment. They are at their wits' end and they are scared of the future, as their son now enters his teenage years.

———

Mark is a five-year-old ground rocket. He is smart, bold, and instantly attracted to action. If there is no action around to attract him, Mark creates some. He enjoys getting a rise out of others, and seems to know intuitively the surest ways to do this. Indoors, he sees, he touches, he breaks. Outdoors, he runs away, even in unfamiliar places.

Mark has attended three preschools in the last three years. He was asked to leave one of them because he teased and provoked his playmates. The decision for him to leave the other two was mutual. Mark was bored and unhappy, as well as disruptive and physically aggressive.

Mark's parents love their son's strong will and energy, but they are out of patience. Their home looks like a battle zone and they seldom take Mark anywhere. Raising this child is not at all what they expected. Mark's mother feels disappointed and infuriated. Mark's father would rather be somewhere else.

There are times when Mark is a delight. He is fascinated with locomotives, airplanes, and any machine that gives him power and speed. He has an insatiable appetite for new things and places. But just when his parents start to enjoy their son's high spirits, something goes wrong and Mark inadvertently does something destructive.

Mark's mother says that she does not know if she will ever be able to trust her own son. She feels ashamed of thinking this about a five-year-old child. Mark's father feels relieved when he leaves the house. He feels sad that this is true.

———

What do Kate, Brian, and Mark have in common? These children are intensely *divergent thinkers.* Their minds create sparks that ignite wildfires of thought. One single thought lights up many more. This causes them to be creative, innovative, and stimulating. At the same time, it makes it harder for them to think convergently. *Convergent thinking* is focus on a single flame, concentration on a solitary thought. It means resisting the impulse to burn or flare with irrelevant ideas and perceptions.

Kate, Brian, and Mark are representative of a growing number of children today. They are conundrums, children with a profile that is both intriguing and maddening. These children are appealing, daring, and entertaining. Yet they are frustrating, demanding, and difficult to raise.

Typically, they are strongly opinionated, so it's hard to break through to them in ordinary ways. Their temperament and intellectual style challenge even the most devoted parent's patience, resolution, and stamina.

As a practicing psychologist, I have worked professionally with free-thinking, strong-willed children for over twenty years. I have observed these qualities become more prominent in our younger generation. These children have the *Edison trait,* an innate style of boundless, individualistic, divergent thinking.

THE EDISON TRAIT

Thomas Alva Edison was a prolific inventor who, by the time he died, held 1,093 different patents. He was divergent thinking personified. Edison's innovations ranged from sound recordings to business ventures. His work lit a path for many, both literally and figuratively.

Edison-trait children, like Edison, are naturally creative. They enjoy adventure and prefer new territory, especially when it comes to their own mental landscape. Like Edison, they are highly original, unconventional, and inventive. They are the mavericks, pioneers, and artists. Because they are disposed to divergent thinking, it is an uphill battle for them to concentrate on only one idea at a time. In view of this, their school years, like Edison's, may be filled with pain and frustration.

CHILDREN WHO DON'T CONFORM EASILY

As a child, Thomas Edison was a misfit in the classroom. His mind was constantly wandering and he couldn't sit still in his seat. He required personalized instruction. He needed to learn in his own style and at his own pace. Only then could he get himself on track, and turn his wild ideas and mischief into brilliance and scientific discovery.[1]

Every year educators report that they see more and more students who fit the Edison-trait profile. These children learn by doing, seldom by listening. They are at home on computer keyboards and probably know more about the equipment in the audio-visual department than most of the faculty do. They are never without questions and they have a story for every occasion. During class time, some are reclusive and some monopolize their teachers' attention. Often they are a source of stress to others.

At home, they surprise, amaze, and incite their parents. They are spirited children who live life with a passion and determination for pursuing what they want. They have a talent for creating upheaval and for provoking parents to nag or burst at the seams with frustration. They have inquisitive, inventive, Edisonian minds.

DREAMERS, DISCOVERERS, AND DYNAMOS

If these descriptions sound familiar, ask yourself these questions: Does your child come up with angles nobody else does—sometimes humorous, sometimes mind-boggling? Does he seem to live in his own personal world, where a quest for novelty and stimulation reign? Is he easily distracted from assigned tasks, but intensely focused on his own?

While Edison-trait children truly are one-of-a-kind people, their attributes do tend to fall into three different types. There is overlap and there are exceptions, but in general these types are: Dreamers, Discoverers, and Dynamos. Here are some quick sketches. Chapter 1 gives more detailed profiles.

Dreamers

Some Edison-trait children (like Kate) daydream. They live in the sky with their heads in the clouds. They are imaginative and artful. Ideas and stories have personal meanings to them. They can become quite absorbed in "inner space." If your child can tell you what star date it is, but not the actual month, day, and year, he may be an Edison-trait Dreamer.

Discoverers

Other Edison-trait children (like Brian) are doers. They must see what happens for themselves, so they "do" first, and ask questions later. They are insistent in their opinions and their inquisitive, adventuresome ways. They are passionate, spontaneous, and often dramatic and entertaining. Like Thomas Edison, they like to experiment, so they test to see how far they can go. They experiment with themselves, with others, and with the rules. If doing things his own way is paramount to your child, he may be an Edison-trait Discoverer.

Dynamos

Sometimes, Edison-trait children (like Mark) also have an inordinately high energy level. These are children who are constantly on the move. Sometimes they have an aggressive streak. Their impulsivity lands them in various kinds of trouble, which usually disturbs those around them more than it does them. They can be dauntless. They like power and speed and a personal challenge. If your child can't pass up a race or a dare, he may be an Edison-trait Dynamo.

WHAT'S RIGHT AND WHAT'S WRONG

Your Edison-trait child has an inventory of positive qualities:

- Openness to multiple sights, sounds, and thoughts
- A daring or wandering imagination

- A global perspective
- Creative urges or compelling attraction for new ideas
- Intense focus on his own pursuits and interests

These are attributes of his outstanding gift for divergent thinking. Now reconsider this list. This time, I'll rephrase his strengths as weak points in convergent thinking. Your Edison-trait child

- Is easily distracted
- Lives in a state of disorganization
- Neglects important detail
- Doesn't follow things through to completion
- Won't obey or comply

See how these strengths got transformed into deficiencies? This is how others, for example, many teachers in overcrowded classrooms, see your child. This is what you often hear at parent-teacher conferences. And it is understandable. It is the teachers' job to train your child to use convergent thinking skills. So they tend to overlook his divergent thinking strengths, and see only his weakness in convergent thinking.

As teachers and other professionals start to name your child's problems, they begin to identify him with the things he doesn't do well. As his parent, you may be anxious, resentful, and habituated to seeing his failures first, too. What happened to Edison happens to him: His strengths are not recognized or encouraged by others, especially in the classroom, where convergent thinking dominates. His problems multiply. His self-esteem erodes.

Dreamers, Discoverers, and Dynamos is a manual for you to help your child reclaim his strengths. It gives you the vocabulary and tools you need to help him reconstruct a positive self-image and a blueprint for success. It can help you recognize and make the most of his best qualities, in a world that doesn't see them or understand their worth.

IS THE EDISON TRAIT THE SAME AS ATTENTION DEFICIT DISORDER (ADD)?

No, it is not.

While just about all children who have ADD have the Edison trait, not all children with the Edison trait have ADD. In fact, most do not. ADD means that *there is serious impairment and dysfunction,* in addition to an Edison-trait mind and temperament.

To have ADD, your child's behaviors must first of all match a list of criteria for the diagnosis. This list is similar to the list of weaknesses in convergent thinking that you just read about. (These criteria are described in more detail in Chapter 13, "What Is ADD?") Then, to warrant the diagnosis, your child's behaviors not only must match the list but must also be excessive and disruptive of his functioning and not be explained better by other causes, such as stress or anxiety.

There is a common misperception about the diagnosis of ADD. Many people think that if a child's behaviors match the list of criteria, the child has ADD. This is inaccurate. The criteria are actually behaviors typical of *all* children, especially divergent-thinking ones. To qualify for the diagnosis, a child's behaviors *must be dysfunctional.* His functioning must be impaired to an extreme that is more severe than the ordinary problems of approximately 95 percent of children his age, for example, if he is chronically failing in school.

An unimpaired child who is more divergent than convergent may have the Edison trait, but he does *not* have ADD. This includes the child whose behaviors do not exceed the most extreme 5 percent, and the child who is coping adequately and therefore lacks "significant impairment," a legal requirement for the diagnosis.[2]

WHY THE CONFUSION?

The rise of an intensely divergent-thinking style is relatively recent. We don't yet have many words to describe divergent thinkers who are functional. So we overuse and misuse the words that we have, even if they suggest dysfunction. This can be harmful, both to children who qualify for a diagnosis of ADD (because we discount its seriousness to them) and to children who do not (because we incorrectly revise our expectations and treatment of them).

We have coined plenty of words to describe what is *wrong* with our children. We need words to describe what is *right*. We call Edison-trait children inattentive. Are they "*in*attentive" or are they attentive—to what is important to them, not us?

There is mounting evidence that ADD is overdiagnosed in professional health care settings today.[3] Chapter 13 covers this issue. By current sources, at least 20 percent of all children have the Edison trait and this number steadily grows. In contrast, only 3 to 5 percent of all children qualify for the diagnosis of ADD.[4]

UNDERSTANDING OUR CHILDREN

As the population of Edison-trait children increases, we are becoming more aware that as parents and professionals, we need to take a closer look at what is happening in our homes and schools. Why do so many children now struggle to learn, especially when it comes to particulars like detailed directions, rules of grammar and spelling, and math facts? We need better explanations than naming and blaming our children for having deficiencies. Could it be that to a degree, our mind-set and educational format have outlived their usefulness? Every day we expect children to adapt to our way of thinking. Is it time to update our thinking and be more open to the potential of theirs?

Robert B. Brooks, Ph.D., a psychologist and popular lecturer, asks us to look at each "total child" and search for that child's "island of competence." What can he *excel* at doing because he is the way he is?[5]

Russell Barkley, Ph.D., another expert in the field, notes that the children we call inattentive are also "wild, funny, effervescent. They have a love of life." As adults they "can be incredibly successful" and gravitate into creative fields or make good salespeople.[6]

Martha Denckla, M.D., director of the Department of Developmental Cognitive Neurology at the Kennedy-Drieger Institute at Johns Hopkins, says, "Think of an absentminded professor who can find a cure for cancer but not his glasses in the mess on his desk. These are the inventors, creators, poets—the people who think creative thoughts because they don't think like everyone else."[7]

For years, in my own private practice, children who have attentional problems have been teaching me all along that their symptoms are by-products of their creative and energetic nature. One of my clients is a promising young writer; several are clever cartoonists. Many have a knack for computer games. I have gone to see a few of them star in local theater productions. By chance, I happened to meet one at a nearby skating rink where, as we skated side by side, he convinced me to let go of my fear and resistance, so I could learn to cross one leg over the other. As we sped along, it occurred to me,

Barkley was right. This child could well be headed for an illustrious career in sales.

THE GIFT OF BELIEF

In an important long-term study, researchers Gabrielle Weiss, Ph.D., and Lily Hechtman, Ph.D., asked young adults who had had attentional difficulties as children what had helped them the most.[8] What truly had made the difference to these children? The answer was: having someone who believed in them, an accepting and supportive parent, teacher, or other adult.

All children benefit from having a supportive adult, but the Edison-trait child *needs* one. It is critical for him to have a believer and harder for him to get one. That's because it isn't easy to put your belief in an Edison-trait child.

In this world, your child's behaviors often elicit disapproval or pity from others and sometimes even from you. How can you sustain an overriding confidence in his abilities? You watch as he sidesteps his homework. You overhear kids tease him. You wonder if you're being manipulated. You get angry at things he does. You worry about him and his future. Can he learn to succeed as a student without losing his creative spirit? Sadly, he reads your doubts and fears. Soon they become his doubts and fears, too.

Yet you must find ways to replace your worry with trust. This is crucial for your child's well-being. An Edison-trait child is a child at risk, and he needs your conviction that he is going to make it.

He needs to hear you say things like "I'm so glad that you are you." . . . "It's amazing how you come up with ideas that no one else does." . . . "I know you can do this. You've solved problems like this before." He needs to hear you say these things and know you mean them, even—no, especially—when he's in the middle of a mess he's just made.

Your child wants you to think of him and think "possibility," not deficiency. You may not approve of the things he does, but he needs your approval of him as a person.

Your child's innate way of thinking is an intrinsic part of him. To him, it's the only style of thinking he's ever known. He yearns for you to accept him and to see in him a trait that says strength, not weakness.

You can learn to do this. As you read and learn more about the Edison trait, you will find yourself seeing your child in a different way. When you look at him, you will see more potential than before. It will feel natural and right for you to keep his treasury of abilities *central* to you and to him.

EDISON-TRAIT SOLUTIONS

Children who have the Edison trait are not easy-to-raise children. As the parent of an Edison-trait child, you probably spend a lot of time feeling exhausted, discouraged, and angry. Parenthood isn't what you pictured it would be.

If your child is a Dreamer, you may feel utter frustration. You'd like to light a fire under his seat. The harder you try, the less he does. You fight the feeling, but sometimes it seems he acts so lazy, you resent him for it. You feel helpless, befuddled, and chronically annoyed. "Wake up!" you want to scream. "Get yourself in gear. Now!"

If your child is a Discoverer, you may spend enormous stores of energy trying to control your own temper. Every day brings arguments and fights. You dread outings and parties that should be happy events. Any point of disagreement can escalate into warfare. In public, you feel embarrassed. What do people think? Other children listen and cooperate. Why doesn't yours? You feel ineffective, disillusioned, and exasperated. Why must every little thing be a major production?

If your child is a Dynamo, you may feel drained and bedraggled. It's hard to keep up with a child who seldom pauses. You feel trapped, because you must watch him closely every minute. You don't want to take him shopping or even to visit friends: He touches everything he sees, and is especially drawn to breakables. You feel frazzled, nervous, and on the threshold of your tolerance. He does not sit still. He does not listen. He gravitates toward danger. You're giving 100 percent to try to discipline your child, yet you suspect other parents think you let him go wild. Stressed and overwhelmed, you long for quiet and solitude. You spend a lot of time wishing you were somewhere else.

You have probably tried many approaches and techniques. Chances are, you've been experimenting—with your child's diet or vitamins, or with behavior charts or "time-out" procedures. But the changes, if any, don't seem to last. You wonder, why don't these efforts produce better results?

Many methods have validity and the best ones will be discussed in this book. However, stand-alone methods are cut flowers that die in their vase. Successful methods are the blooming flowers of a living plant, the natural outgrowth of understanding how your child thinks and feels, and connecting with him and his abilities, strengths, and motivations.

This vital process is what *Dreamers, Discoverers, and Dynamos* is all about: how to see and experience the world *from your child's point of view.* It is a generative process that results in effective communication and problem solving.

As you read *Dreamers, Discoverers, and Dynamos,* I encourage you to be like your child—an independent thinker, a discoverer. Be open to how you, or your spouse, may manifest Edison-trait qualities yourself. It is, after all, an inherited characteristic.[9] Your self-knowledge is a valuable asset in creating new ways to reach your child.

Throughout this book, I have made an effort in my own writing to apply the techniques I recommend that you use with your own children. My goals have been to

- Speak clearly and directly
- Parse content into brief, concise messages
- Use storytelling, imagery, and metaphor

As your Edison-trait child would surely do, see what you think for yourself.

IN THE CHAPTERS AHEAD

I sincerely hope that *Dreamers, Discoverers, and Dynamos* helps you and your child achieve your goals. However, no book takes the place of a personal consultation with a properly qualified health care provider. I recommend you discuss your concerns with your child's pediatrician or psychologist, psychiatrist, or counselor if he is seeing one. (In Chapter 14 you will learn more about getting an evaluation.) What you learn as you read *Dreamers, Discoverers, and Dynamos* can help you make the most of professional services you may use.

Throughout this book, I use male pronouns in some chapters and female pronouns in others. In the Notes at the end of the book are explanations and references to technical information and research studies for your consideration.

In Part I of *Dreamers, Discoverers, and Dynamos,* you will learn more about this intriguing profile, and what it means to your child to grow up with it. You'll gain insight and understanding into the nature of your child's divergent thinking. You'll learn how the norms for perceptual style have changed over the course of the last hundred years or so, and why even if you are an Edison-trait adult, your child's typical way of thinking still differs from your own. You'll learn about different types of attention and which are best suited for particular kinds of tasks.

In Part II, I will guide you step by step through a program to develop the most helpful perspective and actions to reach your Edison-trait child. In "Step One: Believe In Your Child," you'll learn how to build trust and a positive attitude. In "Step Two: Watch What You Say," you'll get tips on how to choose words that promote health and success. In "Step Three: Build a Parent-and-Child Team," you'll find out how to dissolve battle lines and create a strong alliance with your child. In "Step Four: Encourage Your Child's Interests," you'll learn how to nurture your child's penchant for creative, exciting experience. "Step Five: Teach Your Child Self-control" shows you specific ways to discipline your child. "Step Six: Coach Your Child to Learn How to Achieve" teaches you to build on your child's strengths, for example, his abilities to hyperfocus, multitask, and creatively visualize. "Step Seven: Take Care of Yourself" teaches parent stress-management skills. "Step Eight: Take Care of Your Family" covers basics like sibling rivalry and special situations like adoption and two-household families.

Part III explains how to obtain professional services for your child while maintaining your ability-centered approach. You'll get ideas for helping your child succeed in school and suggestions you can discuss with his teacher. You'll read about ADD, its relationship to the Edison trait, and what is known and unknown about the brain chemistry of children who have different styles of thinking. You'll find out what psychological testing can and cannot detect, how test results are interpreted, and how diagnostic and treatment decisions are made. You will learn about medication, its cost-to-benefit ratio, and current trends in prescribing. And you'll hear about some nonmainstream approaches, like the Feingold diet, neurofeedback treatment, and a research program that uses computer games to train fast minds to slow down and hear details.

Part IV looks to the future, and how the Edison trait gives your child a leading edge in our fast-paced global society. It enables him to take command of the power and speed of technology. As a divergent thinker, he is equipped to adapt to myriad new situations. He can assess new conditions and meet new demands.

Your child's Edisonian mind gives him a distinct advantage in the business world of today. He can handle abundant incoming data, and scan it for opportunities, like new markets. He can turn innovation into profit, which is exactly what he needs to succeed in our accelerated, entrepreneurial twenty-first-century workplace.

WE ALL LEARN AS WE GO

The people and stories I describe in this book are based on my clients and their experiences. (I have changed names and details.) Like you, the parents you'll read about are beset by the recurrence of problems they did not intend, cause, anticipate, want, or ask for. Parenthood is a journey with unexpected turns in the road. We didn't put those curves there, but we must travel them nonetheless.

No parent, no expert—no one—has the answer. It is important for you to keep this in mind. Don't expect the impossible from yourself or your child. Instead, acknowledge and commend yourself and him, for your hard work and efforts. There will be ups and downs, breakthroughs and setbacks. Regardless of the outcome, when you've done your best, take a moment and let yourself feel good about that.

In Chapter 10, I offer some suggestions for how you can rejuvenate your good feelings about parenting. Here's a preview. It's a healthy reminder you can give yourself as often as it helps: *I am thankful to be a parent. The responsibility is great but the rewards are greater.*

We are just beginning to understand and appreciate the complexity of our children. If we can remain open-minded about what makes us all different, then from our children we shall learn.

Author's Note

Since the first publication of *Dreamers, Discoverers, and Dynamos* (formerly titled *The Edison Trait*), I have been touched by the responses I have received from readers. People have shared stories with me that show how substantially life can change when you shift to a strength-centered approach. Parents have described the improvements they have seen when they apply "time-in," speaking in metaphor, using Socratic dialogue, replacing demands with "the empowering question," and other practices from the book.

As this paperback edition goes to press, I have decided to write this note to address an important question I am asked frequently: "Are my child's problems chemically based?" The answer is "Yes . . . *and* they are psychologically based, too." Mind and molecule interact for all of us. Here's how:

A neurotransmitter is a brain chemical that is both the cause and the result of a particular behavior pattern. The neurotransmitter, dopamine, mediates goal achievement. When you succeed, you boost your dopamine *and* that dopamine drives you further. Self-induced dopamine is the biological mediator of the adage "Nothing succeeds like success."

Now, consider what happens when an Edison-trait child starts school. Like other five-year-olds, he's off to explore his new world, driven by dopamine, and serotonin, too. (Serotonin is the neurotransmitter of security and well-being.) However, compared to most other five-year-olds, a young Edisonian thinks more divergently. He soon finds out that school is the land of convergent thinking. Teachers whose job it is to maintain order and standards are bound to correct him. His original, imaginative answers get labeled "wrong." The child begins to associate classwork with the pain of disappointment. He experiences fear of failing and feels put down in front of status-conscious peers.

Insecure and embarrassed, this child is now driven by a divergent brain chemical: norepinephrine, the neurotransmitter of stress. Norepinephrine triggers fight-or-flight behavior. The child becomes defiant (fight) or avoidant (flight). Adults react with criticism and punishment, which perpetuates the cycle of stress.

We can force a child to perform, but this will not change his brain chemistry or lead to self-motivation. Monkeys will perform a task whether they are rewarded with fruit juice or punished with noxious puffs of air in their faces. However, *only the reward* increases the dopamine in their brains. A child will perform if we force him. But he will remain norepinephrine-driven, acting out (fight) or tuning out (flight), when he is left on his own. To act as self-motivated students, our children need to be driven by dopamine and serotonin, *not* norepinephrine.

There are many ways to break the fight-or-flight cycle, with or without prescription drugs. Stimulants such as Ritalin and Adderall typically produce the fastest results, by helping to regulate dopamine. However, the action of these drugs is temporary and does not replace the skill building a child needs to succeed and self-induce dopamine. Each situation is different, which is why I call the chapter on medication (Chapter 15), "A Personal Decision."

Dreamers, Discoverers, and Dynamos *teaches parents how to raise their children to be self-motivated learners, driven by dopamine and serotonin, not norepinephrine.* The Edison-trait child who fights or flees schoolwork shines brightly in other places. We can guide this child to bring that light with him to the classroom. When we commit to a strength-centered approach, we raise our children to be the heroes, not the victims, of their lives.

PART I

Your Child's Inventive Mind

CHAPTER 1

~~~

Does Your Child Have the Edison Trait?

If a man does not keep pace with his companions, perhaps it is because he hears a different drummer. Let him step to the music which he hears, however measured or far away.

—Henry David Thoreau

AN INVENTIVE MIND

He was a boy who learned only by doing. At age six, he had to see how fire worked and accidentally burned his father's barn to the ground. The next fall he began school, where he alternated between letting his mind travel to distant places and keeping his body in perpetual motion in his seat. Because he was distractible and restless, he did not last long in a formal classroom. His teacher called him "addled." Eventually, his mother had to home-school him. As an adult he would recall: "My father thought I was stupid and I almost decided I must be a dunce."

The core of his learning was his passion for experiments. As his new teacher, his mother gave his talent free rein. At the same time she infused him with the disciplines of study. With time and determination, he mastered his runaway mind. He grew up to become a prolific inventor, bringing the magic of electricity and sound recording into the world. He either invented or improved hundreds of practical conveniences. It is said that Thomas Alva Edison succeeded where others failed or never tried, because it was his nature to dare.[1]

Today, a growing number of children have that nature to dare. Like young Edison, they are easily distracted and disorganized, but also wildly imaginative and inventive.

They have minds that are at home with meanderings and leaps of vast proportions. They make unexpected, sometimes startling, connections.

QUALITIES OF A CREATIVE MIND

There was once a man who drove a truck on a road through a town and got stuck under a bridge that had a low clearance. The men of the town gathered around the wedged truck to think of ways to dismantle the truck or the bridge. Finally, a young boy came up and asked, "Why don't you let some air out of the tires?" That is what they did, and the truck went on its way.

This was a child who had the Edison trait. He saw an element of the scene that no one else saw, because they were busily and systematically focused on what to them was relevant to the solution. An Edison-trait child:

Expects the Unexpected

A child with the Edison trait makes sudden, astonishing connections. Because his inner critic disallows neither the ridiculous nor the sublime, he can be innovative, ingenious, and fascinating. He can see ordinary things in extraordinary ways, which is the very essence of creativity.

His sense of humor is disarming. It stems from keen perception and the ability to see things from a different perspective. Sometimes he exhibits the kind of straight-from-the-subconscious humor that makes successful stand-up comics so funny. He blurts out ideas that are just under the surface, things that most others would have automatically censored.

Thinks Autonomously

This is a child who stands up for his own ideas, especially when they are uncommon or nonconformist. He is an independent thinker and does not rely on the opinions of others to form his own judgments. In a matter of personal interest to him, he stands firm with conviction, even in the face of strong opposition.

Hyperfocuses and Persists

When the Edison-trait child is intrinsically motivated, he has formidable mental power. If he is working on a project that is his own brainstorm, he is determined, tenacious, and persevering. As if by magic, he can work for hours involved in what he is doing. He finds ways to overcome barriers; his passion sees him through. In matters of his own choosing, he has inner direction and resolve.

Is Diverse and Intense

Edison-trait children are pluralistic, nonconforming, and multifarious. Once they begin to speak on a topic of their choosing, clear your calendar . . . you'll be here for a while. Flights of fancy are common. One thing leads to another, though sometimes the connections are not apparent to the rest of us.

Has a Mind That Is Holistic

The Edison-trait child notices and reacts to things from any and all directions, so he is likely to have a global sense of places he has been. Take this child to the shopping mall and he'll probably be able to lead you back to your parked car.

Lives on His Own Schedule

Time passes slowly for this child when he is not engaged in an activity of interest. Otherwise, watch out! When an Edison-trait child works on a project of his choosing, he is dedicated and determined.

Loves to Come Up with Ideas

Some do this slowly and dreamily. Others are like kernels of popcorn popping. Many do both. They have qualities of being both a whimsical Dreamer and a high-charged Discoverer or turbulent Dynamo.

DOES YOUR CHILD HAVE THE EDISON TRAIT?

All children are imaginative and enjoy make-believe, but children who have the Edison trait live even closer to their imaginations. It is their lifeblood.

Children manifest the Edison trait in various ways. Some are quiet and reserved and live in their own worlds. Others are loud, interruptive, and bold.

Your child may be a Dreamer, a Discoverer, or a Dynamo. Or he may combine features of any or all of these patterns.

- **Dreamers** drift from place to place, on a schedule of eternal time.
- **Discoverers** have to find things out for themselves and do things their own way.
- **Dynamos** are always in motion, with a flair for surprises, power, and speed.

If your child has the Edison trait, you'll find that some passages in this book will sound as though I wrote them with him in mind. Others won't fit at all. To see how closely your child's patterns match the profile of children with this trait, take a moment and think about him since his earliest days. Then ask yourself these questions:

*If your child is a **Dreamer***
1. Does he get absorbed or intensely involved in his own ideas much of the time?
2. Is he prone to saying things out of the blue?
3. Does he procrastinate to an extreme?
4. Are his interests and activities eclectic?
5. Does he start at least three projects for every one he finishes?

*If your child is a **Discoverer***
1. Is he easily attracted to sights and sounds around him?
2. Is it vital for him to express his opinion?
3. Does he crave novelty, power, and excitement?
4. Is he always ready to speak, especially if you're talking?
5. When he wants his own way—which is almost always—is he relentless?

Or, if your child is a **Dynamo**
1. Does he get aggressive or intensely emotional about his own ideas much of the time?
2. Is some part of his body always in motion?
3. Are chances to run and climb as vital as the air he breathes?
4. Does he have boundless energy, enough for about three children his age?
5. Do you find yourself wondering if he lacks common sense?

The more "yes" answers you gave to these questions, the more reason there is for you to read on.

DREAMERS

Noelle's teacher calls her "a fairy-tale princess." Noelle lives in her own delicate world, which makes her vulnerable to the stress of classroom demands and playground roughhousing. "She has the soul of an artist," her mother observes.

Noelle is a bright child, but gets teary-eyed and withdraws whenever there is a math test or classwork that must be finished by the end of the work period.

Noelle loves music. She tried to take piano lessons, but this did not work out. Noelle told me, "I couldn't get the notes in a row, the way the teacher did, and I knew that's what she wanted." Noelle dances with extraordinary grace. Also, she likes to draw. At times, when engaged in these activities, she becomes totally absorbed, intensely focused.

I was not surprised when I learned that Noelle likes to paint in watercolors. In getting to know her, I'd come to realize that she thinks in watercolors, too.

Dreamers are mind wanderers. These Edison-trait youngsters seem to be lost in timeless space. From time to time, they have blank expressions on their faces or may look a little dazed. Actually, they are floating through one or several ideas in another realm, a world of their own.

> *I dwell in Possibility*
> *A fairer house than Prose,*
> *More numerous of windows,*
> *Superior of doors.*

Like Emily Dickinson, the author of these words, Edison-trait Dreamers are self-styled visionaries and poets. They have an ephemeral quality, a digressive style of thinking, and an inclination to see things from an unusual, even quixotic angle. In the classroom, after a lesson is taught, the Dreamer may not give the expected response, so others presume he just didn't "get it." But ask him and you'll find out that if he was tuned in, he probably "got it" all right—in an entirely unintended or uncommon way. He produces the kind of answer that makes you think twice.

Dreamers like sensory experience. They are drawn to color, sound, texture, taste, and fragrance. Often, Edison-trait Dreamers remember odd and seemingly unrelated facts and details, knowledge of an idiosyncratic nature. Seldom can they say exactly why they are drawn to these particular thoughts or recollections, but their fascination can become intense. What appears as spaciness to us is felt as absorption by them.

ANNE MORROW LINDBERGH
PORTRAIT OF A DREAMER

Poet, pilot, and dreamer, Anne Morrow Lindbergh was ahead of her time. Her books are still read and beloved today. Airlines still fly international routes that she and her famous husband scouted and mapped together.

Throughout her school years, Anne's imagination was both her friend and her foe. She saw images and stories everywhere and wrote fairy-tale plays for others to act in. But rote learning was her nemesis, particularly multiplication tables, and as an adult she acknowledged, "I never passed an arithmetic examination in my life."

As a freshman at Smith College she failed Greek and mathematics. In a letter to her mother she wrote: "I do wish I had some alibi for such inefficiency . . . but I haven't any excuse. . . . I look at a birch tree through a mist of gym shoes, course cards, alarm clocks, papers due, writtens, laundry boxes, choir practices, bills, long themes, and exams. . . . it makes me discouraged and when I'm discouraged I can't do anything [April 22, 1925]."

Later that year, Anne discovered her passion. In response to the dean's suggestion that she change her schedule to take Home Gardening, a rebellious and self-determined Anne decided instead to enroll in literature courses that appealed to her imagination. The tone of her letters home improved dramatically: "I can't begin to describe the classes . . . so <u>rich</u> and so <u>stimulating</u>. It is the most glorious world—I feel like a Magellan! . . . Some powers have no hold on me as they seemed to have before—I feel like saying, 'Let them not have dominion over me!' *[October 10, 1925].*"

Anne graduated from Smith, began an illustrious career as a writer, and achieved fame as Charles Lindbergh's copilot, navigator, and radio operator. Motivated by a sense of adventure and purpose, the Dreamer who never passed an arithmetic test in a classroom successfully performed complex mathematical calculations in the cockpit of a plane, often under high-risk conditions. She and her husband broke the transcontinental speed record, and they were the first to fly many uncharted routes, like the Great Circle route from New York to China. Their work made it possible for commercial airlines to establish passenger service.

Anne Morrow Lindbergh wrote five books of diaries and letters, and eight books of prose and poetry. Her perennial best-seller, Gift From the Sea, *is still widely read and appreciated. The most recurring symbol in this eloquent Dreamer's literary works is the unicorn— a one-of-a-kind imaginary steed of natural beauty, strength, and wonder.*[2]

DISCOVERERS

From the moment he was born, Gregory was an explorer. "He'd climb out of his crib, go into closets, empty the cabinets, get past any lock. When he was three, he walked out the front door and down the block. Then he was mad at us when we stopped him!" Gregory's dad spoke with a curious mix of exasperation and pride.

Gregory's mom's voice sounded worried. "Once when I was driving, he leaned over and took the wheel right out of my hands. Suppose he had done that on the freeway?"

At school Gregory is known as a child who tests limits. His teacher says he is smart, but does not want to do his work. She says, "He's always looking for some excuse, for some way to get out of doing it. And he's constantly on the lookout for excitement. If there's a ruckus anywhere, that's where you'll find him."

Gregory likes to trade things and find ways to make money. Baseball cards are his passion and he has made some profitable deals. At school he sold candy and gum, until the principal ordered him to stop. In sixth grade, when yearbooks came out, he thought up clever inscriptions, then sold them to his classmates to use.

Discoverers are Edison-trait adventurers who must blaze their own trail. They are high-spirited and have to see "what would happen if . . ." They are spontaneous and they must do things their own way.

Discoverers are multisensorial, usually with a strong preference for visual input. This is a child who craves, and often creates, the stimulation of power, surprise, or diversity. He wants to explore his own ideas and express his own opinions. He wants life to keep him interested. If he does not find people stimulating, he will stimulate them, usually by provoking laughter or anger.

Discoverers like to live in the moment, without giving too much mind to what will happen in the future. Typically, they are not planners. Discoverers live with the attitude that they'll discover what's going to happen when it happens. That's what makes life interesting.

When a Discoverer is on the trail of an idea or project of his own, he feels a sense of urgency or impatience. During these times the Discoverer may "hyperfocus." He pays attention to what he is doing with an unusual degree of intensity and to the exclusion of all else. Discoverers also "multitask." Multitasking means doing more than one thing at a time. Dreamers and Dynamos hyperfocus and multitask, too. But Discoverers do it more.

HENRY FORD
TALES OF A DISCOVERER

The man who made the automobile an affordable reality saw into the future with the open eyes and mind of a discoverer. As an adult, Ford stated his personal philosophy: ". . . all life begins here and now. Other men will tell me things which they claim to be facts, but I must not believe them. I will not accept things as true unless I, myself, prove they are true."

As a child, Henry was high-spirited and strong-willed, and he spent many hours on the "bad boys' bench" at school. Once, he directed his classmates to dam a drainage ditch so he could build a water wheel, which he then attached to a coffee mill to see how many things he could grind; pebbles were fun because they gave off sparks. Unfortunately, it rained while the ditch was still dammed, and this flooded and ruined a farmer's crop. Another time, Henry concocted a steam turbine, using the school fence as a support. After getting about

3,000 rpm from the engine, it blew up, injuring several children and setting fire to the school fence.

In the classroom, Henry was a doer, not a listener. His mother had to teach him how to read at home. He liked to figure things out, but he was poor in spelling and penmanship. He had a gift for invention and an aversion for convention.

An enterprising young Ford refused to accept the status quo that cars were only for the rich. He was determined to make and sell family cars. First he built a practical gas-powered engine. Then he set his entrepreneurial drive in motion. He attracted financial backers by challenging the world's racetrack champions—and winning. Twice he began companies and twice his companies failed. The turning point came when Ford realized that he needed a business structure that would free him to work on his own. He needed to be able to construct his own timetable and to account only to himself. He recalled this historic moment in his own words: "In March, 1902, I resigned, determined never again to put myself under orders."

Ford then built the "999," a remarkable race car. He and several loyal workers toiled in an unheated warehouse, designing and testing parts. They donned boxing gloves for antic midnight matches to restore the circulation in their hands. When they were done, they had built a car that had four upright seven-inch cylinders and, according to The Detroit Journal, made "more noise than a freight train."

The 999 beat all contenders and set a new speed record. As a result, twelve investors came together to back the Ford Motor Company. With the innovative style of a Discoverer, Ford developed the assembly line to mass-produce automobiles. He made himself and his investors into millionaires. And he gave America the keys to the car.[3]

DYNAMOS

"I call him 'my child who flew.' It was the very first day he got his bicycle. He came tearing down the hill, and, with the bike at full speed, he stood up on the seat! What was he thinking of? He wore a cast for months, but did he learn? No. He'd do it again in a minute. He does not have a strong relationship with gravity."

Ty's mom, a best-selling novelist, has a knack for describing Ty's life in the danger zone. Referring to the popular comic strip character, she says, "My son is Calvin."

Dynamos are fuel-injected speedsters. They have erratic spurts of energy. They overexcite easily, and when this happens, trouble is on the way.

In some ways, a Dynamo is also a Discoverer. He is impulsive. He acts first and thinks later. Like the Discoverer, the Dynamo loves power and speed. And like the Discoverer, the Dynamo is strong-willed and immovable in his position.

The distinguishing feature of the Dynamo is his boundless physical energy. Dynamos keep their bodies in motion, one way or another, almost all the time. They walk, run, skip, kick, climb, jump, bounce, leap, bound, pounce, bolt, dash, race, sprint, dive, swim, splash, and fly.

Dynamos act with gusto and zest. They are risk takers and daredevils. And they are constantly entertaining. Life in their company is never dull.

JESSE OWENS
TRIUMPH OF A DYNAMO

At the 1936 summer Olympics in Berlin, the dynamic Jesse Owens won four gold medals and set one world and two Olympic track records. He did this against a backdrop of Nazi hatred, threats, and racism. With the determination of a champion, he insisted on his own history-making version of reality—and he prevailed.

As a child, James Owens was accident-prone and impulsive. Once he stepped into a steel hunting trap his father had just set. Another time he got too close, and was run over by a cotton drag. He often got into scrapes and brawls. There is not much to say about him at school, because there was not much schooling for blacks in the 1920s in Alabama. James liked to "spin yarns," a source of conflict with his dad, who feared that his son's ideas and ambitions were too unrealistic.

In junior high school, Owens found what every Edison-trait child needs: an adult who understood and believed in him. That adult was his running coach, Charles Riley. Coach Riley painted mental pictures for Owens. When he wanted Owens to run lightly, he told the athlete to move "like the ground was a burning fire." Riley helped Owens improve his attitude. He taught him how to step back, take a look, and act, not react. James became known as Jesse during this period, a new name for a new life.

When Owens arrived in Berlin in 1936, the Olympics were marred by world tensions. The Third Reich now occupied the previously demilitarized Rhineland, sending shivers of fear throughout Europe. At the stadium, Adolf Hitler's daily presence cast a perceptible chill. Throughout Germany the tenet of Aryan superiority reigned. Blacks were considered a "subspecies." Nazis denounced their "use" in the games and lodged a formal complaint to prevent "nonhumans" like Owens from competing.

Owens not only overcame this pressure, he turned it around to make sports history. His Dynamo ability to make things go his way gave him the winning edge. In the long jump, for example, Owens had become rattled when officials called two immediate, controversial fouls on him. One foul away from elimination in his best event, Owens created a new scenario for himself on the field. He stopped and spoke with his rival, Lutz Long, a tall, blue-eyed, blond German. The two began to joke about how much Long looked like a prototypical Aryan male.

Owens went on to qualify for the event, and his first jump in the finals set an Olympic record. An inspired Long then jumped farther then he ever had in his life. But Owens kept his lead. In the fifth and sixth rounds, Long matched Owens's jumps exactly. Each time, Owens responded by leaping even farther, breaking the Olympic record he had set the round before.

In the end, Jesse Owens won the gold and set an impressive Olympic record. The first person to congratulate him, in full view of Adolf Hitler, was the picture-perfect Aryan, Lutz Long.[4]

THE EDISON TRAIT IS LIFELONG

The Edison trait is a personality characteristic. It endures. As Edison himself did, people with the trait have to make good matches between their aptitudes and their life work.

Mr. Richards is a forty-three-year-old investment broker. When he learned about the Edison trait, he related to it immediately. He says that looking back over the course of his life, he can see a parade of events leading him to understand and accept his nature.

For years Richards went from job to job until he built a successful business of his own. His first marriage failed, due largely, he says, to his ignorance of how he was given to impulsivity. Today, he is happily married.

Mr. Richards enjoys considerable personal and financial success, which he attributes to the kind of risk that he, unlike many others, is willing and inclined to take. Mr. Richards says the Edison trait has caused him "a heap of trouble" but "it's what gives my life creativity and energy."

TURNING THE LIGHTS ON

As the parent of an Edison-trait child, you have probably asked yourself some variation of the following question: "If my child can recall the entire roster of the 1955 Brooklyn Dodgers, why can't he remember that eight times seven is fifty-six?"

To better understand your youngster, picture him wandering through an empty house alone. Most of the rooms are dark. One or two are well lit. When your child enters a bright room, he is filled with enthusiasm to explore. He remembers those bright rooms and develops a strong preference for them. Of course, the way you see it, he should be able to turn the lights on in any room, if only he would use the light switch. When you ask him to and he doesn't, a strain of tension develops between you.

From his point of view—and this is his house—his lights are wired differently. In the past, your Edison-trait child has tried to use the same kind of switch he sees others use, but to no avail. He senses that he doesn't operate the same way. He has a different configuration. Problems start getting solved when you work from his blueprints, not yours. You empower him to figure out his own circuitry, and the rules and methods to turn his lights on.

CONVERGENT, NO—DIVERGENT, YES

Having the Edison trait makes some things easier for your child and some things harder. The things that come easy are

- Thinking up wild or unusual ideas
- Standing up for, feeling strongly about, and getting involved in those ideas
- Making things up, and imagining the future
- Trying things out
- Starting new projects

The things that come hard are

- Focusing on someone else's ideas
- Letting go of his own ideas

- Remembering things he's been asked to do
- Practicing skills repeatedly
- Finishing things

The things that come easy are divergent thinking skills. In divergent thinking, one thought stimulates many others; thinking branches out. The things that come hard require convergent thinking. In convergent thinking, many thoughts reduce to a single one; thinking funnels in.

Read the lists again. It is no surprise that Edison-trait children will not shine in a typical classroom, or on the playground, or in most forms of organized sports. In settings like these, their chemistry sets them apart. They are the exceptions to our implicit rules of how children should think and perform, rules that say they should behave like uniform convergent thinkers.

CONVERGENT THINKING AS THE NORM

It is a natural human tendency to assume that all minds work the same way. We tacitly agree that all minds should naturally be able to follow through on one idea at a time, from beginning to end, with attention to detail. We call convergent thinking the norm and we presume it's what comes naturally if a brain is "normal." Divergent thinkers are viewed as having "attentional problems."

We label convergent thinking as right and divergent thinking as wrong. We base the methods we use to train our children on this premise. We expect children to focus in a linear fashion for as long as we say they should. This is true at home and at school. And at school, as class sizes get larger and children get more diverse, a teacher's tolerance for a student's divergent thinking necessarily diminishes. The same curriculum gets taught to all students in the same way and at the same pace.

The brains of Edison-trait children are misunderstood, *not* inferior. As students they are attentionally disadvantaged because we punish, and fail to appreciate, their unique creative slant. They get blamed for not completing desk work in the allotted time. They are scolded for not staying in their seats until recess. They are forced to work at an unsuitable tempo, and then get graded down for poor handwriting, and errors in grammar, spelling, and math facts. These outcomes are inevitable artifacts of a mismatched approach.

We teach to their weaknesses, not to their strengths. We insist that they see things our way, but we won't see things theirs. These children are stunningly divergent. They are on a quest for discovery, exploration, and stimulation. Surely we can be flexible and accommodate their style. They can and will develop convergent skills, but only if their desire to learn is protected and kindled with success.

WE CAN HELP EDISON-TRAIT CHILDREN
DEVELOP SKILLS

We Can Guide Them to Motivate Themselves

"I remember what it used to be like," said Kyle, a tall, lanky seventeen-year-old who has the Edison trait. Kyle was referring to the time he was failing junior high school. "I felt like I lived in a maze with glass walls. I could see the way out, but I never could get there."

Now a college-bound high school senior, Kyle had come back for a visit. His metaphor reminded me of the words of psychologist Russell Barkley, Ph.D. He says that a struggle like Kyle's is "not a problem of knowing what to do. It is a problem of doing what you know."[5]

Many times, after being shown what convergent thinking skills are, children who have the Edison trait do not apply these lessons. Dreamers forget what they were supposed to do. Discoverers and Dynamos know they should plan or wait, but they act too soon or stop too late.

Like Kyle at age fourteen, Edison-trait children can see the right path, but keep running into walls on the way there. Since they have to work harder at patience and self-control, these children need more impetus to try. Conceptualized this way, their problem is one of *motivation*. Chapters 4 through 9 describe specific ways to keep their motivation high.

These children need extra incentive and stimulating rewards. They need to experience success so that they can believe in it. They need reasons compelling enough to keep up the extra effort to get through the glass maze.

We Can Communicate—Think and Talk—in Their Language

A child with the Edison trait needs to feel he's in control. He will accept help only if it does not threaten his autonomy. He is prone to feeling crowded and seeing adults as overbearing.

The Edison-trait child is easily overwhelmed. For this reason, he needs clear direction, phrased in brief, concise messages. He needs his workload assigned in manageable portions. He needs structure, simple categories, and prominent visual cues.

For this same reason, he needs frequent breaks and relief from tension. He responds best to a calm and steady voice, devoid of emotional charge.

The Edison-trait child thinks in images and stories. He needs instruction that is attractive and captivating. He responds to metaphors and identifies with characters he likes. Creative approaches work best. Humor is a strong ally.

In Chapters 5, 6, 8, and 9, you will learn more about communicating with your child, including effective ways to correct him. You'll learn to listen more than you talk, and to think in "Edison-trait dialect," using mental pictures to connect his world and yours.

Your goal is to value your child's divergent thinking, while at the same time teaching and encouraging him to think convergently. With guidance and support, he will learn how to concentrate, shift focus, and do things in sequence. He'll make his own ways to organize his thoughts, words, papers, time, and money, to follow through, plan, schedule, and stay on track. He will come to appreciate conventional wisdom and the merit of reflective thought.

BRIDGES, NOT FENCES

Pretend for a moment that when babies are born, they already know how to talk. Right from the cradle: "Hello, Mother. Hello, Father. Please feed me. I'm hungry."

Now let's say 80 percent of the babies in the United States are born speaking English, but you're a parent of one of the 20 percent who speak a foreign language. You know you must help him to learn English somehow, so he can get along with everybody else. But it's clear your little guy likes his language better than yours.

He learns barely enough English to get by, but no more. He prefers the sound and the flow and the feel of his own tongue. He doesn't know how much of your language he can learn, even if he tries. And why should he try, when everyone acts as if he already should speak English fluently, and people make a bigger deal over his failures than his efforts?

At first, you forbid your child to speak his language. That doesn't work.

Next, you reward him when he speaks only English. That works some, but it's a strain on everyone.

Finally, you make a commitment to learn and appreciate the language he speaks. You enter his world—through his sounds, his words, and his expressions. You don't insult his language; you find what is beautiful and useful about it.

At the same time, you acknowledge every attempt he makes to speak English—regardless of whether he succeeds or not. You let him know you recognize his efforts and his desire to communicate with you. You tell him that you see his courage and his hard work.

And then, a funny thing happens.

The more good you see in his world, the more good he sees in yours.

You build bridges, not fences.

You become enriched by your knowledge of his language. And he grows in his motivation to learn yours.

~m~

Children Who Are Divergent-Thinking-Dominant

The universe is made of stories, not of atoms.

—Muriel Rukeyser

CAN CRITICS LEARN TO CREATE?

I went to graduate school at Arizona State University in the mid-seventies. As was true at most traditional university settings at the time, the clinical psychology program was a "scientist-practitioner" model.[1] We were there to become good therapists and, at the same time, to conduct research to test our methods. It was no accident that *scientist* was the first word in the name of that model. We were there to hone our critical thinking skills. Convergent thinking reigned supreme.

As fledgling scientists, we searched for brilliant research ideas, especially when dissertation deadlines loomed in front of us. One fall, the department held a symposium to teach us a new technique called "brainstorming." This process had been developed by a "think tank," a group of cognitive scientists who study ways to solve problems. They had been examining methods used by innovative people, like Thomas Edison. At that time, brainstorming was catching on in business and industry as well.[2]

BRAINSTORMING

We arrived at the appointed time, with notebooks and pens in hand, prepared to do what we all did best: listen dutifully and take copious notes, as a respected authority lectured on what rules we should follow and why.

Instead, the instructor stood up and told us that for the next thirty minutes, there was only one rule to follow. The rule was this: There are no rules. No rules, no criticisms, no judgments, no limits, no stopping. We would do nothing but think freely, even wildly, and say the first things that came to our minds.

I looked around and saw a room full of skeptical faces. The instructor then asked: "How can you improve a pencil?"

Skepticism turned to puzzlement on more than one face. Several moments later, a few brave souls began to respond:

"How about an attachable ruler and compass."

"Have a 'free-flow' graphite option, for filling in spaces when sketching."

"Aromatic graphite, for writing in different scents."

We were allowed to build on, but not to tear down, one another's ideas.

"A fluorescent attachment for writing in the dark." . . . "How about 'glow-graphite'?"

I looked around the room. Most students and faculty were, in fact, chiming in. Free-thinking was turning our brainpower on, like city lights at dusk.

I still remember my personal favorite of the day: a pencil that could be used to prevent writer's cramp. It had a battery-driven vibrator option for massaging the weary hand. Of course, a decade later came word processors, making writer's cramp obsolete. Wait—how about a mouse with a vibrating option?

THE CONVERGENT THINKER'S VIEW

Convergent thinking is a necessary and satisfying brain function. It is essential for accomplishing goals. There is great satisfaction in doing it well.

The person who is convergent-thinking-dominant counts and calculates with ease. She likes to observe and report. And she is particularly good at finding mistakes that need to be corrected. Numbers matter, as do details.

The convergent thinker is exact, literal, and orderly.

- Facts alone matter.
- Measurements are quantitative.
- Thinking is analytic.

Ask a convergent-thinking child to tell you about her day. Typically, she'll reply: "I woke up about seven a.m. Then I got dressed and ate breakfast. Then I got ready for school and walked there with my friends. When I was at school, in the morning, we worked on a script. We're making a play out of a book we've been reading. We talked about parts and decided on some. After recess we did math. Then there was lunch and social studies and P.E. After school I had a piano lesson."

The convergent thinker naturally starts at the beginning. She'll tell you the first thing she did, then the next, then the next. She is *sequential,* that is, she links her thoughts in a "straight line" with a logical order that determines what comes first, then second, then third.

The convergent thinker perceives discrete units of thought. In other words, *she lives in a universe composed of atoms.*

The convergent thinker is a natural at critical thinking. Like all humans, she is prone to criticize what she understands the least. So the convergent thinker tends to be critical, even incredulous, of divergent-thinking processes.

THE DIVERGENT THINKER'S VIEW

The divergent thinker lives in a natural state of "brainstorm." She sees life through a kaleidoscope that is set in perpetual motion.

- Patterns change frequently.
- Experience is described, not measured.
- Thoughts are multicolored, multishaped, and hard to hold in one place.

Ask the divergent-thinking child to tell you about her day. Her reply will go something like this: "I'm going to be Mrs. Arable in

Charlotte's Web! I'm also going to learn Fern's part, in case Linsey Adams gets sick. I wanted to be Fern, but so did Linsey and four other girls, so we picked names out of a hat. We picked Linsey's first, then mine. Jackie Forrest will be Charlotte and Tim O'Connor will be Wilbur . . ."

The divergent thinker instantly recalls the most exciting event of the day. Then she'll tell you the most exciting parts about the most exciting event. Then she'll tell you her most exciting associations to those exciting recollections. Her thoughts bubble to the surface like water gurgling in a brook.

The divergent thinker whirls with ideas and images. She lives in a universe made up of stories.

Critical examination does *not* come naturally to the divergent thinker. She does not understand it, and tends to take it personally. She gets defensive when criticized by a convergent thinker. She feels convergent thinkers believe she is not as smart as they are.

Divergent thinkers hold to their free-thinking outlook on life. If the Edison-trait child had the literary skills of an accomplished writer like D. H. Lawrence, she might express this attitude as he did, when giving his divergent thinker's view of the moon: "It's no use telling me it's a dead rock in the sky! I *know* it's not."[3]

A UNIVERSE OF STORIES *AND* ATOMS

In reality, there is a divergent thinker *and* a convergent thinker in each of us. To a large extent, these modes of thinking correspond to, or at least approximate, the specialized functioning of our right and left brain hemispheres. In a manner of speaking, we think divergently, in far-fetched fantasy, by means of our right brain. We think convergently, in one-step-at-a-time progression, courtesy of our left brain. (Neuroscientifically, this is an oversimplification. Nonetheless, these correspondences are close approximations and provide a useful model of our children's styles of thinking.[4])

In reality, human experience is the result of right- *and* left-brain functioning. Both modes of thinking have complementary survival value. Right-brain divergent thinking picks up patterns and connections that left-brain convergent thinking would instantly dismiss. Left-brain convergent thinking can check on reality, in case the right brain has detected patterns where none exist.

In *The Dragons of Eden,* Carl Sagan responds to D. H. Lawrence's opinion of the moon:

> Indeed, the moon *is* more than a dead rock in the sky. It is beautiful, it has romantic associations, it raises tides. . . . But certainly one of its attributes is that it is a dead rock in the sky. Intuitive thinking does quite well . . . but . . . must be willing to accommodate to the insights that rational thought wrests from Nature.[5]

The universe is a whole-brain experience, made up of stories and atoms.

PARTICIPATING CONSCIOUSNESS

In *The Reenchantment of the World,* the historian Morris Berman speaks of "participating consciousness," which is the mode of thinking that prevailed long ago, in the days of folk tales, legends, and affinity with the earth:

> The view of nature which predominated in the West down to the eve of the Scientific Revolution was that of an enchanted world. Rocks, trees, rivers, and clouds were all seen as wondrous, alive; and human beings felt at home in this environment. The cosmos, in short, was a place of belonging. A member of this cosmos was not an alienated observer of it but a direct participant in its drama.[6]

Children who are divergent-thinking-dominant are resurrecting this approach to life. It is an endearing, but sometimes maddening, Edison-trait characteristic. They delight in the imaginative, and can sniff out adventure in a nanosecond. But because it is *their* adventure, they seldom, if ever, take advice from others. *They* must experience things for themselves. They make and test their own laws of nature.

In today's techno-magic world, children see only the magic— satellite photos, holograms, and microwave dinners. They have no way of connecting this magic with the rigors of the convergent thinking that was necessary to produce it. It takes time for them to appreciate the merit of others' opinions and the sustained efforts of scientists who have preceded them.

On the upside, their mind-set gives them unshakable confidence when they are at the controls of their favorite form of technology. Watch your very young child take charge when she plays her favorite CD-ROM. Watch your older child's ease and fluidity at the joystick of a video game. Does your son or daughter at college write you letters or send you E-mail?

Divergent-thinking children expect machines to respond to their commands. Their intuition says no to grunt work. *Life is their personal adventure.* They are active, assertive cast members of Berman's "participating consciousness," in a new universe that now incorporates computers, electronics, and other technological vehicles of power and speed.

A WHOLE-BRAIN EXERCISE

One day, when Jeni, my younger daughter, was in the fifth grade, she came home and asked me enthusiastically what "robbing Peter to pay Paul" meant. A few minutes later, she reappeared: "How about 'when the chickens come home to roost'?" I was tempted to follow her back to her room to find out what she was up to, but curiosity killed the cat, I remembered, so I didn't. When she returned and asked me to explain "a horse of a different color," I could contain myself no longer. I asked her to spill the beans. I did not want to be left out in the cold. And so, she let the cat out of the bag.

Her class had just been given an assignment by their teacher called "The Idiom Project." The requirements were:

1. List as many idioms as you can, as long as you know the meaning of each.
2. Select five that are "lessons for life" and write a half-page description of each.
3. Select ten to illustrate in pictures: On the left side draw the literal meaning and on the right side draw the actual one.
4. Create a four-box cartoon that tells a story or makes a joke, and include as many idioms as you can, sensibly.

5. Make up five original idioms, explain their meanings, and illustrate one in pictures.
6. For extra credit: Research five foreign idioms and give their literal translations and actual meanings.[7]

Judging by the phone calls and snippets of conversation I overheard in the weeks that followed, Jeni's classmates were as enthused about the project as she was. It woke up divergent *and* convergent thinking functions. It was a "whole-brain" assignment, and it reached *all* the students.

On open-school night, the students' completed projects were on display. Each booklet showed the high energy and hard work of its young author. Every child had listed at least several hundred idioms. I got goose bumps from reading some of the "lessons for life." The pictures were the quintessence of visual communication. Some were poignant, some humorous, and some uncanny.

Often, on open-school nights, convergent-thinking students shine and divergent-thinking students spend the night wishing it were over. That night, pride and self-esteem extended to every child in the room.

DIVERGENT THINKERS LIVE AND WORK WITH IMAGINATION

What would happen if we were to give a similar class of fifth-graders a worksheet of idioms, with directions to write out the meanings of each one, then grade them, taking points off for misspelling or poor handwriting?

A convergent-thinking child might whiz through the exercise and get an easy "A."

A divergent-thinking child might . . .

1. manage to complete the task, but lose points for infractions, get a low grade, and see in this yet another confirmation that she is not as smart as her friends
2. space out somewhere in the middle of the assignment, and hand in incomplete work

3. space out, bring the work home to finish, but lose it on the way
4. bring the work home, and after hours of procrastinating, day-dreaming, and cleverly outwitting her parents' best efforts to keep her on task, get the job done, but forget to hand it in the next day.

The divergent thinker has no *ownership* of convergent-thinking assignments. She does not feel they belong to her, or that they have much to do with what she wants out of life. If she was to tell you her honest reaction, it would be something like "What's the point?"

However, when you invite this child to play with the pictures in her mind, the divergent thinker says yes. This kind of learning makes sense to her. She fires up her imagination, takes charge, and is in full command of her mission.

DIVERGENT THINKERS USE MENTAL PICTURES TO COMMUNICATE

"No, no, you can't come in." Gina, an eight-year-old Dreamer, said to her mother in a tiny voice. Gina, her mother, and I were in the midst of a counseling session. As she spoke, Gina cupped her left hand and made it talk like a mouth forming words.

Gina's mother sat in a chair facing her. A minute ago, her right hand had knocked on an invisible door between them. Now it fell to her lap as she heaved a sigh. She looked in my direction.

"Gina is mad at me. She still takes everything I say the wrong way. It can be almost anything and she'll get upset and say that I'm mean."

"You think I'm stupid!" Gina exclaimed.

"No, I don't," her mother replied.

I'd been working with Gina and her mother long enough to understand the source of their conflict. Gina's mother, a convergent-thinking single parent, ran her home by the clock. Gina was a sensitive, divergent-thinking child whose only interest in clocks was to get to the movies on time.

When Gina's mom corrected her daughter or urged her to hurry up, she felt that her comments were justified. She saw her behavior as a reasonable way for a parent to act. But in Gina's world, her mother's corrections and reminders hurt her. The words stung. Gina felt put down and small. She thought that no matter how hard she tried, her mother would never be pleased.

We had talked about all this before. Gina's mother said she wanted Gina to trust her, and she would listen and respect Gina's feelings. She wanted Gina to try again too. She wanted Gina to see that she was not trying to hurt her. But it was hard for Gina to open the door. We needed some Edison-trait talk, some new mental pictures, to help rebuild mutual trust.

"Sentry," I called in a soft voice, cupping my hand like a mouth. "Sentry, you are right to be cautious about giants at the gates. There are some giants who eat little children. But this is a friendly giant, like the BFG.* Ask her some questions and see for yourself."

"Giant, why are you here?" Gina's cupped hand spoke in a stronger voice than before.

"I want to be your friend," her mother's cupped hand replied gently.

"How do I know what you're saying is true?"

"I give you my word."

"Sometimes," I interjected, "giants squash little things they don't mean to. It's because they are giants and may not notice teeny things."

Gina readily agreed. Her sentry had a list of tips for giants to watch where they step. The giant listened attentively and promised to be careful. The sentry let the giant through and Gina and her mom got a fresh start on their friendship.

A picture is worth a thousand words to anyone. It is worth a thousand volumes of words to an Edison-trait child. Pictures make words come alive for Edison-trait children. They respond to analogies, metaphors, and images because they think in those ways.

As adults, we are accustomed to speaking in literal terms, especially to discuss important matters. The more serious the problem, the less playful we are in our talk. We tend to think of imagination as a way to escape from our problems, not as a solution to them. This forms a sharp contrast with the outlook of an Edison-trait child, who uses mental pictures to give words their meaning. This child feels trapped and overpowered when adults speak too directly.

In my practice, I often see examples of this in family therapy, especially in the initial sessions. When parents first come in, they have a no-nonsense approach to solving family problems. They expect their children to face the issues as seriously as they do.

* The BFG is the Big, Friendly Giant in a popular children's book by Roald Dahl.

If their child acts silly or withdraws in silence, the parent usually feels hurt or angry, assuming the child's behavior means she does not care. In most cases, this is untrue. The child cares very much. She needs some mental pictures to attract her mind's eye, and draw her into the communication.

John checked the clock, making sure we all noticed.

"John, I want you to pay attention to what Dr. Palladino is saying."

John shot a stony glare at his father, then looked back at the clock.

"You want us to know that you don't want to be here," I said to John.

"I don't care," John mumbled.

"You see what I mean? We care, but he doesn't." John's father spoke sternly.

"John, you mean that you don't care about being here or not?" I asked.

"I don't care," John repeated.

"I think you care about your family, but you feel like a prisoner here," I ventured. As I spoke, John's tension eased a little bit.

"It probably feels like you're in prison lots of the time, not just here." I paused. John was listening. It was a start.

John and his parents continued in family therapy. Several sessions later we faced another common problem that parents have with their Edison-trait children. Edison-trait children often act without realizing how much they hurt others. Thoughtless acts are a natural expression of their spontaneity. They get caught up in the moment. When this happens, if you try to say that your feelings are hurt, your Edison-trait child is apt to get defensive. Reason with her and she counters your every argument.

But something different can happen if you use mental pictures to say how you feel. The right image or analogy can end a stalemate or avoid a fight.

John sat staring across the room, steaming. "Yeah, okay, so I said, 'Shut up.' So what? I said I was sorry. What's the big deal?"

I looked over at John's parents and asked, "Are your feelings still hurt?" They nodded. I went on. "You've said that it hurts when John says, 'Shut up.' Describe the hurt. Is it like a slap, or a bruise, or a paper cut?"

John's father looked thoughtful. "It's like a slap, but it's a slap in the face. There's the sting of the slap, but there's the insult, too. It's hard to forget."

John's mother said, "For me, it's like a knife cut on my finger. It bleeds and I feel sad."

We all fell quiet for a while. John stared out the window. It was the end of the session and we said our good-byes.

In subsequent sessions, we did not resume this dialogue. However, John stopped saying "Shut up" to his parents.

Mental pictures work outside the walls of the therapy office, too. At one of the schools where I consult, an Edison-trait fourth-grader was getting a reputation for creating scenes on the playground. She domineered and belittled others, making herself an outcast. Adults talked with her to no avail, trying to explain the reason she was becoming disliked. The girl continued to blame others for her growing unpopularity.

One day, the girl just stopped her bullying. Her teacher commended her and took a moment to ask her why she had changed.

The fourth-grader looked at the teacher. Then she looked at her own hand, which she held up, finger pointed in an accusing manner. "You see this?" she asked. "When you point your finger at someone else, there's three fingers pointing back at you. Gerry's sister told me that. And it's true." A mental picture had gotten through to her when nothing else had.

THE ART OF METAPHORIC LANGUAGE

A metaphor is a figure of speech or an idea told as a story. Edison-trait children think primarily in patterns and images. So metaphoric language is truer to their mode of thinking than literal, factual talk. Metaphoric language includes the use of idioms, analogies, metaphors, myths, allegories, aphorisms, parables, fables, and anecdotes. It is rich in symbolism and persuasive power.

Experts in hypnosis phrase hypnotic suggestion in the form of metaphor. They recommend that when you are deeply relaxed or in a trance, you imagine metaphors for achieving your goals. For example, if you are learning to use trance as an anesthetic, you might imagine that your hand is immersed in ice water until your fingertips actually start to feel numb. The use of metaphor is particularly effective when you are in a state in which you have increased access to your subconscious mind. (Some say the concept of a "subconscious" mind itself may be a metaphor for right-brain functioning.)

Metaphor and imagery are used extensively in sports psychology to help athletes enhance their performance. A gymnast might see herself as a gazelle, or a runner might imagine herself as a cougar.

Metaphoric language is a primordial form of human verbal expression. Some of our earliest known writings, like biblical parables, are examples of metaphor. Some philosophers and writers have argued that metaphoric language represents an *original* form of human thought. They say it "harkens to our genes."[8] It is also a possibility that metaphoric language (as in the fifth-grade idiom project decribed above) harkens to our corpus callosum, which is the connection between the left and right brain. In response to metaphoric suggestion, our left- and right-brain hemispheres communicate and function as one. This is known as a whole-brain response. Elite athletes and star performers call it "being in the zone."[9]

Metaphoric language is the divergent thinker's preferred mode of communication. This sometimes distresses the convergent thinkers around her. They prefer direct and literal meanings. They may regard metaphoric language as pointless or dishonest, or even consider an Edison-trait child as a chronic liar because of it.

"You wish I was Benjamin. You always have." Charles was referring to his cousin Benjamin. Charles and his mother were having it out during a family therapy session. As they faced this core issue in their relationship, feelings intensified between them.

"Charles, how can you say that? Name one time, just one time, that I have compared you and Benjamin." Charles's mother, an extremely logical woman, glared at her teenage Edison-trait son.

"Come on, Mom. It's there all the time. Benjamin got a scholarship. Benjamin won an award. Benjamin writes so well. Tough luck. He's your sister's kid, not yours."

"Name one instance, just one instance, Charles. When did I ever say I prefer Benjamin to you?"

Charles could hardly speak. He was paralyzed with pain and anger. He felt that what he was saying was important emotionally. To him, his mother's logical arguments said she didn't want to listen. He felt rejected and resentful.

Charles's mother felt pain and anger too. She felt unjustly accused by her own son, and confused and agitated by his relentless insistence on an illogical argument.

"Just for a moment," I suggested to them both, "let's agree to use Benjamin as a symbol. Let's say he stands for outstanding achievement in school, for winning trophies, for high status. Let's say he stands for someone who is recognized for what he has done."

Fortunately, both Charles and his mother were amenable to this proposal. They accepted the image of Benjamin as symbolic and communication began to flow. It didn't matter whether or not Charles's mother had ever actually compared him to Benjamin, Charles was attuned not to her logic, but to his fear of inadequacy in the face of an achiever like his cousin. After some further dialogue, they arrived at a place where Charles's mother could sense her son's vulnerability and need for acknowledgment.

"Charles, I'm glad you are my son. I want you as my son. I love you for who you are."

Charles looked at his mother in an entirely different way after that. He finally got what he needed—to hear unambiguous words of acceptance from her. The situation relaxed considerably, and Charles was able to see what his mother had been trying to say, too.

This convergent-thinking mother did indeed have a valid point. To get along well in the world, her son has to know how to use his left brain and see another person's point of view. He needs to be able to check that his feelings are justified and appropriate to the reality of his situation.

But timing can be everything. With feelings so raw, this mother made a good decision. By accepting the use of his metaphor, she could hear his cry for help. By identifying his need, she could satisfy it.

CREATING NEW SCENARIOS

"I know all the doors and the windows are locked. I still feel scared. And I don't want to be alone."

Lauren has come to see me because her bedtime fears have gotten out of hand. As is true of many Edison-trait children, Lauren lets her imagination get the best of her at bedtime. Her parents try to reason with her almost every night. Some nights, however, she feels terrified and refuses to sleep in her room by herself.

"Show me where you sleep now," I ask. We have rearranged some of the office furniture to resemble Lauren's bedroom. We are on the floor playacting bedtime. Lauren is curled up in the far corner.

"And this is where your window is, where you're afraid someone will break in?" I ask. Lauren nods despondently.

"Lauren, what would it take for you to feel protected right now?"

"You're here right now, so I'm not afraid."

"I see. So when someone else is here, it helps you feel safe. Where do you want me to be, so you feel the safest?"

"Right behind me. Over here. So they can see you from the window."

"Okay. This is great. . . . Lauren, remember how you told me you loved The Wizard of Oz?"

"Uh-huh."

"And we sang the song about the rainbow?"

"Uh-huh. And the Munchkins?"

"Yes. Well, do you remember Glinda?"

"The good witch. She was beautiful."

"I feel like Glinda. Do you feel like Dorothy?"

Lauren laughed and nodded yes.

"Can you imagine Glinda standing right where I am, right now?"

"Uh-huh."

"Let's draw a picture of you and her in your bedroom. You're over here and Glinda is over your shoulder."

"Right over here. She was all white. And she had a crown and a wand."

Lauren is an extremely bright child. She is fully capable of understanding that her fear of a nighttime intruder is a metaphor for her fear of frightening, intrusive thoughts that show up at her window of consciousness when she is alone, in the dark. Being an Edison-trait child, she feels vulnerable to graphic, unwanted images that are difficult for her to manage. She and I will talk about this another time, but not now.

This is not a left-brain moment. It belongs to Lauren's right brain. As Lauren develops an effective metaphor that gives her the courage to face her own fear, she develops the skill that she was meant to get from working through this problem. In other words, she creates the solution that works the best *for her.* Later on, feeling safer, she can also see the convergent thinker's path to the same place: left-brain checking. Reminding herself that the windows are locked, that the house is secure, etc. *is* a useful skill. And Lauren will learn how to apply this mode of thought, too, all in good time. But tonight she needs a mental picture that's brighter, clearer, and stronger than the dark images of her unwelcome imagined intruders. Tonight she needs Glinda, the good metaphor.

EDISON-TRAIT CHILDREN ENJOY PLAYFULNESS AND A SENSE OF HUMOR

Research supports the notion that joy and play enhance creativity. In one study, people who "felt good" after seeing a humorous movie solved problems more creatively.[10] In another, people who saw problems as games came up with more creative solutions than those who considered the same problems to be work.[11]

Edison-trait children enjoy novelty, make-believe, and a good laugh. It's a vital part of their natural bent toward creativity. Often the best way to get through to them is with humor.

Many times, when a parent brings a child to see me for a first visit, that child is stone silent. Sometimes the child feels punished by having had to come, so she is furious or resentful. If this is the case, the child's bad feelings must be addressed first. But more often than not, the child is just trying to stay safe. And usually the best way to break the ice is with humor.

A session might start off with the child ignoring anything that is said to her. In a playful way, I might walk over to the child as if I'm about to look in her ear.

"Hmmm. May I take a look? Well, I see what's going on. Look at all this stuff in here. I see a bicycle and a television and a computer, a puppy, a helicopter, and an entire set of the *Encyclopaedia Britannica*."

Usually the sillier the better. And the sooner the child participates, the better, too.

"Want to take a look and tell me what you see?" I'll ask right away, turning my head so the child can easily "peer in" through my ear.

"Jelly beans."

"Words."

"The stuff you dreamed about last night."

These are just a few of the things Edison-trait children have seen in my ear. We go on from there.

Young children can tell us things in play that they might not otherwise know how to say. For example, a four-year-old Dreamer looked into her mother's ear and said: "There's nothing in here but clocks. Hurry up. Hurry up. Hurry up."

Playfulness and the world of pretend are keys to communicating with children. Sometimes, in family therapy sessions, it is easier for the child to talk to someone else "on the phone."

In my office, I use a variation of the basic tin-can-on-a-string phone system. A seven-year-old Discoverer helped me invent it. I issue a paper cup to each family member. I have one too. These are cordless phones. (I am very modern.)

The person making the call dials her cup and identifies the person she is calling. She "rings" until she gets an answer. The person talking speaks into her cup, while the person listening holds her cup up to her ear.

Using the phone system reduces interruptions. Also, it promotes attentiveness and listening skills. It is nonthreatening, so it makes it easier for a child or parent to do things like deliver an apology if one is due. It lends itself to spontaneity. And it usually leads to some laughs, which is good.

Edison-trait children are on a constant quest for novelty. The phone system holds interest for about one to three sessions. Then it's time for beanbag catch (where only the person with the beanbag can talk) or draw-and-tell (in crayons, markers, or colored pencils). The ideas that work best, of course, are the ones that the children themselves come up with.

Once the tone is set for play that is lighthearted and fair, much can be accomplished. Playacting and role reversal can be fun and revealing. But the playing field must remain on level ground. If your child senses that you are trying to trick him, or lead him somewhere without his permission, these strategies will not work at all. The goal is to join your child honestly in the land of imagination, in the open field of possibilities.

EDISON-TRAIT CHILDREN DISCOVER THROUGH DIALOGUE

Edison-trait children are fiercely independent. They do not like being told what to do. They want to think and act for themselves.

They like to experiment, explore, and discover. They talk better than they listen. And they come up with ideas that are fresh and revealing.

The Socratic Method

The Greek philosopher Socrates taught by asking questions. Socrates lived in the fifth century B.C. and his teachings were recorded by his student Plato. According to Plato, Socrates engaged in dialogue with his students; in the course of a dialogue, a subtle understanding of the topic emerged. The teacher did not pose a question with one specific, "correct" answer in mind. Rather, teacher and pupil conducted a genuine exchange of ideas with the next question and answer building on what came before. It was a true process of discovery. Neither Socrates nor his student understood the topic at hand as fully before the dialogue as they did after it.

Socratic dialogue is an especially effective method for understanding and redirecting the divergent-thinking child who is caught up in a fiction. Your goal is to listen and learn as you go along, not wring a canned answer or confession from your child. If you confront an Edison-trait child with a lie, she will deny and defend herself to the end. But if you engage her in an honest inquiry about the matter, she is far more likely to allow the truth to come to light.

Jason, an eight-year-old Edison-trait Dynamo, was "losing" his homework assignments several times a week. This is common behavior for an Edison-trait child and Jason had worked on this problem before. But this time things were more serious. Jason was building a wall around himself.

At school he was being made to stay in at recess to make up the work he didn't hand in. This did not help him at all to remember his homework. Every week he had a new story about why he didn't know what the assignment was.

One day his father decided to reverse course with him and try a Socratic dialogue. Instead of scolding him, he stayed calm and asked quietly, "Jason, you're a smart kid. I believe there is a reason why you bring home some homework assignments but not others. We just don't know what it is yet. What do you suppose is different about the assignments you remember and the ones you forget?"

Jason said that he did not know. His father remained unperturbed. He did not get exasperated or lose his temper. He just seemed puzzled and wanted to know more about it. He asked questions gently and gave Jason some space.

Eventually Jason admitted that he knew that on some nights there was something about his homework that he didn't want to do. With that information, Jason and his dad figured out that Jason "forgot" his homework when he had word problems in math to do. Jason didn't "get" them, so he reflexively avoided them. With that knowledge, the "forgotten assignment" problem became much more solvable.

A CHARIOT DRAWN BY SIX WILD HORSES

A highly successful entrepreneur once told me of a metaphor that he has found, and continues to find, useful in his life. It is vivid, playful, and invites a person to take responsibility for himself. "Having the Edison trait," he said, "is like having a chariot led by six wild horses. Each one pulls in a different direction. You feel an upsurge of power, force, and urgency. There's an irresistible quality. But the horses go everywhere at once, so the chariot and you go nowhere.

"Occasionally the horses align themselves. You get a taste of high speed and intense focus. You get to feel what it's like on that galloping chariot ride. Once this happens, you make it your life's work to figure out how to align those horses, and drive that chariot where you want it to go."

Thoughtfully, he added, "What if, instead of trying to force these kids to do their work, you could somehow get them to look on it as the task of getting all their horses lined up in the same direction at the same time?"

The metaphor sounded like a good fit to me the first time I heard it. Once I started to use it in my practice, my Edison-trait clients taught me more about it. By the way, Discoverers and Dynamos have wild horses; Dreamers have restless unicorns and winged horses. One of my clients doesn't relate to the chariot as a metaphor, but has a leopard in whose presence she feels and trains her inner power and raw energy.

The essential aspect of the metaphor—horses or unicorns or leopards—is the feeling of empowerment. First and most important, every Edison-trait child *needs to experience success.* She needs to feel the sense of command that comes with driving the chariot. Every Edison-trait child has a personal interest—a passion—that she can get totally absorbed in. When she pursues this self-fulfilling passion, she is most likely to encounter her first real success.

But even then, the Edison-trait child may feel that her success—staying focused and getting things done—is something that happened on its own. She does not yet know what she did to harness her own energy, so she does not yet realize that she can "will it" to happen. To use the metaphor of the well-lit room, the Edison-trait child does not know how to turn on the light switch, so she does not realize that lighting the room is up to her.

So what the Edison-trait child needs next is to believe in herself. She needs to accept the fact that she can command her horses, even when it is hard for her to do so. The power lies in her. But if she is engaged in battles with convergent-thinking parents and teachers, she is not free to discover this power within herself.

Finally, the Edison-trait child needs permission and encouragement to explore and experiment with her own Edison-trait ways. The convergent-thinking adult wants this child to line up each horse, one by one. The child knows that by the time she has lined up the sixth horse, the first one is off again, bound for meadows or sky. The divergent-thinking child needs to try out her own ways to command the power of her thought. She needs to develop skills like hyperfocusing and multitasking. As she does, she learns to *lead* her team of wild horses. And she no longer has to fear that without her knowing it, they will lead her everywhere and nowhere at the same time.

In "The Ransom of Red Chief," O. Henry writes about a ten-year-old nineteenth-century boy who sounds like an Edison-trait Dynamo. Sitting around the campfire at night, the boy talks excitedly, with the equivalent of about six wild horses' worth of unbridled mental energy.

> "I like this just fine. I never camped out before; but I had a pet 'possum once, and I was nine last birthday. I hate to go to school. Rats ate up sixteen of Jimmy Talbot's aunt's speckled hen's eggs. Are there any real Indians in these woods? I want some more gravy. Does the trees moving make the wind blow? We had five puppies. What makes your nose so red, Hank? My father has lots of money. Are the stars hot? I whipped Ed Walker twice, Saturday. I don't like girls. You dassent catch toads with a string. Do oxen make any noise? Why are oranges

round? Have you got beds to sleep on in this cave? Amos Murray has got six toes. A parrot can talk, but a monkey or fish can't. How many does it take to make twelve?"

What a chaotic surge of thought power! Now consider the following account of a focused Edison-trait adult, who has trained himself successfully to keep his wild horses at his command.

HYPERFOCUS: IN COMMAND OF THE SIX-HORSE TEAM

In researching the ideas for this book, I discovered that flying is a popular domain of Edison-trait people. Pilots like to command those "big horses." In the cockpit, they condition themselves to keep their ability to hyperfocus under their direct control. They train their mental steeds to stay in line, with the right heading. The more horsepower they feel, the stronger they hyperfocus in response. In moments of danger, their ability to hyperfocus magnifies. They are able to keep a steady flow of intense concentration. At the same time, they can multitask and keep track of many things at once.

These mental skills were at work in the thinking of an F-4 pilot on a mission he flew in Korea. Here is his description of what happened:

> It was a dark, cold, rainy morning with a low overcast that was near minimums, which meant it was about as bad a weather as they would allow us to take off and land in. I had a double malfunction. Both my BLC valve and my flaps failed. The procedure to correct the valve failure was to put the flaps down, but the flap failure prevented this. The valve failure meant hot air in the wings would melt the circuitry within 30 seconds. Shortly after that, the hydraulics would melt, then the structural components.
>
> I had people on the ground trying to talk to me, to figure out what was going on. There wasn't time for that. I had to focus. I knew what to pay attention to and what to filter out. I brought in all the important clues, and only the important clues. It happened fast, yet it flowed. It was all one continuous motion.

It started right after takeoff. I got an immediate hard roll of the aircraft. The plane tried to roll upside down. I corrected for this, and discovered the split-flap problem. I tried to put the flaps back down, and the BLC light came on. The airplane could be unflyable in a minute or two. I was flying through clouds and rain, but I knew there were villages below. I declared an emergency and asked for the most experienced ground controller to get on the line. The voice changed. I tried the flaps again. Nothing. A full pattern to land would take a long time, a tight one is hard to stabilize on final, and if you blow it, you have to take it around again. I asked for a very tight pattern and short final. The controller was good. I got my backseater ready to eject. I dumped fuel, got down to minimums, broke out, took it down, and just barely stopped on the runway.[12]

Compare this jet pilot to O. Henry's ten-year-old talking at the campfire with six horses' worth of mental energy, going in six directions at once. The pilot had the same force of mental energy, but using skills like hyperfocus and multitasking, he kept all his horses lined up and going in the same direction. This is the kind of mastery—of power, speed, and adventure—that your Edison-trait child has the potential to reach.

CHAPTER 3

〰

The Nature of Attention

Human beings have adapted amazingly, to the Himalayas, to
the desert, to the forest, to the seashore, to São Paulo, to
Prague. This extraordinary diversity is why our mind is so disorganized, so full of conflict, so diverse, and so difficult to analyze simply.

—Robert Ornstein,
The Evolution of Consciousness

DIVERGENT THINKING THEN AND NOW

On November 19, 1863, when Abraham Lincoln concluded the
Gettysburg Address, one of the most beloved speeches in the history
of the United States, he was greeted with total silence. ". . . and
government of the people, by the people, and for the people shall
not perish from the earth." Nothing.

Why? Because his audience was waiting for more. Edward
Everett, the orator who preceded Lincoln that day, had spoken for
two hours. In 1863, a two-minute speech (the total length of the
Gettysburg Address) was unheard of.[1]

I mentioned this fact to a school media specialist. She told me she
had once ordered a CD-ROM of famous speeches in American history. She thought it would be interesting to have some of her students read them out loud. But when she did, she admitted
sheepishly, even she couldn't keep her mind on these lengthy ora-
tions for very long. She would start to think of all the things she had
to do back at her desk instead.

What has happened to the nature of our attention since 1863? The
norms for divergent thinking appear to have changed over the course

of the last hundred years or so. The degree of divergent thinking in the general population has increased dramatically. Back in 1863, most people enjoyed two-hour speeches. Today, most people enjoy twelve-second channel surfing. What has accounted for this change?

Why Divergent Thinking Is Increasing

We all have some potential to think either convergently or divergently. When our culture places a premium on one kind over the other, people respond to what is being rewarded.

Back in 1863 (and before), there were fewer people on earth. They lived in a simpler, slower-paced world than the one we live in right now. The culture rewarded convergent thinking, the ability to listen and concentrate for long periods of time on a single subject, like on Edward Everett's speech.

Through the years, our population has increased and our level of technology has risen. Our culture—business, communications, entertainment—now places a premium on a faster, more global kind of thinking, namely divergent.

In today's complex, fast-paced society, we are changing the nature of our attention to meet the demands of our environment. To keep up with information as it grows and circulates rapidly, we, as a population, are becoming more divergent in our thinking.

The Divergent-Thinking Continuum

To help us see how we are changing the nature of our attention, we can picture a normal, bell-shaped curve to show the distribution of divergent thinking in the general population. Behavioral scientists use the normal curve to show the distribution of many characteristics in the population. It shows how individuals differ along a single dimension. The normal curve that represents IQ is an example. In this typical bell curve, there are a few individuals with very low measurements at one far end of the spectrum, a few individuals with very high measurements at the other end of the spectrum, and most of us, whose measurements fall somewhere between these two extremes, humped up in the middle of the curve.

As individuals, we all vary in how much or how little we are inclined to think divergently. Each person has a different propensity for it. Imagine giving each person a divergent-thinking "score," just as we might for IQ. This score marks the person's place on the curve. The least extreme divergent thinkers are on one end and the most extreme—those of Edison-trait magnitude—are on the other. Most people are on the "hill" in between. Their scores would be about average. They are the average norm.

This normal curve can represent the population of any time. Let's first consider how it would represent the population of 1863, when most people enjoyed listening to a two-hour oration. Perhaps those on the least divergent end hoped the speaker would go on for three hours, while those who were most divergent—the nineteenth-century Edisonians—wished for a concise one-hour talk.

Next, let's make the curve represent the population as we exist today. Most people today probably think the Gettysburg Address is about the right length for a speech—two minutes. Those on the least divergent end might be pleased to listen for about another ten minutes, while those who are most divergent—the Edisonians of today—will probably listen to a speech only if it is on the inset screen of a picture-in-picture TV, so they can watch the Discovery Channel at the same time.

The Divergent-Thinking Continuum over Time

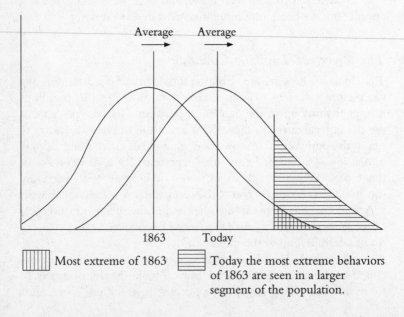

Average   Average

1863   Today

Most extreme of 1863   Today the most extreme behaviors of 1863 are seen in a larger segment of the population.

Everyone on the curve today is *more* divergent thinking than those on the 1863 curve. Our divergent-thinking "scores" are getting higher. The average norm for divergent thinking is changing. The entire curve is shifting to the right. Divergent thinking behaviors considered to be average today would have been thought of as extreme in 1863. Behaviors now considered extreme would have been considered extremely extreme.

My friend the media specialist summed it up nicely. She said, "If we—you and I—lived back in 1863, they would think something was wrong with us. We'd have ADD."

Why We See the Edison Trait in Our Children Today

If the "average scores" or norms for divergent thinking are changing through time, why haven't we noticed the gaps between generations before now? Why didn't our parents see us as noticeably more divergent thinking than they were? Why is the Edison trait, a primarily inherited predisposition, becoming more prevalent today?

The answer lies with the fact that divergent-thinking norms are not only changing, they are changing *at an accelerated rate,* not a steady one.

We are seeing a new form of the generation gap. Before today, there has never been such a contrast in the span of one lifetime. Before today, there has never before been a single gap so large, due to the rapid rate of change itself, between any two generations.

Think of it this way: When Abe Lincoln's family wanted to make soup, they started by asking young Abe to go out back and split some logs to start a fire. A few hours later, after they had picked, washed, and cut the vegetables, kindled the fire, and simmered the soup, they sat down to eat.

Over the course of the next several generations, things changed, but not that drastically. Abe, his children, his grandchildren, and his great-grandchildren all exercised about the same length of sustained attention to make soup. Sure, the wood-burning stove was an improvement over the open hearth, and the whole neighborhood showed up on the day the Lincolns of the 1920s got their first gas stove. But basically, these four generations of Lincolns began to cook dinner at least an hour before they knew they were going to feel hungry.

In contrast, let's now consider the generations of Lincolns alive today. The oldest living generation of Lincolns today were children in the 1920s. Like the generations who preceded them, they prepared and ate home-cooked meals all their lives. They grew up in a culture that, overall, rewarded patience, predictability, and the virtues of convergent thinking.

Today's middle generation or baby-boomer Lincolns were raised mostly on home-cooked meals, with occasional TV dinners. Later in life we learned to make soup by opening a can. Now we microwave water to make instant cup-of-soup. (Recently I ran out to a specialty store to get a new kind of microwave cup advertised to reduce by thirty seconds the time it takes to boil water.)

Today's youngest generation, our children, began life expecting instant soup. Our children—the Edison-trait generation—don't understand why our kitchens don't come equipped with food replicators, the way they do on board the USS *Enterprise*. Today, the size of the divergent-thinking gap between our oldest and our youngest generation is unprecedented.

Why is the pace of life accelerating? Our accelerated rate of change is a direct expression of our accelerated population growth. In biblical times, the population of the world was less than the population of the state of California is today. Neuropsychologist Robert Ornstein explains: "The pace of change is increasing: producing the first billion humans required about a million years; producing the most recent billion, fourteen years."[2] As the world population explodes, our stores of information increase exponentially. We do what we must to keep up.

Social scientist and author Alvin Toffler says we now live in a "blip" culture: ". . . the ninety-second news-clip intercut with the thirty-second commercial, a fragment of song and lyric, a headline, a cartoon, a collage, a newspaper item, a computer printout." Toffler points out that these "modular blips of information" come to us in "packages" that are "oddly shaped, transient, and disconnected." He describes today's sharp rise in divergent thinking this way: "Instead of merely receiving our mental model of reality, we are now compelled to invent and continually reinvent it."[3]

Psychiatrists and authors Edward Hallowell and John Ratey call our present-day culture "ADD-ogenic. . . . The fast pace. The sound bite. The quick cuts. The TV remote control clicker."[4] It is the culture of a generation that is making a radical departure, at an accelerated rate, from those that preceded us.

The gap between generations is now wider than it has ever been in history. It is so wide, it has become a gap of misunderstanding. Today we live with school policies and cultural expectations of "normal" that were set by our oldest generation and the convergent-thinking generations that preceded them. But it is our youngest generation—from across the widening gap—that goes to school and gets judged by these outmoded norms. That is why it appears that there are more and more children with the Edison trait. And that is why we need to revise our thinking about our children and the nature of their attention.

DIFFERENT TYPES OF ATTENTION

In 1863, Lincoln's listening audience was held spellbound by a two-hour oration. They specialized in convergent thinking because it was adaptive to their time and place to do so.

Let's transport that nineteenth-century audience to the display room of a late-twentieth-century electronics superstore. Do they have the kind of attention necessary to work the demo program on a personal computer? Picture them face-to-face with a giant wall of TV screens. While they are trying to sort out the chaos and keep whatever focus they can, the Edison-trait child standing next to them can effortlessly report on every program on every channel in the room.

The Edison-trait child multitasks easily, paying attention to more than one thing at a time. He is a specialist in divergent thinking, because that's what he needs to be adaptive to his time and place.

In *Growing Up Creative,* Teresa Amabila describes the following experiment in adaptation and survival: Take two clear glass jars, put ten live flies in one, and ten live bees in the other. Cap the jars, then lay the jars on their sides, with the jar bottoms facing a prominent source of light, like the sun. Remove the caps.

Return the next day, and you will find one empty jar and one jar of ten dead bees. The flies escape but the bees do not. Why?[5]

Instinctively, both flies and bees fly directly toward light. In their respective jars, both types of insects go for the light but fail, because their path is blocked by the clear glass bottom of the jar.

Now the bees will fly and refly the same path, until they perish. You might say they are well focused on their goal and the path they should take to get to it. The bees use a strategy that is akin to convergent thinking. They pay undivided attention to what they are supposed to do.

The flies, on the other hand, will fly and fail for a while. Then they will circle and explore. Eventually the flies will try the path that is directly opposite to the logical one they should take to reach their goal. They will live and be free. The flies use a divergent-thinking strategy. They pay attention to multiple stimuli—different directions, the air space, their survival, and the way out.

PHOTOGRAPHER'S ATTENTION

Behavioral pediatrician Dorothy Johnson, M.D., counsels young divergent thinkers by telling them the difference between photographer's attention and student's attention.[6]

To explain photographer's attention, she asks them to imagine that they are in Yosemite Valley. "If I give you a camera and ask you to take pictures, I know you'll take the most fascinating photos humanly possible," she says. "I know you see things most tourists do not. You'll probably get a picture of a treetop in the clouds, or of the spray off a waterfall, or maybe a pattern of textures on a cliff wall. You might catch a close-up of a wildflower, an unusual bird, or a curious chipmunk. Or you might capture a smile or a tear on the face of a baby or an old man." Edison-trait children like to hear her describe their own special talent—seeing and thinking the unusual.

"This is because you excel in photographer's attention," she explains. "But in school, you see, you need student's attention. Student's attention is where you stay on track, do what you're asked to, and make yourself think *only* of the next thing you're supposed to do.

"Student's attention will get you good grades," she advises. "Of course, if you use student's attention with your camera at Yosemite, you'll get a pretty dull set of pictures. 'Here we are at the first scenic view. And here we are at the second.' You know what I mean."

The Edison-trait child who is talked to in this way does not worry about having a "deficient" amount of attention. He understands that his divergent thinking, his talent for photographer's attention, is recognized and appreciated. He senses it will not be devalued in the process of his learning more about convergent thinking. This understanding makes it safe for him to learn student's attention.

A HUNTER IN A FARMER'S WORLD

Another metaphor that describes different types of attention has been proposed by author, entrepreneur, on-line systems operator, traveler, risk taker, and innovative thinker Thom Hartmann.[7] Hartmann refers to divergent thinkers as Hunters and to convergent thinkers as Farmers.

Hunters have qualities that are adaptive for hunting. Hunters . . .

- constantly monitor what they sense around them
- jump into the chase at a moment's notice
- make quick decisions about new headings and strategies
- hyperfocus and drive hard when in pursuit
- are independent, take risks, and crave excitement and adventure

Farmers, on the other hand, have complementary attributes, suitable to accomplishing farming goals. Farmers . . .

- keep focused on the work in front of them
- sustain steady, dependable effort
- stay organized and purposeful, and follow through on long-term plans
- pace themselves and exercise patience
- are cooperative, cautious, and security-minded

Hartmann notes that most schools are run by and for Farmers. Problems occur when Hunters are treated like substandard Farmers, instead of like Hunters capable of learning what they need to.

Hartmann also suggests that perhaps the Hunter/Farmer distinction is more than a metaphor. These personality types are genetically based.[8] And there appears to be a correlation between the prevalence of these types and the predominance of agriculture in a given society.[9]

Hartmann proposes that today's Hunter and Farmer types might actually be true descendants of ancestral hunters and farmers. In other words, our individual preferences for different kinds of attention may have their roots in our basic survival instincts.

DISCOVERERS AND DYNAMOS AS HUNTERS

"When he was five years old, we lived on a ranch in Colorado." Tommy's mother has known for some time that her son is an Edison-trait child. "Some bears had been bothering our horses. Tommy knew what was going on. The grown-ups had been talking about it every night. The other children were scared.

"So Tommy turns up missing. He's gone for two hours. And so is one of the dogs. I had begun to organize a search.

"Then we get a call from a neighbor at a ranch almost three miles away. Tommy's there with the dog, a stick, and a glass jar. 'Poaching bear' is what he told the neighbor.

"The stick was for defending himself. The jar was for knocking the bear out. Tommy remembered that a bear can be stunned by hard impact directly on the nose. He once heard that's how come electric fences work, because the bear hits it first with its nose. He was going to take aim and throw that jar right at the bear's nose. Amazing how he can't remember simple things he's been asked to do, but he remembers how to stun a bear.

"Is Tommy a 'hunter'? Yeah, I'd say so."

Both Discoverers and Dynamos are Edison-trait children who exhibit Hunter qualities. They explore. They are independent. They seek stimulation. They move quickly and decisively on what they want. And they take risks.

If they see a rabbit they like go by, they are likely to jump into action. They don't want to hear about, discuss, or study rabbits. They want to see them, chase them, and catch them.

DREAMERS AS GATHERERS

"If Candice put one tenth the effort into her schoolwork that she puts into remembering who played what role in what movie, she'd be a straight 'A' student. She recognizes a face, even if it's on the screen for two seconds. She is a walking catalogue of Hollywood stars and films. She can also tell you her favorite scenes from the movies. She'll remember the darndest things about them. If it didn't make me so mad, I'd really admire her."

Although Edison-trait Dreamers are explorers, they don't quite fit the profile of the Hunter. They do not have quick-to-accelerate and given-to-the-chase Hunter qualities. While they seek new places and new experiences, they do so at their own self-styled pace. They are wanderers set on their own inner course.

Edison-trait Dreamers do have the qualities of ancestral food gatherers. For example, they follow their instincts, act on their own, and go after just what they want. They are highly visual and responsive to myriad sights around them. They like to collect things, especially objects of nature, and they seem to be pulled toward certain themes that they like and remember.

CAREER PATHS FOR DIVERGENT THINKERS

Interestingly, Edison-trait adults almost all say that their school years were far more demoralizing and failure-prone than life *after* they entered the workforce. This makes sense when you think about it. Your child's world, the world of school, strongly favors the Farmer mentality. But in the workplace, as Thom Hartmann noted in a *Time* magazine interview, Hunters "can be found in large numbers among entrepreneurs, police detectives, emergency-room personnel, race-car drivers and, of course, those who stalk the high-stakes jungle known as Wall Street."[10]

Today, when your child struggles with the demands of school, it may be hard for you to picture him as a mature, responsible, productive adult. Yet when Edison-trait children grow up, many can and do attain enormous success. Those who learn how to capitalize on their strengths and compensate for their weaknesses tend to gravitate toward work for which they are well suited and, in many cases, very well paid. Here are some examples:

THE VISIONARY DREAMER

Edison-trait Dreamers make good designers of just about anything, providing that something has truly captured their interest. They may be found designing parks, houses, office space, cars, clothing, jewelry, art exhibits, stage sets, special effects, costumes, store displays, media ads, music videos, dance routines, and gala events.

Liberated from burdensome measurements and calculations now performed by personal computers, Dreamers can easily create physical representations of their ideas, like scale models and prototypes. With desktop publishing, they can print reports and brochures. This makes it possible for Dreamers to communicate their visions and sell their concepts and products to others.

Those with good spatial abilities make gifted architects. Those with a knack for composition and color flourish as painters, photographers, and graphic artists. Almost every facet of the entertainment industry favors the creative edge of the Edison-trait Dreamer. Today's Edison-trait writers can let their creative juices flow, then easily correct and edit later, because of word processors that have features like spell-check.

The fashion industry is a haven for Dreamers. One Sunday, the "Style" section of *The New York Times Magazine* ran an article entitled "The Restless Ones."[11] It was a humorous slice-of-life piece on how the industry attracts those with ADD. The article said, "The traits that make it so hard for people with ADD to get on in the world are the very traits that make people get ahead in the world of fashion." It went on: "Intolerance of boredom, frequent search for high stimulation, impatience, mood swings, impulsive behavior. . . . Where else but in an industry that seizes on the hippie look one minute and moves on to diamond bracelets and drop-dead glamour the next can a person make a virtue of a short attention span?"

Well, actually, the answer is: in quite a few industries. And the reference to a "short attention span" is actually a misnomer for the ability to shift focus rapidly. Nonetheless, the point is well taken.

Fashion, a multi-billion-dollar industry, is a province of Edison-trait imagination and divergence. Although the article may have been written tongue in cheek, it points to a prevailing truth. In any industry, those who ride the crest of the wave have the best view. They can see ahead to create new markets, which in turn means profit and growth.

THE ENTREPRENEURIAL DISCOVERER

Edison-trait Discoverers are usually good at starting and building their own businesses. They are natural-born entrepreneurs. They have a knack for finding a niche in the market and filling it. They have panache. They make persuasive salespeople, deal makers, and agents.

I counsel a twelve-year-old Discoverer who comes to see me, as he tells it, "so I can help my family adjust." He attends a small private school, where he owns and publishes a classroom newspaper, which he sells for a profit. When his teacher found out what was going on, she scheduled a conference with him to discuss the matter. The next time we met after the conference, I asked him how things went with his teacher.

"No problem," he replied. "We hired her."

Thom Hartmann profiles the skills and accomplishments of numerous entrepreneurs who are classic Hunters.[12] He also cites a reference by psychologist Edna Copeland, Ph.D., who studied a sample of entrepreneurs and found that they had Hunter qualities.[13]

Edison-trait Discoverers have a penchant for invention and innovation. Some have a natural aptitude for and attraction to computers and other tools of high technology. They design hardware and software, multimedia presentations, video games, and Internet home pages. They spawn novelty. They create new markets. They thrive in a field that is advancing at an astronomical rate.

Thomas Edison himself was a determined entrepreneur and a pioneer industrialist. Because of his phenomenal success as an inventor and scientist, most people overlook this. Edison helped to launch the General Electric Company, which was originally named the "Edison General Electric Company." He also began numerous electric utility companies. Many of them, like Consolidated Edison in New York City and Southern California Edison in Los Angeles, still bear his name today.[14]

THE RISK-TAKING DYNAMO

Edison-trait Dynamos react swiftly and decisively in the face of risk or adversity. They make good fighter pilots, foreign news correspondents, and emergency medical personnel. They become elite athletes and record-breaking competitors.

Like Discoverers, they excel as entrepreneurs. They are more aggressive than Discoverers and more willing to act without hesitation on the spur of the moment. Some make and lose fortunes several times over the course of a lifetime. Many have already begun their own businesses by the time they graduate from high school. They are the movers and the shakers. The higher the stakes, the greater their motivation.

Dynamos are the most enterprising and bold Hunters on Wall Street. They are the pirates of industry. They buy and sell commodities, futures, and nouveau high-risk ventures.

In his best-selling exposé, *Liar's Poker,* author and bonds broker Michael Lewis describes the frenetic action of Edison-trait Dynamos on the trading floor of the New York Stock Exchange. "Most of the men were on two phones at once. Thirty seconds was considered a long attention span."

According to Lewis, the entire culture of Salomon Brothers, the brokerage firm where he was initiated, was one that rewarded daring, even ruthless, behavior. Some people had the temperament for it and some did not. Those who succeeded had a taste for it right from the start. They had a predatory nature. Lewis said, "It was in their blood." Alexander, a pseudonym for Lewis's mentor at Salomon Brothers, made his first killing in the stock market when he was in the seventh grade.

Michael Lewis himself has the résumé of a Dynamo. An art major at Princeton, Lewis's life experiences include writing books and skydiving. He describes himself as someone who tends "to move too fast for the organizations I join." He was known as a bond salesman who cut "multi-million-dollar deals in the blink of a computer screen."[15]

WHO WILL YOUR CHILD BECOME?

I include these glimpses of a promising tomorrow to reassure you as a parent today. There are many bright futures open to your Edison-trait child. The profiles I sketched here are only a few of them.

As his parent, you know your child—his strengths and his weaknesses. As you learn more about his Edison-trait nature, you can guide him to become his best self.

PART II

※

Eight Steps to Help Your Edison-Trait Child

Part II takes you through a step-by-step course to reach and teach your Edison-trait child. The eight steps are:

Step One: Believe In Your Child
Step Two: Watch What You Say
Step Three: Build a Parent-and-Child Team
Step Four: Encourage Your Child's Interests
Step Five: Teach Your Child Self-control
Step Six: Coach Your Child to Learn How to Achieve
Step Seven: Take Care of Yourself
Step Eight: Take Care of Your Family

CHAPTER 4

Step One: Believe In Your Child

If there is anything we wish to change in the child, we should first examine it and see whether it is not something that could better be changed in ourselves.

—Carl Jung

STAY CONNECTED TO YOUR POWER AS A PARENT

The *Los Angeles Times* once printed this anecdote sent in by a woman who overheard her grandsons getting ready to play:

> "Let's play Power Rangers," five-year-old Grady said. "I'll be Jason because he's the boss."
> Two-year-old Corey thought for a moment. "Then I'll be Jason's mommy."[1]

As a parent you form a powerful image in your child's life. Sometimes it feels as though just the opposite is true. You talk to your child but nothing seems to get through.

When you are not listened to, you feel unimportant. You wish that you would matter to your child as much as his favorite video game or TV show.

The truth is that you matter a great deal to your child. See yourself through his eyes. He depends on you to meet his needs. You can survive alone in the world. He cannot.

If your Edison-trait child disregards you, it is *not* because you are unimportant. It's because what you are saying lacks personal meaning for him. You want him to write neatly. He could care less about penmanship. You look at his room and see chaos. He looks and sees a functional relay station to drop off and pick up stuff.

It is wrong for your child to ignore you, and in the steps to come, you will learn ways to deal with this problem. For now, however, practice just this much: When your child disregards the things you say, do not take it personally. Your child does see you as an important and powerful figure.

In fact, you and your child probably get into power struggles precisely because you are important to him. When your child "pushes your buttons" emotionally, he's like a two-year-old fascinated with a light switch. He is exploring and exercising power, and *you* are the power he's playing with. He is attracted to the firepower of your anger. Unaware of what he is doing, he looks to see what your response will be.

"Dad, Sara is such a dweeb. She wears those dorky pigtails," Nick informed his dad.

Nick's comment caught his father off guard. He turned to his son and said, "Nick, why are you teasing Sara? She's not even here."

Bob, Nick's older brother, answered for him. "That's easy, Dad. Because it always makes you so crazy."

NEUTRALIZE YOUR THOUGHTS

Your Edison-trait child is strong-willed and imaginative. In addition to being attracted to power, he is likely at times to do things that seem manipulative and deceitful. He wants to get his way, and he'll try almost any maneuver. He bends the truth in his direction. To him it's just a blurring of the line between what is real and what is imagined.

Be alert to ascribing ulterior motives to your child. He is not out to get you. He does not want to hurt you (except, perhaps, if he feels you hurt him).

"Brett, you promised me. You said if I trusted you to take the phone in your room, you would not make prank calls."

"Mom, it didn't start out as a prank call. It was a call that forgot what it was doing."

Yes, Brett is impulsive in his quest for stimulation and power. No, it's unlikely he planned to disobey. Edison-trait children are not given to premeditation.

"Brett, why did you go to Frank's? Your homework isn't finished yet."
"But Mom, you said I could go."
"I said you could go if you finished your homework."
"But I am going to finish my homework."
"Come on, Brett. I meant after you finished your homework."

Yes, he'll go as far as he can. No, it's not to aggravate you. It's only to get what he wants.

"Brett, I spoke with Ms. Carter this morning and she told me that you and Frank were the only ones to get detention for what happened on the playground yesterday. Didn't you tell me that all the boys in the class were involved?"
"They were. Only it was just me and Frank that got caught."

Yes, he chooses his own version of the truth. No, it's not because he wants a lie to come between you. To him, it is a means to an end. He anticipates criticism or punishment if you know the truth. So he creates a fiction to protect himself.

When you feel provoked by your child's responses, try not to take it personally. Stay as calm and neutral as you can. Before you summarily judge him guilty of lying, try to see things fairly through the eyes of your child.

Here is an exercise to help restore your faith. Take a deep breath, close your eyes, and relax. Now cradle your arms as you did when you held your child as a baby. Think back on what it felt like to hold your infant child. Pretend you are holding him right now. Let his innocence touch you and help you remember. That innocence still lives inside your child today. Look for it now. It's there. You'll see.

EXPECT THE BEST

In sports psychology, the concept of the self-fulfilling prophecy is well accepted. The way an event turns out, positive or negative, is directly influenced by whether the athlete's expectations and abilities are positive or negative. Here's how:

Expectation

		+	−
Ability	+	+	−
	−	−	−

Notice that only one of the four possible outcomes is positive. To get a positive outcome, you need both positive expectation *and* positive ability. Notice also that positive ability can be canceled out by negative expectation. In other words, if an athlete has the ability to do something but does not *believe* it is possible for him to do it, he doesn't succeed.

In the same way, your expectation influences your child's progress. If you expect the best, you'll help your child achieve the best he can.

One night, at a parents' support meeting, one mother stood up and related this story:

Learning to read was a nightmare for Sean. He just couldn't work out the phonics. He wouldn't read his schoolbooks. It was a losing battle.

Then we found out about books on tape. It was a blessing. We could get all his textbooks on audio. So we did. Things went smoothly from there. We felt an enormous relief.

Then, when Sean was in the third grade, I started to wonder if we were doing the right thing. People said, "Leave well enough alone," and "If it ain't broke, don't fix it." But I had to find out for myself. So, I tried.

Every night was torture. It was horrible. For a long time, one of us ended up crying. We fought and screamed. Some nights I wondered if the neighbors were going to call the cops. I longed for how easy it used to be.

Well, things got better and by the fourth grade, Sean could read his schoolbooks by himself. Was it worth it? Yes. For me it was.

Sean's mother made a conscious decision to expect Sean to learn how to read. She disrupted the comfort of her fatalistic attitude and took on adversity and risk.

Like Sean's mother, you too can decide to expect success. In doing so, be realistic, yet positive. Of course, there will be obstacles, setbacks, and struggles. But keep your mind on future possibilities, not past defeats. When you expect the best, you risk more, yet you gain more too.

STAY CENTERED ON YOUR CHILD'S STRENGTHS

Mental Exercise 1

Think of three things you like about your child. Now write them down on a piece of paper. For example:

1. Full of energy
2. Bounces right back
3. Takes matters into his own hands

Go ahead. Think of three specific qualities in your child that especially appeal to you. Write them on a piece of paper and keep this paper in your wallet or calendar book. Glance at it often. Take it out when you catch yourself feeling discouraged or frustrated.

Mental Exercise 2

What is your child's name? Think of one positive quality about your child that starts with the same letter as her name. For example:

Mary—musical
or
John—joyful
or
Chris—creative

Your turn:

_____   _____
      your child's name   *a positive quality*

Now repeat this over and over again to yourself all the rest of today. It's your mantra. Close your eyes and see your child's smile as you say it.

Mental Exercise 3

Think of something your child did that you feel proud of. Write it down or draw a quick sketch of your child doing it. (Stick figures are allowed.) For example:

Mother's Day morning, when she made me breakfast in bed.

Now think back and write or draw a scene from your memory:

Take a moment to close your eyes and visualize your child doing this good deed. Give yourself permission to see him as capable.

Be proactive in keeping the right mind-set. The next time you start to see your child as a villain or a victim, use your awareness as a cue to change your way of thinking. Do one of the mental exercises you just practiced. Think up new words and images. Or take out the papers you just wrote on, and reread them again . . . and again, as needed.

FIND CAUSES THAT LEAD TO CHANGE, NOT BLAME

Psychologists have demonstrated that the way you explain the cause of an event affects the odds of its recurrence. This is called attribution theory. A single event has many contributing causes. We choose the causes we want to acknowledge, usually out of habit.

Kirk's mother heard a plop and a splash. She looked up to see Kirk staring as milk flooded over the counter and onto the floor.

"Kirk, you are so careless. You do that every time you lift a full container of milk to pour. You never learn."

Kirk's mother has chosen to explain Kirk's behavior in a way that makes it more probable that it will happen again. She is creating negative expectation in herself and her son.

What if Kirk's mother said instead, "Wow, Kirk. What a mess! It's hard to handle the milk container when it's full. It's got a different feel to it. But I guess you figured that out. And now you'll know it for the next time."

This response does not create blame or pessimism. It attributes what happened to something Kirk *did,* not to a weakness or flaw in his character. This time, Kirk's mom stays open to the fact that Kirk can learn, and creates positive expectation for the future.

In Step Five, you will learn more about holding your child accountable for the things he has done. Whatever cause you attribute his behavior to, he is still responsible to set things right. Attributions are not excuses. Your child still needs to correct his mistakes.

"Kirk, I like how you do things for yourself, like the way you got your own cereal and milk here. So, what's your plan for cleaning this mess up?"

Positive Attributions

When you correct your child, isolate the mistake to "this time only." Don't bring up past mistakes and burdensomely discourage your child. You want it to be easier, not harder, for your child to prevent it from happening again.

Here are some more examples. In each one, something has happened that can be interpreted in at least two ways:

A. Using an attribution that leads to recurrence
B. Using a healthier, more promising explanation that stops the spread of the problem and limits it to a present, correctable mistake

1. Your child missed a deadline for handing in a paper.
   A. He does this constantly. This is just like him.
   B. He was preoccupied at the time.

2. Your child lost his temper and hit a friend.
   A. He gets out of control so easily. His friends don't like him very much.
   B. He went over the line. Things must have been building up for him.
3. Your child said something that hurt your feelings.
   A. He always blurts things out without thinking about how others feel.
   B. He must have been under a lot of stress to have lashed out as he did.

Children's Attributions

Children usually learn their style of attribution from their parents. If you make attributions that lead to progress and growth, your child will learn to make healthy attributions, too.

The effectiveness of adopting an optimistic mind-set has been demonstrated repeatedly by psychologist Martin Seligman, Ph.D.[2] He has shown that when children believe their failings will last, they are at risk for depression, they develop fatigue, and they demonstrate less effort. Whereas when children believe that a failure is an isolated incident, they resume a high level of responding, which then increases their chances for success.

Your child's belief in himself begins with your belief in your child.

---*nv*---

Step Two: Watch What You Say

The notion of giving something a *name* is the vastest generative idea that was ever conceived.

—Susanne K. Langer

CHOOSE HEALTHY WORDS

Words evoke feelings, ideas, and images. Words are suggestive. Words increase the likelihood that one behavior will triumph over another.

In a recent study, eighty-five adolescents ages sixteen to nineteen were asked their feelings about the terms commonly used to describe students who have learning differences. The only acceptable word to them was "exceptional." They had clearly negative reactions to words like "impaired," "deficit," "disorder," and "disability."[1] Adults hear these words and think of them as diagnostic terms. Children hear them as insults.

Do not allow your child to feel stigmatized by the words adults use to describe her. Train yourself to choose only neutral or positive terms to describe your child's problems.

- *Is she "lazy" or "a mastermind at finding the easy way out"?*
- *Is she a "scatterbrain" or "a widely divergent thinker"?*
- *Is she "mean" or "single-minded about getting her own way"?*

Here are some more examples of choices to consider:

Defiant		strong-willed
Unyielding		determined
Slow	can be	thorough
Sloppy		overlooks the unimportant
Out of it		imaginative

When you name your child's behavior in a positive way, she is more likely to hear you. Feeling accepted and not put down, she is also more likely to try a new behavior you suggest.

THINK IN HEALTHY WORDS

Words structure our reality. The words we choose in the privacy of our own minds determine our trend of thought. As one Discoverer's mother told me during a counseling session: "I looked at him and thought, 'How can you do this to me, you selfish little brat?' Then it hit me. 'I sound just like my own mother.'

"So then I thought, 'Well, at least I'm not saying it out loud.' But what does that mean? I'm more of a hypocrite than she was?"

This mother realized that her thoughts have impact on her attitudes and actions toward her child. She resolved to give her son the benefit of the doubt, even in her mind, and even when she got mad.

Another mother told me this story:

The school district sponsored a meeting about children with attentional problems. It was supposed to be for parents only. The auditorium was full and we were discussing our children. The language was pretty one-sided, you know, people saying how their kids are stubborn, hostile, defiant.

I kind of knew we weren't being completely fair. But the truth is, it felt good to hear other parents talk about their kids. I felt like maybe I wasn't such a bad parent after all. Maybe it wasn't my fault, but his.

We started to watch a video about ADD. Then it happened. We got to a part in the video where the father was supposed to take his son on a camping trip with the Boy Scouts. The father said something like "Would you want to spend three days in a tent with him?" And the whole auditorium cracked up laughing—loud and long. I looked down the aisle where I was sitting. There was a little boy, I don't know, six or seven years old, I'd guess.

His eyes were glued to the screen and he had tears streaming down his cheeks.

Watch what you say at the most fundamental level—the things you let yourself think. Then your words and actions will flow with truth and ease.

PRACTICE THE 80/20 RULE

Let positive statements make up at least 80 percent of what you say to your child. Positive statements are acknowledgments of your child's views, efforts, and right actions. Let corrections and re-minders make up no more than 20 percent of your parent-to-child communications.

This is a challenging rule for parents. Edison-trait children are given to repeated mistakes and inefficiency. Their behaviors are likely to frustrate even the most patient of parents. *"Do you realize what time it is?"* . . . *"Didn't I just ask you to do that?"* . . . *"Stop in-terrupting me now!"* . . . *"I just finished telling you not to do that."*

You *can* change your habits of speech, but first you must listen carefully to yourself. Take a step back and detach yourself from your words. Make yourself hear what you say in the same way your child hears you. Record data as if you were an objective social scientist. Here's how:

Block out a ten-minute time period when you and your child are together. Have a paper and pencil on hand. Draw a line down the center of the paper so you have two columns. Put a plus sign on top of one column and a minus sign on top of the other. Your paper should look like this:

+	−

Every time you say something to your child, classify it as "+" or "−." Make a tally mark in that column. Examples of "+" comments include compliments and thank-yous. Examples of "−" comments include criticisms and don'ts.

At the end of ten minutes, add up the tally marks and compare the two columns. Most parents are surprised at how many "−" marks they recorded. One mother concluded, "No wonder he tunes me out."

Your goal is an 80/20 ratio, or 4:1. This means four "+" comments to a single "−" one. Every time you find it necessary to point out something unsatisfactory, you must already have observed, or you now need to observe, four satisfactory things. Start looking for the good right away!

To succeed at the 80/20 rule, you need to keep track of what you last said. Since it is impractical to carry your tally sheet around with you (except perhaps in your head), here's another method that works:

Listen to yourself talk. Every time you correct or nag your child, turn your ring around one-half turn on your finger. Keep it turned around until you have made four positive comments. Or slip your watch off one wrist and onto your other. Keep it there until you've observed four good things.

Be Authentic

There is always some good to be found somewhere in a situation. Notice your child's efforts or acknowledge the intelligence behind her motivations.

Dean is a juvenile offender. He is in therapy because the court has ordered him to come to therapy as a condition of his parole.

Dean says his father is a jerk, yet he often talks about him. Dean recalls, "When I was little, I busted up the door of his Chevy Impala. We stopped for gas and I swung it open right into the pump.

"Man, he lost it. He yelled and cussed and made me work to pay for it." Dean paused. "That wasn't so bad. What I hated was his stupid rule that from then on, when the car stopped, I had to ask his freakin' permission to unbuckle my safety belt. Every time. With people in the car and everything."

"It was humiliating?" I asked.

"Yeah, I'd say. And you know what? Mr. Perfect never asked me why I banged the door open to begin with," Dean continued.

"Why did you?"

" 'Cause I was gonna hop out and clean the freakin' windshield."

How to Do It

To say something positive, think up sentences that begin like this:

- I like the way you . . .
- Thank you for . . .
- I understand what you were trying to do to. You were trying to . . .
- You gave that a good effort. I saw you . . .
- I noticed how you . . .

Don't "Undo" an Acknowledgment

Don't cancel out your compliment. After you have commended your child, resist the temptation to reverse what you just said. Stop yourself *before* you begin the next sentence with the word "but . . ."

The 80/20 rule serves several purposes. It gives your child a high rate of reinforcement, which keeps her motivation up. It curbs nagging, which keeps your motivation up. Your child listens more. And you naturally become more discriminating about what is important enough to correct and what you can let go.

TELL STORIES OF PAST SUCCESSES

Sometimes the best way to apply the 80/20 rule is to remember a time when your child was in the same type of situation she is in right now, but she had a better attitude or she succeeded at what she was doing. So, for example, if your child is having a hard time getting started on her homework, remind her of an afternoon she sat down and got it done. If she acts aggressively with her sister, remind her how nicely they played together yesterday. If she's struggling with math, remind her how well she handles money at the store.

These stories of past successes help restore your child's confidence in her own abilities. They also bring back the mood your child was in when she was successful.

Sheri slammed her backpack down on the table. "I can't believe it. Ms. Myers says the social studies project is due on Monday, no exceptions. I'll never get it finished by then. And we lose a half of a letter-grade for every day it's late. She's mean."

Sheri's mom chose to ignore the bang on the table. "You're pretty mad, huh?"

"Yeah, I'm mad. It's so unfair." Sheri was agitated, yet her mom remained calm.

"It seems to me you said the same thing about your science project last month. And you did a great job with that. Remember the pie graph?"

"I'm going out for a walk." A walk was one of Sheri's methods to adjust her attitude.

Success stories are good for all children to hear. Retelling them is especially effective for Edison-trait children. Your Edison-trait child thrives on storytelling and imagery. Travels through time suit her style. An image of her own success from the past renews her hope and belief in the present.

Tell your child these stories with sincerity and in good faith. Do it for love and without expectation. If she thinks you're flattering her to get what you want, she will brush aside the things you say. Only things you say from your heart have a chance of entering hers.

Become a repository of your child's successes. As soon as she has done something you want to remember, jot it down in a memo pad or on a piece of paper you stash in a box or a drawer. Include everyday instances of good behavior, like being ready on time, as well as major projects like running a successful lemonade stand. Include recent ones, like cleaning up her dishes this morning, as well as oldies, like how she told a funny joke to a roomful of people when she was only three years old. One of the best times to tell your child success stories about her past is right before she goes to sleep.

MAKE THIS A DAILY HABIT:
REMEMBER THE BEST THING YOUR
CHILD DID TODAY, AND TELL HER
TONIGHT AT BEDTIME.

What you say to your child becomes what your child says to herself.

—⁓—

CHAPTER 6

Step Three: Build a Parent-and-Child Team

We must all hang together, or assuredly we shall all hang separately.

—Benjamin Franklin

BE ON THE SAME SIDE

"Everything is such a battle with Daniel."
"He was my second child, so I knew it was him, not me."
"I have a cannon. My mom has a popgun. I don't care if I get my homework done. She does."

You are *not* the enemy and neither is your child. You and your child are allies against a common enemy, or rather common enemies. They are the enemies we all face: fear, stress, intolerance, misunderstanding, discouragement, exhaustion, disappointment.

You must break the mental image that you and your child are waging war between you. This attitude and approach is as destructive as any other war on earth. No one truly wins.

- Understand, don't blame.
- Cooperate, don't intimidate.
- Act, don't react.

The moment you feel a power struggle starting to build, take a step back, break the pattern, and create a new and healthy way to see things. Interestingly, one of the most effective things you can do is to physically walk over and stand side by side, next to your child. Or pull up a chair and sit right by his side. Look in the same direction he is looking. Reflect on—and do not challenge—the last thing he said.

"I hate this. It's dumb. I'm not going to do this anymore."

Chuck's mom could hear the words forming themselves in her brain: "Yes, you are, young man!" But instead, she stopped and chose silence. She moved a chair from the head of the table, next to the place where he sat. They both stared into the same corner of space. Chuck's mom said, "You feel like quitting, huh?"

Chuck nodded. They sat in silence.

In the quiet, Chuck's mom got in touch with her intuition. "Time for a break?" she asked. It turned out that it was. When Chuck returned to work, he had a better attitude.

The most critical time to find a point of agreement with your child is right at a point of disagreement. When you can't give your child what he asks for, give him what you can—for example, respect, attention, understanding, and a friendly spirit.

Tina wanted to stay up until midnight. Instead of gearing up for battle, her mom decided to try a new approach. She gave Tina her full attention while Tina told her how she felt. Then she spoke gently to her daughter. "I understand it's a very grown-up feeling to stay up with us. I understand why you want to. I like it when we're together too. Right now it's time to be in your own cozy bed. Do you want to play a game of Go Fish when you're all ready?"

Imagine you and your Edison-trait child as two leaders of separate nations. Create peace, not war. Use care and diplomacy when differences crop up between you. If you jump to enforce your will, he will jump to enforce his. Instead, aim to create a shared vision, one that is acceptable to both of you.

In actual fact, each of you is a respected and powerful *leader*. You *lead* your own life. And he *leads* his.

You want to communicate with your child in a way that promotes cooperation yet respects his autonomy. A good book to help you do this is *How to Talk So Kids Will Listen & Listen So Kids Will Talk* by Adele Faber and Elaine Mazlish. This book is based on the premise that there is a direct connection between how children feel and how they behave.[1]

EMPOWER, DON'T OVERPOWER

There was once an old man and a boy. The boy wished to outsmart the old man. He captured a small bird and cupped it in his hands. He approached the old man.

"Old man," said the boy, "what do I have in my hand?"

"A bird," the old man replied.

"Old man," the boy asked, "is the bird dead or alive?"

Now the old man was a wise old man, and he knew if he said "alive," the boy would kill the bird to prove him wrong. He knew if he said "dead" the boy would free the bird and feel so triumphant he would surely play this trick on others, at the expense of small birds.

The old man thought about the boy's need to feel smart by outwitting his elder. So in a kindly voice, the old man said to him: "The bird is in *your* hands, my son."

Prevent control battles between you and your child. Acknowledge your child's right to make choices and your right to live your life in peace as well. Enjoy the fact that your child thinks and acts for himself. Like the old man, don't be fooled or manipulated. Like the bird, your child's life lies in his own hands.[2]

PRACTICE "TIME-IN"

By now, most parents are familiar with a method commonly used to help calm or discipline a child, called "time-out." (For more about time-out, see Chapter 8.)

"Time-in" is an exercise that reduces the need for time-out. It is an all-time favorite of Edison-trait children. In time-in, you dedicate time and attention exclusively to your child. You don't make or take phone calls or half read the newspaper. This is one-on-one time. You and your child think and act freely together. There are no "have-to's." The goal is mutual enjoyment, to be, not to do.

Kerry's dad accepted an important new position that required him to travel a lot. As a child, he had been ignored by his workaholic father. So he desperately wanted to reassure his sensitive seven-year-old Dreamer that he was not abandoning her. But the more he spoke about his feelings, the more restless and insecure she became.

When they came to see me, we talked about things Kerry liked to do. We decided to take out markers and paper and begin to draw. Without looking at each other's papers, Kerry and her dad drew very similar pictures. When they discovered this, they began to talk and laugh freely. Kerry's father exclaimed, "This is fun!"

Now, at home, they make time to be together with no pressure allowed. Since they both like to draw, they often do. When Kerry's dad had to be out of town on her first day back to school, he sent her a fax. It was a picture of him thinking about her in her new classroom, in a cartoon bubble above his head.

During time-in, if something comes up spontaneously that you both want to do, go for it. Otherwise, just be. We are, after all, human *beings,* not human *doings.*

Time-in is a child-centered activity. So when you practice time-in with a divergent-thinking child, be prepared to spend a lot of it listening to his whirlwind of ideas. Often, time-in with a Dynamo requires that you be in motion, too. Be prepared to walk and run and play.

Be an active and friendly listener. Get involved in your child's thinking. Do *not* point out flaws, teach a lesson, make suggestions, give advice, or try to fix anything. Do nothing that implies judgment. Remain silent and show interest. Or do the following:

- Reflect back what your child has said.
  "So what you're saying is . . ."

- Ask friendly questions.
  "So then what happened?"

- Share a similar story about yourself, but keep it short. (*Relate, don't teach.*)
  "When I was ten . . ."
- Show appreciation.
  "Hey, that was cool."

It is optimal to have at least ten minutes of time-in every night. This may be hard to do at first. Our fast-paced, hard-driving culture does not promote it. According to one estimate, the average amount of time that parents in the United States spend with their children has dropped 40 percent in the last twenty years.[3]

When we do take time from our busy schedules to be with our children, it is usually for a specific purpose, for example, to read to them or help them with their homework. That is why, until you begin to reap its benefits, time-in may feel nonproductive. If this happens, remind yourself that you are investing in your child, weaving the fabric of your relationship.

If you are striving to be a good parent *and* climb the ladder of success in your career, there may be a clash in the qualities, not just the time, you need for each. In *Children of Fast-Track Parents,* Andree Brooks names some of these conflicting qualities.[4]

Qualities Needed to Succeed in Chosen Career	Qualities Needed to Meet Needs of Growing Child
Efficiency	A tolerance for chaos
A constant striving for perfection	A tolerance for repeated errors
A goal-oriented attitude toward the project at hand	An acceptance of the seemingly capricious nature of child-raising
A stubborn self-will	A softness and willingness to bend
A controlling nature that enjoys directing others	A desire to promote independence in others, even if their ways are not your ways
A concern about image	A relaxed acceptance of embarrassment
A feeling that nobody is as smart as you	A true respect for your child's abilities free from comparison with your own

Time-in gives us a chance to develop the qualities we need as parents. It forms the basis for a strong parent-child team.

Is "just being" the same as "doing nothing"? Hardly. First of all, it dissolves predetermined mind-sets. You get to encounter your child outside a circumscribed role. For example, you get to see him as other than a reluctant student or a rebellious teen. Also, you become open to the present moment and a flow of fresh, new ideas.

Perhaps most important, when you spend time *being* with your child, you spend time getting to know him. You learn what things look like through his personal window on the world. You honor him as a person.

BEFRIEND YOUR CHILD

See your child as a "partner in growth," not a subordinate to be managed. If you yourself were raised in an autocratic household, you'll probably feel some resistance to this concept. You may hold the view that you as the parent have a natural authority. You have the responsibility to make rules and carry them through.

You are right. You are the authority in your home. But this is not the only role that you have. You also have a role as an equal human being. Each family member—baby or father—has this same role. Each family member commands and deserves respect. This respect does not depend on the person's age, income, or position in the family. It is natural human respect.

Mutual respect and consideration are what makes closeness and intimacy possible between parent and child. You can be a responsible parent who sets limits and follows through, *and* still enjoy closeness and intimacy. You can exercise authority *and* not dominate or domineer. You can be your child's teacher *and* your child's friend.

Every child wants a parent he can confide in. As your Edison-trait child becomes an Edison-trait teen, his need for your acceptance may become critical. Adolescence is a time when your child will experiment with the world outside your home and values. It is every teen's developmental task to test and see what his limits are, as he tries his wings.

Edison-trait children experiment with more risk than most. They dare to go higher and faster and further than other teens do. As your child explores issues like sex, power, and drugs, how do you want him to think of you? Do you want to be a parent he has learned to trust through the years, someone he can turn to if he's made a mistake or lost his way? Or do you want to be someone who has enforced the rules so well that there is no open door in the wall that divides you?[5]

There is a story in the Talmud about a king who had a son who became estranged from his father. The son received a message: "Return to your father." The son said: "I cannot." Then his father sent a messenger to say: "Return as far as you can. And I will come to you the rest of the way."

Let go of the need to be perfect, and give your child the same freedom. Find joy in watching your child grow and share that joy with your child freely. Meet the task of raising your Edison-trait child with creativity and resourcefulness, and these traits will flourish in both of you.

FIVE WAYS TO TELL YOUR CHILD "I VALUE YOU"

1. Respect Your Child's Anger

Pete was furious. It was Jim's birthday and he was not one of the four friends Jim chose to go to the ball game with him. He ranted about times he stood up for Jim in front of the other boys, and how Jim chose popular boys to go with him, not true friends.

His father and I just listened. We didn't try to fix it, or talk him out of it, or help him see another side. We stopped what we were doing, gave him our undivided attention, and just listened.

2. Enjoy His Jokes

This is not the story of a parent. It is an example drawn from a time I tested a quintessential Edison-trait child.

I was administering the WISC-R, a standardized intelligence test. One of the tasks requires the child to put together puzzle pieces to make a picture of a child. Each leg is a single piece of the puzzle. After finishing the puzzle, Jake, a Discoverer, took the two leg pieces and made them run across the table. "Oh, oh, where do I go?" he asked in a falsetto voice, as he made the legs scurry about wildly. Then he sent them soaring high, landed them in their box, and shut the lid. The two of us laughed out loud together.

The standardized instructions say that under the circumstances, I should direct the child not to handle the test materials unless I have told him he may do so. All I could think of was "If only this test had a scale for originality." I have given WISC tests hundreds of times. This child's response was endearing and one-of-a-kind humorous.

3. Resist Correcting Minor Infractions

Don was just leaving for the park. He was in a great mood. He'd made breakfast that morning for the family and had even cleaned up after himself. It had turned out really well. He knew it and felt it.

I opened the dishwasher to empty it. Instead of clean dishes, there was pancake batter caked on almost all the things. Don had not rinsed the bowl and spoons well enough. For the next twenty minutes I'd be soaking and scrubbing. But I held myself in check and never said a word to Don about it.

4. Speak Respectfully

"I don't care what you think. Get to your room. You're not going anywhere." I thought it but I didn't say it. Instead I managed to say, "Linda, can I speak with you privately?"

In her room, in a calm voice, I said: "Linda, I know you disagree. But we've discussed this before. You need to pick up your things from the family room before you can leave the house with your friends. Thank you for listening."

5. Expect Excellence

Gary got interested in science fiction. It started with his dedication to Star Trek: The Next Generation. He put up posters in his room and started to collect memorabilia. He liked to make up stories about the way the world might be in the future.

In his social studies class, he received an assignment to write a research report on a time period other than the present. He asked if he could write about stardate 3800. It was certainly not what his teacher had in mind, but she said yes, and he went to work.

He wrote a lengthy, well-organized report, including the status of religion, science, art, intergalactic politics, and interstellar exploration in the future. He illustrated the report with sketches, diagrams, and maps. He based his observations on Star Trek reference materials and on electronic correspondence with Trekkies on the Internet. The final product was so impressive it was put on display in the school media center for the remainder of the year.

As you value your child, your child values himself.

◆

CHAPTER 7

Step Four: Encourage Your Child's Interests

There is always one moment in childhood when the door
opens and lets the future in.

—Graham Greene,
The Power and the Glory

KNOW YOUR CHILD

From the moment Nancy Edison found her lost toddler sitting on a
nest of goose eggs to test the theory of hatching, she suspected her
young son had a passion for scientific inquiry. What is your child's
passion?

Is your child a Dreamer? Dreamers usually have talents in drama,
music, writing, fine arts, and practical arts. The same child who repeatedly confuses complete and incomplete sentences choreographs
a complex dance that wins the school talent show. The child who
daily asks you how to do the next step in long division creates jewelry that rivals the latest designer trends.

Is your child a Discoverer? Discoverers are intensely curious and
enterprising young people. Like Edison, they enjoy carrying out
their own original experiments. Ironically, they may dread science
class, where they have to carry out planned experiments in a prescribed manner. They want new experiences and they want them
on their own. Discoverers will make home videos, play interactive
computer games, or develop an interest in backyard rocketry. They

are entrepreneurial, starting up businesses like delivery services, pet sitting, and car washes. They like to make a profit.

Is your child a Dynamo? Dynamos have lots of physical energy. They favor nonteam aerobic sports like bicycling and swimming, and daredevil sports like skiing and skateboarding. They like aggressive team sports like roller hockey and football, but find it hard to pace themselves with others to engage in team play. Dynamos are drawn to power and speed. They like to make things go fast and they take things to extremes. They may get fascinated with trains, race cars, or jets. Like Discoverers, they are also entrepreneurial. They like to take risks in their business ventures and they are excited by competition. They get stimulated by the prospect of winning, which they sometimes confuse with dominance.

Ask your child what she wants to do. But remember, Edison-trait children are easily attracted to novelty. She may speak excitedly about the latest trend, but her interest in it may wane quickly. You'll probably learn more by observing your child and noticing what honestly gives her joy.

What comes naturally to your child? When is she happiest and most absorbed? An activity you think will be good for your child is not as beneficial as the one in which your child shows a genuine interest. For example, some parents have heard that martial arts is a good sport to help a child learn how to focus and sustain attention. It can be. But a better one is any sport in which your child *wants* to pay attention.

Getting your child to agree to what you think she should do is not the same as finding out what she wants. Nor is channeling her to do something that you used to love doing as a child. There are more than enough things she *must* do at school. Let extracurricular activities be her very own.

The best way to identify an authentic aptitude in your child is to observe her doing many different things, then take note of what she is doing when she becomes hyperfocused or intensely involved. Her hyperfocused state is like an arrow. It points to the kind of work she is most likely to succeed in.

When she becomes hyperfocused, she won't need much encouragement from you. She will be drawn to and stimulated by what she is doing. She will want to do it more than anything else in the world. She has found her passion.

BE FLEXIBLE, OPEN, AND TOLERANT

Claire never finishes what she starts. It's an endless procession of this lesson or that. First she wanted to learn to play the piano, then it was dance, now it's Suzuki violin. What next?

Some parents become frustrated because it seems their Edison-trait child's interests change so quickly. But Edison-trait children are divergent thinkers, so naturally they have eclectic interests.

Dreamers are prone to drift from one activity to another. Discoverers crave novelty, so they hunger for new activities. Dynamos need new forms of stimulation at a fairly rapid rate. This can rattle the parent who wants to see his child make a commitment and stay with it.

Think of your Edison-trait child as an explorer, not as a quitter. She has the courage and initiative to try out new things. Commend her for her willingness to dare.

As adults, we lose sight of the delight and excitement new experience brings. Educator John Holt says that "the greatest difference between children and adults is that most of the children to whom I offer a turn of the cello accept it, while most adults, particularly if they have never played any other instrument, refuse it."[1]

Sometimes Edison-trait children will not find their passion until they are adults. For example, a Dynamo would have no way to know if she had an aptitude for flying planes until she is old enough to learn how to fly.

Take heart if the activity your child chooses for herself is not the one you would have chosen for her. You are not alone. Keep in mind that your purpose is to help her find *her* path.

When she finds the kind of work that suits her talents best, this becomes the seed from which her future success germinates. As Holt observes, it is "interesting, but not surprising [that] the things we learn because, *for our own reasons,* we really need to know them, we don't forget."[2] In the words of Kahlil Gibran in his poem "On Children":

> *They come through you but not from you,*
> *And though they are with you yet they belong not to you.*
> *You may give them your love but not your thoughts,*
> *For they have their own thoughts.*[3]

SUPPORT, BUT DON'T PUSH

Encourage your child's self-expression and desire for personal mastery. Think of the last school play or baseball game you attended. Some of the children were relaxed. They enjoyed their moment in the sun. Some of the children were nervous and uneasy. They looked like they wished it was over.

The relaxed children were there for their own personal reasons. Performance came naturally to them. The tense ones lacked inner motivation and joy. They were more concerned with appearance than experience.

Here are some ways to help you distinguish between performance-for-others and self-expression:

Performance-for-others	*Self-expression*
Externally motivated (trophy, applause, approval)	Self-motivated (personal interest)
Fear of failure prevails	Desire to succeed prevails
Results are most important	Learning is most important
Goal-governed	Goal-guided
Progress is measured by comparisons with others	Progress is measured by personal growth
Advance at a set rate	Advance at your own rate
Compete to win over others	Compete to improve yourself
Others judge you (use of evaluative words like good, bad, right, mistakes)	Others give you feedback (use of descriptive words like loud, soft, to the right, to the left)

In *The Ultimate Athlete,* George Leonard says, "Numbed to everything except results, we are likely to miss the dance."[4]

REPLACE WORRY WITH TRUST

Russ is a twelve-year-old Discoverer. He owns a small business that prints booklets of anecdotes and clever word puzzles that require knowledge of local news to solve. Russ realizes that people, his classmates and their families in particular, like to read about themselves. He has "hired" several friends to collect the news, make up the puzzles, design the layout, input, print, copy, and collate the final product. He is in charge of sales.

Last spring Russ ran a booth at a local fund-raiser in exchange for donating 50 percent of his profits. He did phenomenally well. Highly motivated by his success, he immediately began to make plans to rent a booth at a local fair. Russ's parents expressed concern. They realized his customers were buying his product out of a sense of community. How could they get him to understand this without breaking his heart or his spirit?

Russ's parents, by the way, had traveled a long, hard road with their son. Russ has been a strong-willed Edison-trait child since birth. They decided honesty was the best policy with their young business tycoon, and so they planned to sit down with him and explain the reasons for his recent sales success in a direct yet loving way.

Russ listened to what they were saying, undaunted. "I'm a kid," he replied. "What other angle can I use?" He went on to explain that he knew why people bought his product. "People want to help me, and they are."

Russ added confidently, "When I get older, I'll think of something else. It's all in the marketing. People will buy your product if you market it right."

Years ago, a sports psychology instructor once told me, "Worrying is negative goal setting." He went on to explain that every time we name a goal, we see ourselves achieving it. Even though we don't mean it, when we name a worry, we set the same wheels in motion.

When you worry, you visualize an outcome that you *don't* want. When you trust, you name and see the goal *you want* for yourself and your child. You mentally move toward your desired goal just by thinking about it.

Your Edison-trait child has inner resources that you and she have yet to discover. Nurture her talent and you will be pleasantly surprised. There are hidden treasures to be unearthed when you develop trust in your child's creative mind.

"Where did *that* come from?" parents of Edison-trait children are prone to wonder. You don't need to know how your Edison-trait child gets her ideas. When it comes to her creativity, learn to trust her intuition.

Johann Sebastian Bach tried to tell his friends about the effortless flow of musical ideas that came to him. When asked how he found his melodies he said, "The problem is not finding them, it's—when getting up in the morning and getting out of bed—not stepping on them."[5]

Your Edison-trait child wakes up to a steady stream of ideas too. Trust her creative intelligence.

Help your child to discover her own individual talents and strengths.

CHAPTER 8

Step Five: Teach Your Child Self-control

A child's future turns on how his or her mother or father treats
him or her in the privacy of the family.

—Victoria Secunda

UNDERSTAND THAT SELF-DISCIPLINE IS YOUR GOAL FOR YOUR CHILD

All discipline is *self*-discipline. Instinctively we know this. You cannot "control" your child. You *can* raise your child to practice self-
control.

When you try to control your child, you treat him as a thing, not
a person. He may do what you say in the moment, but in the long
run he won't be controlled. He'll find a way to exert his will, to behave like a person, not a thing.

When you raise your child to practice self-control, you honor
him as a person. He'll make mistakes in the moment, but in the long
run, he'll respond as an honorable person. When you show your
child respect, he will show respect to you.

The Edison-trait child is strongly opinionated. At times you are
likely to feel provoked. You will wonder if you are doing the right
thing. Are you strict enough? Do you give in too much? When
your child misbehaves you feel you ought to "tighten your grip."
Consider this parable about the wind, the sun, and a traveler.

One day the wind boasted to the sun, "I am stronger than you are. Dead leaves whirl and flee before me. I make things move. You do not."

The sun smiled graciously. "That is not so, my friend."

"Show me!" the wind roared.

Just then, a traveler came walking down the road.

"Very well," said the sun. "See that traveler down there? Let us agree. Whoever makes him take his cloak off is stronger than the other."

"Agreed," the wind said. "And I will go first."

So the sun slipped behind a cloud and the wind began to blow. The traveler's cloak flapped wildly in the breeze.

But the harder the wind tried to tear the cloak off, the more tightly the man drew it around him.

At last the wind gave up, exasperated. "Have your turn," he said in a contentious voice.

Smiling, the sun appeared from behind the cloud. Steadily, the sun shone warm beams on the traveler.

"How hot it has grown," the traveler said. And of his own volition, he unfastened his cloak and took it off.

HELP YOUR CHILD SEE WHAT HIS CHOICES ARE

Every limit in life is actually a choice. Accept the limit or accept the consequence. Some limits don't feel like choices because the alternatives are either unacceptable or unapparent. When the alarm rings at six A.M. and you wake up and get ready for work, it doesn't feel like a choice. But it is. Wake up or lose your job, an unacceptable alternative. Actually, it's a continuation of the decision you made when you took the job.

Now think about the same situation for your child. When the alarm goes off, his decision to wake up does not feel like a choice to him. He does not recall having made the decision to go to school. You made that decision for him. So you're the villain, the enemy forcing him to get up. The battle lines are drawn. What can you do?

REFUSE TO BE THE ENEMY

Most children show some rebellion against rules as they grow up. Your child, an Edison-trait child, has "rebel" in his bones. An independent thinker by nature, he is going to test just about every rule he can. Accept this fact. Don't take it personally. He is not out to get you.

See your child's strong will as the personal strength it can be. He is going to live by his own rules, not yours or anyone else's. Your rules can become his rules only if he understands and accepts them. To get up with his alarm, *he* needs to decide that *he* wants to go to school and be on time. You can help him come to grips with this, but he is the one who must make the connections.

When he questions the rules, he is not turning against you. He is trying to find his own path. When he won't conform at school, he is just trying to be who he is. To achieve good grades, *he* needs to make schoolwork *his* priority. Don't fight him on this. Try to understand the nature of his fight.

Refrain from judging your child. Instead, make it your goal to teach him good judgment.

CONSIDER YOUR CHILD'S AGE

First take into account your child's age and level of maturity. Keep your expectations realistic.

When your child is about seven years of age, a major change takes place in his ability to reason. Before age seven, a child has only a rudimentary understanding of the relationship between cause and effect. After about age seven, a child becomes better equipped to make this important connection.

It is also true that maturation is gradual and variable. Each child fulfills his destiny on his own personal timetable. Be aware that age seven is the approximate "age of reason," but go by your child's behaviors, not by his birthdate.

Before Age Seven

For your child's first seven years of life, make consistency a top priority. Your child needs a routine that is nearly the same every day. Make his daily schedule predictable. He needs rules that are firm yet fair. Give him the structure he needs and be clear with him about it.

Also give your child lots of encouragement and praise. Edison-trait children need more acknowledgments and rewards than do other children.[1]

Techniques that are useful at this age include:

- *A poster board list of your child's daily routine.* Print times and basic activities in simple words, large letters, and colorful pictures.
- *Daily or weekly star charts.* List only a few behaviors (no more than one per year of age). Use pictures or even photos of your child performing each task, e.g., a picture of him brushing his teeth, getting dressed, eating breakfast.
- *Prizes for good behavior.* Award gifts for stars your child earns on his chart. Also give awards unexpectedly when you "catch your child being good"!

When you set limits, let your child have some say, but do so when rules are being made, not when they are being faced. For example, you and he can talk over what TV programs he may watch. But later that night, when it's time to turn off the TV, the rule is not negotiable. In this way you give your child some ownership of the rules, but you do not allow him to manipulate rules once they have been established.

A pleasant and clear way to communicate this to a young child is what behavioral pediatrician Dr. Dorothy Johnson calls the Y-man technique.[2] Hold your hand with two fingers to form a V. See the V part as the upper part of the letter Y. See the lower half, the remaining part of your palm and fist, as the lower part of the Y.

When the need for a rule arises, make a "Y-man" to your child. Point to the upper part and explain that the two of you will now make the rule, like the two fingers of the Y. Then collaborate with your child and create a rule you both can live with. Explain that once the rule is made, you both agree to accept it. One mother and child I saw in counseling decided to actually conduct a vote when it was time to agree. They would "pass a law" and put it in writing, to make clear exactly what it was they had both agreed to.

Once the two of you agree, the time for rule making is done. Point to the lower part of your hand. "This is where we are with this rule now." The rule is made. There is no further negotiation.

Using the TV example, let's say that following a lengthy discussion of how much and what kind of TV is good for the brain, you and your child have decided he can watch a one-hour educational program and a half hour of cartoons. You pass the law, but that evening after the cartoons, your child wants to watch more. You make a "Y-man" and point to the lower half, to remind him that the rule making is done. It is time now to keep the rule, not rewrite it.

After Age Seven

Once your child reaches the age of reason, it's time to gradually shift more and more of the responsibility for structure, rule making, and rule keeping over to him. Your child's ownership of his rules becomes your most important goal. This means that you need to take the time to discuss and set fair rules, and hold your child accountable for the natural consequences of his own choices. It means you need to create optimal conditions for him to succeed.

Supervise your child consistently so that he gets immediate and accurate feedback. Help him connect choices and outcomes, especially when feedback is delayed. For example, to connect his bedtime with his mood in the morning, you could keep a written record of some of his bedtimes and subsequent morning feelings. Help him discover for himself irrefutably that if he goes to bed on time he feels cheerful in the morning, and if he stays up too late, he feels grumpy.

Make Fair, Logical Rules

To establish good rules, you and your child need to make clear connections between rules and results. Be patient and listen to your child's thoughts about rules. Be respectful as you do this. You are not trying to win a point. You are trying to help him see the logic in his own thinking.

One way to do this is to keep the following format in mind:

If . . .
then . . .
so I'd better . . .

Listen carefully when your child expresses his ideas, then reflect his ideas back to him. Paraphrase what he has said. Use the "If, then, so I'd better" format to stay brief and clear. Here are three examples:

1. "So what you're saying is, '*If* I watch TV all night, *then* I won't get anything else done, *so I'd better* leave time to do other things.' "

2. "Okay. I think I understand. You're saying, '*If* we watch dumb shows, *then* we'll think dumb things, *so we'd better* watch good shows.' "

3. "So what you mean is '*If* you quit watching when you say you will, *then* you'll feel proud of yourself for what you did, *so you'd better* turn the TV off after the last show you're going to watch.' "

Hold Your Child Accountable

Once rules and agreements are made, see to it that your child respects them. Acknowledge him as soon as he makes a right choice. Encourage him if he's undecided. Enforce natural consequences if he errs.

Be calm and consistent and present to follow through. For example, if he's supposed to turn the TV off at eight P.M., be within ear range at that time, so you know if he has done it or not.

If your child does what he is supposed to do, notice and acknowledge it at that very moment. For example, if he has voluntarily turned the TV off, say, "I saw you do that. Good for you."

If your child is undecided, offer support. For example, say, "I know it's hard to turn the TV off, but you can do it." This is an excellent time to remind him of a past success. "Remember on Saturday, when you really wanted to keep watching cartoons, and you turned the TV off all on your own? That was great. It was an act of intelligence and strength."

If your child out-and-out refuses, in a calm and respectful way enforce the rule and its logical consequences. For example, turn the TV off yourself, and ask for an apology for his having ignored you. You may have to deal with an unpleasant confrontation, but you can learn how to handle this type of situation effectively. Most of the rest of this chapter describes methods for you to use.

Please remember, however, that for these methods to work, you need to keep up the work of Steps 1–4: Believe in your child. Watch what you say. Build a parent-and-child team. Encourage your child's interests. The methods in this chapter are power tools—you need to plug them into a source. That source is your attitude and relationship with your child.

Adolescence

Every age brings with it specific developmental tasks. An infant learns to trust that mom disappears and then returns. A child of seven makes cause-and-effect connections for himself. A teenager seeks his own individual identity.

To establish his identity, a teen needs to separate himself psychologically from his mother and father. This process requires that, from time to time, his words and actions oppose his parents' point of view. His behavior must say, "I'm me, not you." It is necessary for his personal growth.

This confuses parents. They do not hear their child's invisible, inner calling to make a statement of independence. They do not know at what moment their child is about to feel and fill a need to say, "I'm me, not you." All that parents can hear is their teen's opposition—for apparently *no* reason whatsoever!

Bob's parents are in counseling to get help with their fourteen-year-old Discoverer. They are intellectual, well-educated people, with a strong belief in the power of reasoning. They are baffled by their son's inconsistent reactions to them lately. Bob has always been a strong-willed child. But now, he will on occasion become adamant about a point that his parents say he knows is illogical.

"I don't understand," Bob's father said. "We were at the dinner table talking, and it seemed like things were going fine and then Bob just started saying things to contradict me. I got so mad I left the table."

I asked Bob's father to imagine that he and his son were on a journey together. They were thinking along the same lines and walking and talking with each other. Then I said that what was about to happen next would surprise and puzzle him. Unbeknownst to him, the terrain would change for his teenage son. Bob's reality would become a desert. He would need water urgently and have to stop wherever he was to satisfy his thirst for "I'm me, not you."

This could cause trouble. It would require trust from Bob's father, since his son's sudden thirst would be invisible to him.

Bob's father nodded. He understood. He remembered traveling through his own desert many years ago.

USE THE SOCRATIC METHOD TO CREATE RULES

The Socratic method (see page 35) can serve as a useful tool when you and your child discuss your rules. Socrates believed in the rule of reason. He thought it was the best way for us to govern ourselves both as individuals (self-control) and as a society (rules and contracts). He believed that in both instances, when justice is coupled with temperance, *all* elements (of the self or of the community) can *agree* on who is to do what. When this occurs, the rule of reason is not a tyranny but the harmonious rule of the happily unified individual and society.[3]

In the Socratic method, you ask your child questions in a friendly, open-ended, let's-look-at-this-together manner. You are not invasive, overbearing, or dictatorial. You approach your child as an intelligent human being, and trust that given the right conditions, he can and will think fairly. You actively guide your child to examine his choices and see where they will lead. And you honestly keep an open mind and listen.

For the Socratic method to work, the key element is your attitude. You and your child need to function as a team with a common goal: deciding what's fair for you and for him, what you need to do as a responsible parent, and what is in his best interest as a growing child. In this spirit, you and your child come together to form the rules you both agree to live with.

Todd is a persuasive twelve-year-old Discoverer. According to his father, if Todd was left on his own, he would watch TV twenty-four hours a day. Todd's father decided to try the Socratic method.
   "Todd, we need a rule about watching TV. Do you understand why?"
   "Yeah."
   "Why do you think, Todd?"
   "Because it sucks you in once you turn it on."
   Todd's father was amazed at Todd's insight.

BE CONSISTENT

To feel safe, children, especially young children, need consistency. It is up to you as a parent to provide it.

As you do this, you may expect your Edison-trait child to test your stamina and your resolve. For example, when it's time for your child to turn off the TV, his efforts to watch the next show may try your patience. Until you have established a routine, you need to be there on time, every time, to see that he turns off the set. You also want to be there to "catch him being good." Do not allow your child to watch another show sometimes, then get angry other times when he tries to do it again.

Remember that Edison-trait children have a strong need to think and act for themselves. This means they want to be in control and will rebel against feeling controlled by you. If your child feels that his behavior is controlled by a rule that is consistently enforced, he will feel less as though he is arbitrarily being controlled by you. He will also feel more in control because he can *predict* what is going to take place. The more self-control he feels, the better behaved he will be. In addition, your consistency decreases his motivation to break rules, because there is nothing new to be discovered about what will happen if he disobeys.

GIVE CHOICES, NOT ORDERS

When a rule is made and it's time to keep the rule, continue to offer your child choices, but offer only those choices that funnel him toward keeping the rule. For example, if he has just finished watching his last program, yet the TV is still on, say, "Do you want to turn the TV off now or after this scene is over?" Then be there, to acknowledge his good decision.

Be careful to offer choices in a sincere manner. Sarcasm is offensive and counterproductive. Communicate trust and the sense of alliance you are building in Step Three.

Here are some more examples of ways to change orders into choices:

Order: Go clean your room.
Choice: Do you want to start to clean your room now, or first thing after lunch?

Order: Empty the dishwasher.
Choice: It's your turn to empty the dishwasher. By what time will you have that done?

Order: Go do your homework.
Choice: Do you want to start on your math or your spelling?

How important is it to give your child a choice? Edison-trait children are determined to do things their own way. And it is a natural human tendency to feel invested in a decision only to the extent that you have chosen it yourself.

To measure how much people value their involvement in their own decisions, psychologist Ellen Langer conducted the following experiment. She sold one-dollar lottery tickets for a fifty-dollar prize. On a random basis, subjects were either handed tickets or allowed to choose their own. Later, Langer's associates tried to buy the tickets from the subjects. Subjects who had been handed the tickets asked for an average of $1.96 for a ticket, while those who chose their own wanted an average $8.67—they valued it more highly.[4]

According to neuroscientist Robert Ornstein, Ph.D., after a choice is made, a person shifts his mind to connect that choice with ideas and images from his own inner life. He claims ownership over the act by making a place for it in his own personal world. Perhaps that is why choice is *essential* to elicit the cooperation of the Edison-trait child, who is a child of imagination, with a rich and compelling inner life.[5]

GIVE CHOICES YET STAY STRUCTURED

Giving choices is not the same thing as being overly permissive. While Edison-trait children thrive on having choices, they do not do well in settings that are overly permissive or unstructured. (This is particularly true for Edison-trait children younger than seven years of age.)

Stay clear about what is acceptable and unacceptable. When you need to remind your child about a rule or if you need to say no to a request, do so in a strong, unwavering tone of voice. Make sure your tone of voice goes down (like a period), not up (like a question mark), at the end of your statement.

After you say no, redirect your child's attention to other choices he has or things you can say yes to. For example, you might say "No, you may not watch any more TV tonight. You *may* listen to one of those new stories-on-tape we brought home from the library or pick out a story and I'll read to you."

Make only those rules you are prepared to back up. If you need more time to think about a rule, say so. Tell your child, "I want to think about this some more. Let's talk again after dinner."

LEARN TO USE THE BROKEN-RECORD TECHNIQUE

What happens if after you make a fair rule and give your child choices, he still refuses to comply? You need to correct your child, and you need to do it in a firm, yet loving manner. The broken-record technique is a good tool for doing this. Here's how it works.

Choose a few words that say exactly what you mean. In a clear, steady voice, say them out loud to your child. No matter what your child says to try to change your mind or the subject, hold your ground by repeating these same few words.

If it's time to turn the TV off, that's exactly what you say. "It's time to turn off the TV." This is what might happen next:

CHILD: But I just want to see the beginning of this show.
PARENT: *It's time to turn off the TV.*
CHILD: I finished my homework—it's only one more show. I really want to watch.
PARENT: I understand how you feel. And *it's time to turn off the TV.*
CHILD: You said I could watch. You said so. You're so mean.
PARENT: I love you too much to let you hurt your brain. *It's time to turn off the TV.*

Remember to commend your child when he does turn it off.

TAKE ACTION AS NEEDED

What happens if your child *still* chooses to ignore you? It's time for you to act. Enforce the rule in a calm and direct way. For example, quietly walk over and turn off the TV.

That might be the end of it, or it might be just the beginning. Your child may react strongly, even wildly, to your action. He may be mad because he feels like *you* took away *his* control.

If your child loses his self-control, now is *not* the time to talk. Before all else, he needs to settle down. You need to stay calm, too.

USE TIME-OUT AS A STRATEGY, NOT A PUNISHMENT

Most parents use or have heard of "time-out" as a method of discipline. Its most popular use is as a punishment, an attempt to assert dominance over a child's behavior. An unfortunate by-product of this use is that your child naturally feels punished. As a rule, when your child feels punished his behavior gets worse, not better.

There is a much better use of the practice of time-out. It is an effective calming procedure. When used with a nonpunitive attitude, it is a tool for your child to regain self-control. Think of the last time you lost your temper. How did you get it back? Did you go to a quiet, private place? Do you wish that you had?

The next time you feel your anger mounting, go to your room and take a few silent minutes to regain your self-control. Let your child see you do this. Explain what you did. Let him know how you used your time-out. You can call it anything you want. "Time alone" is a good name for it.

Then, the next time your child loses his self-control, apply time-out—or "time alone"—as a calming procedure, not a punishment. Here's how:

Direct your child to his room. First, give him a fair chance to go there on his own. One good way to do this is to observe out loud that you both need some time alone to cool down. Say, "Please go to your room and I'll check back with you in a few minutes." If he refuses, and he is still out of control, give him a highly structured choice. "Do you want to go to your room on your own, or do you want me to walk there with you?" If he still refuses, gently but firmly escort him there.

While you are doing this, remain acutely aware of your own arousal level. Your goal at every moment is to reduce it. Don't let your child's anger be contagious.

Calmly tell your child that it's time for each of you to be alone so you can each improve your attitude. Ask him if he thinks it will take five minutes or ten. Tell him how long you think it might take. (A good rule of thumb is to estimate about one minute for every year of his age.) Look at your watch and tell him the specific time you will check back. Make sure he has a clock in his room. If he is too young to tell time, try using a simple kitchen timer.

If you think he will stay on his own, you may leave him. If you don't, stand outside his door and wait.

At the time that you said you would return, knock on his door and see if he is calm. Do this every few minutes until he is. If your knocking provokes him, try slipping a note under his door instead. Write a message like "I'm here and I love you. See you soon." Draw a picture to go with it, like a flower or shining sun. Or if he's too young to read, just slip him the picture.

After you've established the use of time-out as a calming procedure, your child will know what it means and how it works. You can then trust him to calm himself and recognize when he has regained his composure. You can then say something like "Come knock on my door when you are calm." You can also give him options, like going for a short walk instead of staying in his room.

Once you're confident that he will act responsibly when he is alone, you can begin to make better use of your own time-out. In the quiet of your room, close your eyes and relax. Get back in charge of your own emotions.

FIVE THINGS YOU CAN DO TO CALM YOURSELF:
1. *Take three deep breaths.*
2. *Close your eyes and imagine a relaxing outdoor scene.*
3. *Make yourself count backward from one hundred by threes.*
4. *Write your feelings out on a piece of paper.*
5. *Listen to relaxing music, preferably through earphones.*

Prepare yourself for the moment you will face your child again. You want a calm, steady voice, and a firm, loving manner. If it is taking a long time for your child to calm down, you need to check back with him periodically—often enough that he feels you care, but not so often that you distract him from calming himself down. (Once again, a good rule of thumb is to wait no longer than one minute for every year of his age.)

If your child has regained some self-control but is still worked up, ask him if he'd like some company. If he says yes, depending on his age, ask if he'd like you to read to him or tell him a story. Edison-trait children are fond of stories.

When you think it's time to resume talking, continue to give your child a sequence of choices. Use a soothing voice. First, ask him if he would like you there or if he wants to be alone some more. If he wants you there, stay. If not, come back in a short while. Ask him if he's ready to talk yet, or if he'd like you both to be silent for a while and then talk. Do what you think is right, and gauge what you do by his response. If he remains calm, proceed. If he starts to lose self-control, go back a step. If you need to leave his room again, do so.

When your child is ready to talk, listen to what he has to say. Let him tell his side of the story. Be attentive and respectful.

Then, address the problem you are having together in a firm but loving way. Hold your child accountable for his actions. A tantrum *postpones* the moment of accountability for your child. Do not allow him to use it to avoid accountability altogether.

If you sense your child is calm enough to talk but is using the situation to avoid you, give him a choice that funnels him into facing his responsibility. Try this: "We can talk about this now or in about five minutes." Remember, it's not just you he's avoiding. It's his own feelings of self-doubt, frustration, and guilt.

Do's and Don'ts for Time-out
- *Do* stay calm and matter-of-fact.
- *Do* remind your child that you continue to love him, even when he's mad or upset. You might say, "I love you *and* it's time to go to your room and calm down."
- *Do* stay silent most of the time.
- *Do* use the broken-record technique, as needed. Keep a low, steady voice when you do.
- *Don't* catch your child's rage or hostility.
- *Don't* allow yourself to get sidetracked. Don't argue. Don't lecture. Don't threaten.

The main difference between time-out as a punishment and time-out (or time alone) as a way to calm down is this: Time-out as a punishment is an attempt on your part to control *from the outside in.* Time-out as a way to calm down teaches your child self-control *from the inside out.*

Time-out as a punishment makes your child behave for now, but no real learning takes place. Time-out as a learning tool teaches your child a skill that will last a lifetime.

If you have been using time-out as a punishment up to now, begin right away to use it *only* as a calming procedure. And give it a new name, like "take-five" or "time alone."

HOLD YOUR CHILD ACCOUNTABLE

Now it's time to talk with your child. Understand his motives. Accept his feelings. Communicate love and support. Then hold him accountable for his behavior.

Give your child the space he needs to name his mistake. Be patient, firm, and persevering. The truth will come to light.

Do *not* take enemy positions to do this. Stand *with* him as he faces the reality of what he has done. As needed, you may gently guide him to own up to his mistake. But be careful not to accuse, blame, or overpower.

The moment your child admits he is wrong, comment immediately on his courage and sense of responsibility. Do not harp on his faults or elaborate on the error of his ways. Move right into helping him figure out what he can do to make amends.

It is best to ask him first how *he* thinks *he* can fix things. Edison-trait children are highly imaginative and like to think up their own acts of reparation. Help your child get started, then step in as little as possible.

For example, let's say your child refused to turn the TV off and he had a temper tantrum when you turned it off "on him." Having calmed down, he now needs to account for his behavior. For example, he needs to apologize to you for his temper tantrum and clean up any mess he made while he was upset. (If you lost your temper, you need to apologize to him, too.)

Help your child make an apology that is specific to his mistake. For example, a good apology is "I'm sorry I threw the remote. If it's broken, I'll pay for a new one." A younger child might offer to work to pay back the cost, and not use the new one until he does.

An overly general or self-deprecating apology is counterproductive. It evokes bad feelings, not better ones, in your child. For example, your child says, "I'm sorry I'm so stupid. I don't know what is wrong with me."

An effective apology distinguishes between the person and the incident. Your child remains a good person. He made a mistake and he's sorry. A good way to help your child reshape his apology is by modeling one that you give him. "I'm sorry I yelled at you in front of your friends. That wasn't respectful. I'll be careful not to do it again."

As soon as your child owns up to his mistake, acknowledge his courage and right action. Nothing has a higher priority in that moment. Say, "What you're doing right now is a brave and good thing." Make the time to say this even though you may be thinking of what a senseless mistake it was and how angry you still feel about it.

After your child has made amends for his temper tantrum, there is the original problem to deal with. For example, what about the fact that he did not turn the TV off himself? Tell him you do not want to be the TV police. Return to the reason for the rule.

For the child who is younger than seven years or so, you might go back and playact turning the TV off. Re-create the scene as if you were actors in a play. He needs a good, new feeling associated with the act of turning the TV off. In your playful reenactment, after he clicks off the TV, exclaim "You did it!" and give him a hug.

For the child seven and older, go back to helping him make the connection between watching too much TV and what he really wants for himself. Remember the Socratic method. Listen to *his* ideas. Do not lecture.

If he does not think of it on his own, ask your child to promise he won't do it again. Ask him specifically what he will do differently the next time. For example, he could put a stick-on note on the TV to remind himself.

At first you may need to brainstorm with your child to figure out how he can correct his mistakes. But soon he will get used to creating corrective action for himself. Edison-trait children catch on to this quickly, as long as the verdict doesn't come with guilt, your wrath, or a lengthy speech. Edison-trait children easily grasp the concept of making reparation. It is an inventive act.

When holding your child accountable, here are some examples of ways to give him choice instead of an order, so he participates in his own self-correction.

Order: Go apologize to your sister.
Choice: Do you want to say you're sorry to her or do you want to write it in a note?

Order: Clean up this mess you made now.
Choice: Which do you want to do first? Put these things back in your drawers or pick up these papers you tore up?

Order: Pick up the toys you threw in the den.
Choice: Do you want to pick the things up in the den now, or do you want ten more minutes on your own and then you'll come out and clean up?

KEEP A COOL HEAD

Correct your child in a respectful manner. Behavioral pediatrician Dr. Dorothy Johnson suggests using the image of a highway patrol officer as a model.[6] When an officer gives you a ticket, he doesn't yell at you, he doesn't give you a lecture, and he doesn't take your violation personally. He holds you accountable for what you did in a courteous, no-nonsense fashion. This is the style you want to adopt with your child. Follow through with as much authority as you need *but no more.* No drama. No tantrums. No bickering. Just the facts. And corrective action.

DE-ESCALATE

When emotions run high, it becomes more difficult for your Edison-trait child to stay in charge of his actions. He is self-determined, high-spirited, strong-willed, and passionate. Dynamos are filled to the brim with energy. It is up to you, the responsible adult, to tone things down.

- Keep your voice low and steady.
- Watch your word choices.
- Use silence strategically.

Train yourself to respond to your child's state of excitement by concentrating on your own inner state of calm and resolution. Use his rising level of emotional arousal as a cue to lower yours. *Your goal is to keep your self-control, so your child can regain his.*

HOW TO CORRECT YOUR CHILD

Don't . . .	*Do . . .*
Correct in public.	Correct in private.
Delay, if possible.	Correct immediately or as soon as possible.
Jump to conclusions.	Stay open-minded and ask for the facts.
Say, "I'm angry at you."	Say, "I'm angry at what you did."
Talk in an intimidating, resentful, or mocking tone.	Talk in a normal tone.
Lecture or use big words or long sentences.	Tell it straight and short.
Dredge up the past.	Stay in the present.
Micromanage.	Overlook small things.
Say, "I told you not to . . ."	Say, "It's time to . . ."
Nag.	Apply the "law of least reminder" (a small, silent gesture, if possible).

Get the Inflammation Down

When your child creates havoc and gets out of control, it is normal for you to feel anger mount within yourself. Our emotions work much like our bodies in this regard.

Whenever the body get bruised or infected, it creates inflammation to fight the insult or invasion. However, sustained or excessive inflammation aggravates the injury. That is why we ice an injury or take anti-inflammatory medication. The inflammation has its job to do. It delivers the message, "Pay attention. You are injured." After this, further inflammation makes matters worse, not better.

When you are offended or your feelings have been hurt, your anger rises to help you fight the emotional assault. Sustained or excessive anger, however, aggravates the injury. Once your anger has called attention to the fact that something is wrong, reduce your inflammation. It has delivered its message and done its job. Further anger makes things worse, not better.

Todd said no, then called me a bitch. I went ballistic. The more I thought about it, the madder I got. Then I cried, then I got mad again. "How could he?" Then I realized, "Okay, I need to deal with this." I remembered to stop the inflammation. I told myself, "Now, apply ice to the injury." So I was cool. Well, mostly.

DON'T CONFUSE CONSEQUENCES WITH PUNISHMENT

Many parent-training programs and self-help books now advocate the concept of "natural consequences." They do so for a good reason. It works. But to use this concept effectively, it is important to understand just what natural consequences are.

A natural consequence is what follows an action *as a direct or indirect result of the action.* For example, if your child says something mean to you, the natural consequence is that your feelings are hurt. For your child to make up for what he did, he needs, at a minimum, to apologize. An act of kindness would help as well. Now the natural consequence is that you feel better.

A natural consequence is *not* the same thing as a punishment, which is an arbitrary act you enforce as an authority. For example, suppose your child says something mean to you, and in anger, you ground him for a day. Even if you decide you have a good reason to do this, say, to help develop his moral character, it is still a punishment. It is an arbitrary act that is unrelated to the natural consequence of his having spoken disrespectfully.

A "consequence" and a "punishment" may appear to be the same, but a closer look reveals an important distinction. Your child says something mean and unacceptable to you. He refuses to apologize, so you direct him to his room until he is ready to make amends. He is, in effect, grounded. But in this case, your act is a result of his decision, not just yours. He continues to have the power to improve the prevailing consequences by changing his own behavior.

Dan's parents, Jack and Bev, were in a counseling session. Bev was explaining what had happened that afternoon.

"Dan came home from school and he'd lost his wristwatch. So Jack said, 'No TV tonight.' Then Dan asked, 'What's TV got to do with losing my wristwatch?'

"So I got Jack in the bedroom and I asked him the same question. He said, 'Well, the consequences are supposed to be immediate. I had to think of some way to make him feel like he lost something of value, something he really wants. And it had to be something he'd feel right away.'"

Bev concluded, "I can see Jack's point and I can see Dan's."

So could I. What Jack did was better for his son's self-esteem than threatening or belittling him would have been. And the immediacy of his response was good. Nonetheless, Jack's decision to limit Dan's watching TV because he lost his wristwatch is an example of the kind of arbitrary punishment you want to avoid.

Let's assume your child is past the age of reason. If your child lost his wristwatch today at school, the natural consequence is that he now has no wristwatch and he needs to buy a new one. Since he needs one right away, you'll have to buy it for him, and he'll need to repay you. If he doesn't have enough money, he'll need to figure out a way to earn it.

Your attitude is supportive, not punitive. You can help by paying him to do yard work or to wash the car. You can offer an incentive plan, where you match each dollar he earns. Whatever the details, the bottom line is that your child is responsible for replacing his own lost watch. The result is that he develops an inner authority that recognizes the right thing to do.

To make the impact of the consequences more immediate, think of how you can get started right away. Collect whatever money he has or get him to write out and sign an I.O.U. or make a specific plan of what chores he is going to do and when. Perhaps there is a chore he can begin tonight, which means he cannot watch TV. Under these circumstances, *with a logical connection,* not watching TV is a natural consequence, not a punishment.

Without this logical connection, however, depriving your child of watching TV for having lost his wristwatch is a punishment, not a natural consequence. It does nothing to teach your child the value of his property, or allow him to experience a way to recover from the loss.

When you punish, you assume the role of sole authority, so there is no room for your child to develop inner authority. Typically, punishment results in resentment, not restoration. And the original problem, whatever it was, persists.

Sometimes, when children are younger than seven years of age, you need to think imaginatively to enforce natural consequences. If your child hits his sister, he needs to apologize and help her feel better. If he does it again, he needs to find a way to compensate her. Maybe he needs to lend her one of his favorite toys to play with.

If your child's teacher sends a note home about his rudeness to her, and your child agrees it is true, maybe he needs to write her a note to apologize. If he does it again, maybe he needs to write her a more detailed note and buy her a flower with his own money.

The term "consequence" is not just an equivalent word for punishment. It is a different concept . . . with a different and far more productive consequence.

TEACH YOUR CHILD TO DISTINGUISH BETWEEN FEELINGS AND ACTIONS

*"I told Kevin I am not going to stick around when he gets that angry."
Kevin's father is referring to the family blowout that occurred last weekend.*

"Okay, so leave. That really helps. I just get madder, 'cause you're the reason I'm mad in the first place." Kevin's tone of voice is pointed.

They both turn to me. "So you get mad," I say to Kevin. "And you leave," I say to his dad. I sense they would like me to act as an arbiter. What they really need are ground rules that work. They need to agree that they will accept their feelings but recognize that they choose their own actions. I begin. "Mad is a feeling, and leaving is an action. Let's start there."

A basic skill for gaining self-control is to be able to tell the difference between a feeling and an action. This is especially true of an impulse. An impulse is a feeling that is also part urge—for example, anger plus the urge to leave.

An *impulse* is a call to action. A strong impulse feels like a compulsion to act. But an impulse—any impulse—is a feeling, not an action. You choose whether or not to act on a feeling, and if you choose to act, you choose what to do and when to do it. Sometimes you need to slow yourself down, to be able to see all your choices.

A *feeling* is, that's all. It's an incoming message; it gives you information. You want to notice your feelings. If you ignore them, they have a way of coming back at you later.

An *action* is what you choose to do. It's an outgoing message. It gives you and everyone around you information. You want to make good decisions about your actions. They too have a way of coming back at you later, in the form of consequences.

Let's say you get good news:

A happy *feeling* is: You are joyful.
A happy *impulse* is: You have the urge to leave work and go celebrate.
A happy *action* is: You choose to go back to work. You take a short break, call a friend, and plan some fun for tonight.

Or you get insulted:

An angry *feeling* is: You are furious.
An angry *impulse* is: You have the urge to go insult the insulter.
An angry *action* is: You choose to go for a fast-paced walk. As you walk, you come up with an effective, self-satisfying plan.

Here are a few more examples:

Feeling	Action
Happy, smile on the inside	Dance, play my harmonica
Angry, mean on the inside	Kick door, say, "I am mad"

Once Kevin and his dad saw the difference between a feeling and an action, they had a key to unlock the chain of old habits. Kevin learned he could be mad (his feeling) and still talk to his dad with respect (his chosen action). His dad learned he could want to leave (his feeling) and still stay and listen (his chosen action).

Practice making these distinctions and your child will too.

Accept your feelings. Choose your actions.

TEACH YOUR CHILD HOW TO CALM DOWN

You can't fix a leaky roof when it's raining. And when it doesn't rain, it's easy to forget about the leak. Until the next rainstorm.

When your Edison-trait child is having a temper tantrum, you can't teach him methods to relax. And when he's not upset, it's easy to forget you want to do this. Until the next tantrum.

Edison-trait children need to explore ways to regain their self-control. They need to learn how to settle themselves down. Unfortunately, since they also have a strong drive for stimulation, they are likely at first to resist staying quiet long enough to learn relaxation techniques.

When your child is very young, you can plant some seeds for future habits. Learn to notice warning signs that he is about to get agitated. Can you hear it in his speech or see it in his eyes? Reduce stimulation. Read or tell him a story in a soothing voice.

As your Edison-trait child matures, he will become more receptive to trying out methods to prevent himself from getting overexcited and out of control. Some Edison-trait children take walks, go for runs, write out their feelings, play drums, or sketch pictures. Dynamos need plentiful physical exercise every day.

If you have learned a relaxation procedure that works for you, share it with your child. Do this on a good day, when you and your child are on especially friendly terms.

See if your child is willing to experiment with relaxation techniques. Try deep breathing with him, or tensing and relaxing muscles from head to toe. Try self-talk like "I feel calm," or creating mental pictures like a walk on the beach.

Imaginative methods work best for Edison-trait children. Ask your child to close his eyes and think of a favorite place that's out-of-doors. Ask him to describe it to you. At first you may need to prompt him. "Are there any trees? Are there clouds in the sky?" Before you know it, he will take off and describe a rich, lush scene from nature. He may amaze and delight you with his ability to visualize.

Help your child learn to identify his own early warnings that he is getting too excited or upset. Ask him, "What does it feel like inside your body right now?" Look at him closely for signs of tension. In an inviting tone of voice, ask him to explore what it feels like when he's tense. "Does your fist want to punch? Does your forehead feel scrunched? Do you feel hot and mean?" A mental picture is a useful way for him to recognize a cue: "Do you feel like a balloon about to burst? Or a firecracker ready to go off?"

The first time he reads his own signs by himself, acknowledge him right away. If he stops the cycle and calms himself down, let him know that you noticed and admire what he did. Maybe he left and went for a walk or into his room to cool off. Tell him how much you respect his maturity, responsibility, and self-discipline.

Joe, a nine-year-old Dynamo, once gave me this progress report: "I still lose my temper, but now I know some places to look where I can find it."

CHAPTER 9

≈

Step Six: Coach Your Child to Learn How to Achieve

Treat a child as though he is already the person he is capable of becoming.

—Haim G. Ginnot, Ed.D.

BUILD ON STRENGTH

You are your child's first and best teacher. It is up to you to understand her Edison-trait nature and use this knowledge to help her to develop her convergent-thinking skills.

As you already know by now, Edison-trait children are doers. They must find things out for themselves. To learn, they must do. But to do, they must first be willing to try.

Your child won't try things she believes she can't do as well as others. She'll refuse or shy away from caring about school, especially those assignments that slow her down. Why should she force herself to correct grammar or math facts, or make herself finish a low-interest task, only to discover she did not do the job as proficiently as a classmate? She fears the disappointment this would bring.

That's why Edison-trait children need encouragement. They need the *courage* to try things they fear they can't do. And they need ongoing adult support for their efforts and improvement, regardless of their immediate grade or rank among others.

You can best teach your child by being a good coach. Build her confidence. Emphasize her strengths.

Step Six invites you to nurture your child's natural style of thinking so she can grow strong and face what challenges her. In this chapter you'll learn ways to tap her hidden, dormant talents—to awaken her inner drive and potential to achieve.

Feed your child's abilities. Use concepts she relates to and language she understands. Like a nourished tree that branches out to new heights, she will extend her own abilities to reach new goals.

Be a Model, Not a Critic

Your child needs you to be nonjudgmental. If she feels criticized, she will stop trying. To keep your child trying her best, keep trying your best as her coach.

Your child will do as you do, not as you say. In the words of James Baldwin, in *Nobody Knows My Name:* "Children have never been very good at listening to their elders, but they have never failed to imitate them."

Be a good role model for her. Stay motivated, well organized, and on track. And look forward, not down.

GIVE UNCONDITIONAL LOVE

The other day I stopped for a red light behind a car with a bumper sticker that said:

I AM A PROUD PARENT UNCONDITIONALLY

It triggered memories in me of how much I had looked forward to becoming a parent. I recalled my children as babies, their smiles and their babble. I remembered how privileged and thrilled I felt to hear a baby's voice call *me* Ma.

The more commonly seen bumper sticker, MY CHILD IS AN HONOR STUDENT AT . . . , conveys a parent's pride in the child's academic accomplishment. That's a good feeling to have. But I like this other bumper sticker even more. It expresses a parent's unconditional pride in the child's *being.* That makes a powerful statement.

You may not be proud of everything your child does, but your pride and love for her endure. She makes mistakes and provokes your anger, but you continue to love her for who she is. You look for what you can feel proud of. Your unconditional love empowers her now, and for a long time to come.

I was seeing a talented artist in therapy. She was ready to market her paintings, and she knew she had to take some emotional risks to do this. In preparing herself mentally to make business calls, she found it helpful to summon the image of walking hand in hand with her mother, and hearing her mother say, "You can do this." It was an image with roots that went back thirty years.

"It's her unconditional love," explained this adult Dreamer. "If I get on the phone and wind up sounding like an idiot, I'll go back and feel her love. Then it's okay to make mistakes. It's okay to get rejected."

Unconditional love is not the same as blind permissiveness. You can feel and express unconditional love and still hold your child accountable as you must. Love endures. Mistakes are momentary, necessary steps in the process of learning.

Your unconditional love provides safety for your child. When she falls down, she gets up because she knows you are there. Her behavior may be unacceptable, but you accept *her.* What she did may be wrong, but *she* is good.

This is critical for the Edison-trait child because she will make more mistakes than most other children. It is her nature to explore, to think in new ways. Her brain is wired to seek out stimulation and new experience. She lives on the frontiers of her own mind. And it is riskier on a frontier than it is in other places.

CREATE SAFETY

Your Child's Rate of Progress Is Private

Many well-intentioned parents display their children's report cards and graded papers on their refrigerator door. Perhaps you do this too. You feel proud and you want your child to know this. It is a public recognition of her achievement. It also says that you place high value on the accomplishment of her schoolwork.

But what other messages does this send to your child? Does it motivate her to be a better student or a more anxious one? Does it add to or take away from her willingness to take risks in the classroom? At home, does it fuel cooperation or competition between siblings?

Your child's report card is a way for her to chart her own progress to achieve her own goals. At school, her teacher may not divulge her grade to anyone. Her confidentiality is protected by the Right to Privacy Act,[1] the same law that guarantees you confidentiality at work. Would you want your family to post your supervisor's evaluation of your job performance, or your last pay stub, on the refrigerator door?

Your child needs to know how to compete, because the world is full of competition. But it's safer for children to learn about competition playing ball games and board games and cards. Children are not mature enough to appreciate the complexities of academic competition. They are not equipped psychologically to cope with the threat of losing in a competition so closely tied to their sense of self-worth.

You don't have to publicly display your child's grades to let her know you feel proud of her. Instead, tell her yourself. If you want to tell others, first ask her if it's okay. Respect the fact that she owns her grades, not you. She will work harder to achieve them if she feels they belong to her.

Learn to Reframe

"Reframing" is the mental technique of changing the context in which you see something. Nothing about the picture itself changes. But the way you experience it does. Here's an example:

You have just purchased a brand-new car. You can hardly wait to take it home and show your family and friends. As you drive down the road, a rock comes hurling out of nowhere and hits the side of the car. You look around, see the little boy who threw it, and you become enraged. You stop the car, get out, and just as you are about to lambaste the boy, he pipes up and says: "I'm awful sorry I dented your car. I had to stop you. You see my brother just had an accident and he's bleeding real bad and I don't know what to do." Nothing about the picture itself has changed. Your shiny new car is still dented. But your feelings and actions are quite different now.

A classic example of reframing comes from Thomas Edison himself. Edison firmly believed that many small and wrong ideas prepare the way for the occasional useful one. When asked about the progress of his experiments, his favorite reply was to state enthusiastically, "I now know a hundred ways it won't work."[2]

Another term for reframing is *paradigm shift*. Thomas Kuhn explains this concept in *The Structure of Scientific Revolutions*. He describes what is probably the most famous paradigm shift in history: the Copernican revolution. Copernicus's observations led him to conclude that the sun, not the earth, is the center of the solar system. Nothing about the firmament changed, just our understanding of it.

Start to reframe your experience with your child and make it a habit. The most important paradigm shift you can make is to change your focus from what your child *isn't* to who your child *is*.

Teach Your Child to Reframe

Listen to the words your child uses when she talks about herself. Gently rephrase negative things she says about herself. Give her a healthy, new vocabulary to describe her actions. Don't argue with her. Educate her.

LANORE: I hate myself. I can't keep my big mouth shut.
MOM: Lanore, you are an opinionated and spontaneous young lady.
LANORE: What's that supposed to mean?
MOM: Opinionated means that you have an opinion on most things and that the opinions you have are very strong.
LANORE: Okay, that's true. And the other thing?
MOM: Spontaneous means you do things without planning to do them.
LANORE: Like this!
Lanore made a funny face, jumped up, and left.

The next section lists more examples of reframing Edison-trait children's liabilities as assets. When you give your child words to understand and describe herself, you open the way to self-knowledge and self-acceptance. You give her tools to reconstruct what destructive words may have torn down.

BUILD ON YOUR CHILD'S STRENGTHS

The Edison trait gives your child tremendous potential. It is up to you to nurture her distinctive profile of talents. These specific strengths include her abilities to

- Hyperfocus
- Multitask
- Engage in free-thinking
- Visualize
- Generate power and energy

You can reframe many of her problems as strengths when you understand more about them. It's how you start to turn "symptoms" into skills.

Hyperfocus

The Edison-trait child has the remarkable ability to focus with unusual intensity on a project or activity of personal interest to her. Because she can do this under some circumstances but not others, the adults around her may feel frustrated and confused. Is she intractable, incorrigible, and defiant? Or is she steadfast, self-reliant, and bold?

Reframe and keep a view of what your child's personal intensity and drive can accomplish. Here are some ways to see her liabilities as assets:

Liability	Asset
Stubborn	Strong-willed
Uncooperative	Focused on her own mission
Refuses direction	Self-directed
Tunes others out	Isolates self to go within

Multitasking

Multitasking is accomplishing more than one thing at a time. The Edison-trait child uses stimulation as high-test fuel. For optimal performance she's got to go full throttle and mentally move at freeway speeds. If she goes too slowly, her mind sputters and stalls. That is why when she is understimulated—going school-zone speed—her mind starts to think of other things at the same time. The stimulation of multitasking revs her engine up for her, so she can pick up needed speed.

One form of multitasking is called *dyphasic thinking*. Dyphasic thinking is carrying on two lines of thought at the same time. We all think dyphasically on some occasions. Edison-trait children do it a lot. It's a way for them to get themselves up to freeway speed.

If you can manage your dyphasic thinking, you accomplish multiple mental tasks. If you can't, you accomplish none. You get distracted.

Distraction occurs when dyphasic thinking gets too freewheeling. This happens if you take on too much at one time, or if you neglect to prioritize your tasks. The more you label dyphasic thinking as distraction, the less you can see it as anything else. If an Edison-trait child is constantly told she is distracted, instead of improving her ability to multitask she grows up unaware that it is an ability at all.

To illustrate, let's look at two hypothetical Edison-trait girls: Successful Sally and Distracted Diane. Both are Edison-trait children who seek stimulation. Both are healthy, bright ten-year-olds who attend good schools. At their schools, as in all schools, some activities are low in stimulation—for example, assemblies with extended speeches.

When Sally was seven, she began to understand that she was a creative thinker with a divergent mind. Her parents and teachers encouraged her to value this quality in herself. They taught her convergent-thinking skills, but encouraged her to use them in addition to, not in place of, her divergent thinking.

One day Sally went to an assembly that was boring to her. She started to think about other things. When she got back to the classroom, her teacher asked the class questions about the assembly. Sally could not answer them. She said the assembly was boring. Her teacher and parents talked further with her about ways to cope with boredom. Her father, an Edison-trait adult, told her about dyphasic thinking. Sally learned she could pick up the main points at the assembly and also think of other plans and projects. She could successfully keep track of more than one thing at a time.

Today, when Sally goes to an assembly where she feels bored, she multitasks with ease. She stays slightly tuned in, and catches the main points. Meanwhile she also thinks about things like organizing a trip to the movies with her friends, and rehearsing her lines for the school play. At the end of the assembly she has successfully completed three or four mental tasks.

When Distracted Diane was seven years old, she too went to an assembly and got bored. When she got back to the classroom and her teacher asked the class questions about the assembly, she too could not answer. "Weren't you paying attention?" the teacher asked. Diane knew she was not. She began to see herself as a child who did not pay attention. This happened some more and Diane began to think she *could not* pay attention. Meanwhile, in class, she was being taught convergent-thinking skills. "Paying attention" meant paying attention to only one thing at a time. There was no such thing as paying attention to many things at once. That was called "being distracted." Diane decided this had to be true. Classwork consisted mainly of assignments like doing worksheets, where, indeed, the only way she could get correct answers was to do one thing at a time.

Diane got more and more schoolwork that required convergent thinking. She overgeneralized and concluded that convergent thinking was right and divergent thinking was wrong. Today, at an assembly where she feels bored, she tries as hard as she can to concentrate on what is being said. She fails miserably and uses it as yet another proof she can't control her distraction. Children like Diane have no way of knowing they *can* multitask successfully, so they do not even try to develop this skill.

Psychologist and author Sydney Zentall recommends multitasking for divergent-thinking people, herself included. She says that she can think best only when she is sufficiently stimulated. In her purse Dr. Zentall carries small toys to amuse herself when she gets understimulated.[3]

Here is a list of ways to reframe some of the factors that contribute to your child's potential to multitask skillfully:

Liability	*Asset*
Distracted	Attracted to stimulation
Inattentive	Attentive to more than one task
Easily bored	Performs well with high stimulation
Chaotic	Multifaceted

Free-thinking

Free-thinking means coming up with ideas spontaneously. It's a way to use divergent thinking to solve problems creatively.

Edison-trait children like to free-think just for fun. When you spend time-in with your Edison-trait child—when you and she are just being together—you are free-thinking. Maybe a useful idea will emerge unexpectedly, or maybe not.

Sometimes Edison-trait children get put down for free-thinking. Some see it as a waste of time. Successful Edison-trait adults don't see it that way. They say that reserving time for free-thinking is essential, to maintain the flow of their creative juices. If Archimedes had kept his mind only on taking a bath, would he have discovered the principle of the displacement of water?

Free-thinking can be applied to achieve a specific purpose by means of brainstorming, a technique explained in Chapter 2.

Examples of reframing qualities associated with free-thinking include:

Liability	Asset
Doing nothing	Accepting uncertainty
Disorganized	Tolerant of ambiguity
Unrealistic	Visionary
Inaccurate	Fast (not stopping to correct details)

Visualization

Typically, the Edison-trait child is highly visual. She enjoys her sense of hearing and is easily stimulated by music and excited conversation. But listening to words, especially long lines of them, is usually *not* her preferred style of learning.

The Edison-trait child receives information in one glance. She tends to see things holistically, glossing over details. To organize and remember things, she favors pictures, colors, and patterns. If her visual preference is particularly strong, or if she is being taught to read using phonics only, she may be viewed as having inadequate auditory processing skills. This is even more likely to be true if her mind moves so fast that it does not catch auditory details.

If your child needs extra help to develop her auditory skills, talk with her teacher about getting her the help she needs. But don't lose sight of her visual strengths.

Your child's gift for visualization has more than one purpose. It helps her remember things from the past and it helps her to picture things in the future. Successful Edison-trait adults say that *visualizing their goals* is fundamental to attaining them.

Encourage your child to develop this skill, to visualize her personal goals *as already completed*. Ask her, "When this project is done, what will it look like?" Or "Imagine this essay as already written. What point did you make? What things did you include?"

Your Edison-trait child may rebel against *your* suggesting what to visualize to her. That's part of her nature. But she will grasp how visualizing the future can help make it happen. That's part of her nature, too. It is her natural talent.

Ways you can reframe qualities associated with an aptitude for visualization include:

Liability	*Asset*
Poor listener	Good visualizer
Auditory processing weakness	Sees more than she hears
Distracted by what she sees	Stimulated by what she sees
Misses detail	Sees the whole picture

Generation of Power and Energy

The Edison-trait child craves adventure and stimulation. She is attracted to experience that is trailblazing, important, or thrilling. You will find her where the action is. This is especially true of Discoverers and Dynamos, who unfortunately may get labeled as troublemakers when they provoke others for their own stimulation.

Dynamos are daring risk takers. They are motivated by speed, competition, and power plays between people. Because of this they may get a reputation for being reckless, mean, or manipulative.

Look past your child's frantic pace or clever maneuvering. Set firm but fair limits and teach your child to respect others. At the same time, step back and see the big picture. Appreciate how invigorating and life-affirming her high energy level can be.

Some ways to reframe qualities associated with the generation of power and energy are:

Liability	Asset
Makes trouble	Sparks action
Mean-spirited	Competitive
Careless	Daring
Can't sit still	Has energy to burn

SET ATTAINABLE GOALS

Goal setting empowers your child. In one study of second-, third-, and fourth-graders who had problems completing their homework, goal setting was the method that worked better than any other.[4] Goal setting requires that you identify and set goals that your Edison-trait child can achieve.

Be Realistic

When it comes to their personal interests and to imaginative assignments, Edison-trait children like to have challenging goals. But for classroom assignments—in other words, convergent-thinking tasks—Edison-trait children need goals that they know they can accomplish.

Set goals you honestly believe your child can achieve. If she does not reach her goal, break that goal down into even smaller subgoals. If she has to read a three-hundred-page junior classic in a month, can she read ten pages every day? If not, how many can she read? Get her assignment modified.

If her room is a disaster area, make a list of the specific chores you know she can do on her own: put away all her clothes in the next half hour; put her books and tapes away by lunch; clear her desktop before bedtime tonight. Then give them to her one task at a time.

This is a tried-and-true method. Time-management courses teach executives to break down large goals into small, achievable objectives. We all need goals we can see and feel and know are within reach.

The Hierarchy of Learning

This blueprint for success is based on a basic principle of learning theory, called Gagne's "Hierarchy of Learning."[5] Research psychologist R. M. Gagne demonstrated that Navy recruits who could not learn certain types of complex tasks could perform "component tasks." A component task is a simple part or step of a complex task. After practicing a set of component tasks, the recruits were then able to master the larger, complex one.[6]

Gagne then applied his principles to high school students. He found that breaking up assignments into the specific study skills involved resulted in substantial gains in learning. For example, an assignment might be divided into how to use a particular kind of reference source, how to interpret charts, the construction of an outline, and the composition of a summary. The same student who failed to complete a large, amorphous assignment succeeded in completing a series of smaller, specific ones.

The principle is straightforward. Any time an assignment is too hard to do, subdivide it into simpler assignments that the student *can* do with the knowledge and skills she has.

This principle of dividing goals into simpler, doable steps is the foundation of several highly successful formal learning programs. One is called Reading Recovery, a system considered by many to be an educational breakthrough in the fight against illiteracy. This teaching method, developed in New Zealand, targets the bottom fifth of first-graders, those at highest risk to become lifetime functional illiterates. In the state of California, after sixteen weeks, 89 percent of these pupils performed as well as or better than their classmates on standardized reading tests. In San Diego County, the success rate was 93 percent among the 193 pupils who participated.[7]

The structure and methods of Reading Recovery are based on a single principle: *Build on the skills a child has,* rather than trying to make the child use skills she doesn't have. Any sign of good reading behavior is rewarded, even the tiniest steps and subgoals in the right direction. Pupils become motivated readers. Few Reading Recovery graduates need remedial help again.

MAINTAINING THE FLOW OF MOTIVATION

Keep Gagne's Hierarchy of Learning in mind. If your child does not understand something, break it up into smaller parts. If your child feels overwhelmed by an assignment, make up several "mini-assignments" for her. Alternate low-interest tasks with high-interest ones to keep her stimulated. Multitasking, minideadlines, and frequent breaks accomplish this too. Say you look over her math assignment with her. Can she do five problems by five P.M.? If you think she can, say so. Or better yet, ask her how long she thinks it will take to do the work. Suggest that when she finishes, she take a fifteen-minute break, preferably outside to play.

Train yourself to think about the flow of stimulation your child needs, and not just the content of the assignment she must complete. What methods will empower her to stay interested and keep her energy pumped up, so she can continue to work and finish the job? What will help her get her second wind when she needs it? Help her change her mood first; her behavior will follow.

There is a concept in behavioral psychology called "reward sampling." To get a subject to *want* to work for a reward, you give her a taste of the reward *before* she begins. This creates a high motivational state, otherwise known as a good mood.

Play a short game with your child before she settles down to work. Create, but don't try to force, a good mood. You'll find that your child will be more productive—and happier, too.

Reward the Accomplishment of Big and Little Goals

When you break a goal into smaller parts, be sure to reward the accomplishment of each subgoal. If you can't think of a reward, ask your child. She'll let you know.

One popular reward among Edison-trait children is for you to be your child's personal servant for five minutes. During this time she can tell you to hang up her clothes, make her a snack, or feed the dog for her. Try it. "Finish all the math problems on this page and check each one by four P.M., and I will be your servant for five full minutes." Watch her go.

Try subtle rewards, too. While your child is conscientiously doing her homework, walk over and gently stroke her back. The first time you do this she may draw back. Edison-trait children are highly independent and many are ultrasensitive to tactile stimulation. If this happens, in a soft tone of voice, ask her if it is all right for you to do this. Respect her wishes.

BE A FILTER FOR YOUR CHILD

Personalize Facts: For the Child Who Is Younger Than Seven

If your Edison-trait child is under seven, the best way for you to act as a filter for her is to translate what she needs to know into terms she can understand. If your child does not understand what "one half" means, have her divide the toys in her toy box into two equal piles, then the pennies in her piggy bank, and then the food on her plate. If she does not understand what an adjective is, have her look in the mirror and give a "describing" word for every part of her reflection: "brown" eyes, "curly" hair, "baggy" pants.

Use images and stories as much as possible. The letter C is a smile on its side. To encourage your child to try one more time, read her *The Little Engine That Could.*

Rachel was afraid to give answers out loud in the classroom. She had become so emotionally distraught at the prospect that her teacher had agreed to let her answer privately. The teacher knew that Rachel was facing this problem in counseling.

For several sessions, Rachel and I worked on building her self-confidence. I knew that Rachel took dance lessons. One day I asked her to tell me about her first performance.

Rachel remembered feeling scared. She also remembered how she handled it. She imagined that the people in the audience were chickens. It worked. For the moment, she forgot she was afraid.

In the office we playacted Rachel's answering questions in front of the class. She imagined herself imagining everyone else in the room was a chicken. The more we practiced, the sillier things got. Rachel observed that when she laughed at the situation, she did not feel afraid.

Rachel decided to try it in the classroom, for real. It worked. Rachel's imagination and humor proved stronger than her fear.

Once Rachel could draw on her personal experience of overcoming fear, she had a way to deal with feeling afraid in the classroom.

Personalize Facts: For the Child Who Is Seven or Older

Use the Socratic method to encourage your child to make her own new connections between problems at hand and things she already knows. Ask her what she thinks and listen to what she says. Develop the habit of asking yourself every few minutes, "Am I talking or am I listening?" The more you listen, the more your child talks. The more she talks, the more she owns her own desire to learn.

If you are helping your child with her homework, ask her questions that help her converge on the right answer. Don't tell your child flat out that she is wrong. Tell her first she made a good guess. Or better yet, find some way in which her answer made sense, and comment on that.

Gerard needed to know the meaning of the proverb "A stitch in time, saves nine." He guessed, "If you sew something yourself, you can save money."

My first impulse was to say, "No, that's not it." But I stopped myself and said instead, "I never thought about it like that before. That's a good answer. But there's another meaning that most people think of first . . ."

I was just about to tell him, when he yelled, "No, don't tell me. I know!" And he did.

Edison-trait children grasp concepts more easily from metaphors and stories than from lecture and analysis of facts. To hold or renew your child's interest, offer her stimulating interpretations that personalize what she is learning. For example, ask her how the American Revolution is like a teenager having a fight with her parents to leave home. Or how the Civil War is like the conflict that goes on inside one person's conscience.

After age seven, it is time to introduce your child to organizational tools like calendars, schedules, appointment books, prioritized to-do lists, alarm clocks, and timers. Find the methods and items she likes the most, the ones that best fit her style.

Start with an idea you think will work for her. All Edison-trait children like colors and originality. Dreamers usually like artistic things. You might try giving your Dreamer a personal appointment book with a fashionable cover or one that she can design herself. Discoverers need to find or invent their own tools and methods. Encourage your Discoverer to ask people she admires what kind of schedule books they use. Then take her shopping so she can pick out the one she wants. Dynamos need quick and handy tools. You can create a tailor-made book for your Dynamo by making multiple photocopies of an outline or checklist that meets her needs.

Together with your child, build on the ideas that work the best. Your child might like to have a wipe-board in her room for her daily things-to-do list. She might also want a large wall calendar so she can see deadlines at a glance. She might want to make a specific time each night when she checks her assignment book with her wipe-board and calendar.

As much as possible, *she* needs to be the one to design, try out, and continually develop organizational techniques herself. Your goal is to guide her to find, make, and use her own tools, not to do these things for her.

STATE GOALS IN TERMS THAT ARE SPECIFIC, PRESENT, AND POSITIVE

Be Specific

State goals for your child in clear, unambiguous terms. Specify a time by which a goal will be met. In doing so, also remember to give your child as much choice as possible.

Don't say: Go clean your room.
Say: Which do you want to get done by nine A.M., clean up everything that's on the floor or clear the top of your dresser?

Don't say: Do your homework.
Say: Which do you want to start on now, your vocabulary or your social studies?

Don't say: You need to improve your math skills.
Say: Let's practice multiplication any way you want for ten minutes every night this week and on Saturday I'll take you and one friend to the movies.

Be Present

Refer to the past as little as possible. There's nothing your child can do to change it. She *can* act in the present moment. Empower her and stay in the here and now.

Don't say: Why didn't you get this done before?
Say: This has to be done by nine P.M. What is the first step?

Don't say: How many times have I told you not to yell while your sister's napping?
Say: Please play quietly or go outside now.

Don't say: Don't you ever listen?
Say: Please stop what you're doing, look straight at me, and listen, now.

Be Positive

State a goal in words that create a picture of the goal. Describe the behavior you want to see, not the one you want to avoid.

Don't say: I don't want to hear you fight with your sister one more time.
Say: I want you and your sister to get along nicely. Keep your hands to yourselves and use only the kind of language that we allow in our home.

Don't say: Didn't I tell you not to interrupt me when I'm on the phone?
Say: Please be quiet while I'm talking.

Don't say: Don't forget.
Say: Remember.

The Empowering Question

When something needs to be done, ask your child by what time she will finish or start the job. For example, "By what time will you have the things you used for this project put away?" or "By what time will you start your homework?"

Your goal is to teach your child to set and achieve her own goals. The empowering question helps you accomplish this. When your child gives you a specific time limit, she makes a clear, unarguable commitment. This makes it easier for her to achieve her goal. It also makes it easier for you to have a frank discussion with her about the meaning of avoidance and procrastination if she does not.

THE EMPOWERING QUESTION:
BY WHAT TIME WILL YOU . . . ?

CHAPTER 10

Step Seven: Take Care of Yourself

Children grow well when their parents are growing well.

—W. D. Wall

WE ALL NEED REASSURANCE

Janine is the mother of a teenage Dreamer named Crystal. At her first therapy session, Janine, an intelligent, insightful woman, nervously disclosed that she gets upset when her daughter does something she doesn't approve of in front of others. "I hate this about myself. I'm not that shallow," she insisted. "I don't really care what others think. I care about my daughter. So why do I overreact?"

At the next session she told me about a talk she'd had that week with Crystal. "We were sitting at the counter having breakfast. Crystal has such good manners. The other girls her age do not. So I said to her, 'Crystal, you are so polite when all your friends so are rude. Why is that?'

"Crystal said, 'I don't know, Mom, it's just the way I am.' And then I felt agitated. I still am. And I don't know why."

I paused and asked Janine, "What did you want your daughter to say?"

Janine reflected for a moment and then thoughtfully replied. "You know, I think I wanted her to say, 'Because that's the way you raised me.' I need to know that I am a good parent."

Janine realized this was the same reason she got so upset with Crystal in public, too. Her "good parent" status was on the line.

Like Janine, we all need to know we are good parents. And when you are the parent of an Edison-trait child, this question stares you in the face every day. There is the child down the street who gets straight "A"'s, has font-perfect script, and visible shelf space in her bedroom. At stores, there are glares from parents whose children *walk* down aisles and don't reach out to grab items that attract them. And there is the endless stream of thoughtless comments from people offering you advice you don't want or need.

How do you know you are a good parent? Look in the mirror and answer this question: If you were your child, would you want a parent like you?

PARENT STRESS MANAGEMENT

Parenting an Edison-trait child is stressful. To cope, find and practice one or more ways to relax and recenter yourself. Here are a few methods to try.

First, let's assume you actually have the luxury of taking ten minutes for yourself. What will relax you the most? Here are some ideas:

Ten-Minute Methods to Relax
- Take a walk.
- Take a nap.
- Read (not the newspaper, unless it's the funnies).
- Listen to music (preferably on headphones).
- Create (anything).

If you cannot leave the premises, and you have two minutes, not ten, here are some more ideas:

Two-Minute Methods to Relax
- Take three deep breaths.
- Envision you are somewhere beautiful under the open sky.
- Repeat the word *relax* to yourself thirty to fifty times.
- Silently sing your favorite song.
- Talk to God or a Higher Power.

MAINTAIN YOUR SELF-ESTEEM

Protect your private life. Your children grow to value themselves by the example you set. Model self-esteem by respecting your own personal time.

You do need to devote a great deal of time to raising an Edison-trait child. This is a reality. While doing this, however, it is vital that you not turn yourself into a martyr.

Chronic self-sacrifice teaches a child that a person is worthy only by being of service to others. If you let your children use you unfairly, you are setting them on a course to be used by others or to use others unfairly in their adult relationships.

LEARN HOW TO CENTER YOURSELF

There is a diversity of ways to quiet yourself, get rebalanced, and renew your personal strength and mental energy. For example, there are meditation, yoga, prayer, music, and self-hypnosis. There are specialized relaxation exercises such as deep muscle relaxation (the physical tensing and releasing of individual muscle groups one at a time) and "autogenic training" (the repetition of simple statements that self-suggest relaxation in specific parts of the body, such as "my hands feel warm and heavy"). There are books and reputable classes available to learn these practices.

Guided imagery is an effective method that I especially like. In guided imagery, you evoke the feelings you want by imagining pictures and movements you associate with them.

Here are the basics of an exercise that you can use to create a mental vision of sanctuary. The imagery works best when you have your eyes closed. After you use this description the first few times, you will easily recall the images without having to read the words. It takes less than a minute.

MY GARDEN

I close my eyes, take a deep breath, and I am in my garden. I feel calm and serene.

My garden is fully enclosed by a stone wall, seven feet tall. It is safe, protected, and private.

Inside my garden it is peaceful and silent. All around me it is lush and green. There are vibrant plants and colorful flowers. I savor the fragrance as I breathe in the life all around me. My feet are connected to the earth beneath me. Above my head the open sky goes on forever.

I breathe in courage and energy and I breathe out anything it's time to let go of. I feel reverence and joy. I feel centered and clear. I leave my place of sanctuary now, with renewed personal strength.

THINK AFFIRMATIVELY

Ralph Waldo Emerson once said, "Every word is a poem." Every word evokes emotional memories you associate with that word, and in doing so, suggests those moods to you again.

Use this as a guiding principle when you create your own guided imagery and self-talk. Be affirmative. Use self-talk to keep a positive attitude.

Catch yourself when you feel discouraged, disheartened, or self-critical. If you hear yourself say things like "I feel like such a failure," actively argue the point with yourself. Here are some affirmations you may want to try.

AFFIRMATIVE SELF–TALK FOR PARENTS
I am thankful to be a parent. The responsibility is great but the rewards are greater.
I teach my child and my child teaches me.
I find solutions, or I create them.
I am thankful for my children—their gifts and talents and their love.
Enthusiasm and a sense of humor make the best atmosphere for learning.

One of my favorite affirmations comes from Thomas Edison himself:

The surest way to succeed is to try one more time.

REGAIN YOUR PERSPECTIVE

Do you remember the technique of reframing described in the last chapter? Just as you reframe things that you see in your child, you can reframe many things for yourself. For example, if you are looking too closely at imperfections, disappointments, or frustrations, ask yourself, What will this mean to me ten years from now?

My mother tells me she can remember sitting at her kitchen table watching her mother stir a potful of diapers in boiling water on the stove. That's how she sanitized them. Now, as a working mom, I find that some days are tough. Yet when I think about my grandma and her steaming pot of diapers, my idea of what is tough doesn't seem so tough anymore. I would rather be a woman with choices than a woman without them.

APPRECIATION: A HEALTH-PRODUCING HABIT

The late Hans Selye was the first person to identify the stress response. He was a pioneer researcher and leading authority in the field.[1]

Dr. Selye understood what a powerful hold a stress response can have. He believed that the best way to reduce stress was to concentrate on competing thoughts. In other words, you can force stress out by actively thinking of something else. The strongest thoughts for doing this are those that evoke an attitude of appreciation. To replace thinking about demands being made on you, think of specific things you feel thankful for instead. According to Selye, you cannot feel stressed out and deeply grateful at the same time.

What do you honestly feel appreciative of? Your health? Your family? Your home? Take a moment now and make a thank-you list on a piece of paper.

I am grateful for

1. _____

2. _____

3. _____

The next time you feel stressed, take out your list and read it. And may the best thoughts win!

THE TEN-MINUTE VENT

Devoted parents sometimes put so much attention and energy into meeting the needs of an Edison-trait child that they bottle up their own emotions without realizing it. Feelings have to wait for later, but later never comes.

- Edison-trait children exhaust their parents. Do you feel tired, weary, and fatigued?
- Edison-trait children are time-intensive to raise. Do you feel trapped, hurried, or resentful?
- Edison-trait children are conundrums. Are you bewildered, worried, or scared?
- Edison-trait children provoke others. Are you just plain angry?

It is good to vent undesirable feelings. It is not good to dwell on them. A vent with a time limit meets both of these requisites.

To whom do you vent? Since both you and your spouse probably have raw nerves over the same recurring issues, it is preferable to choose a good friend other than your spouse with whom you can safely vent.

Focus on your most intense feelings and ask your friend to listen, that's all. Let yourself go—but for no more than ten minutes.

If your friend is not available, write out your feelings, and write and write. In about ten minutes, you'll probably feel less and less like writing. If you want to vent more, return for another ten-minute session later.

Why only ten minutes? So you contain your stress response. *Containment* is an important concept in stress management. According to Dr. Selye, "An essential feature of adaptation is the confinement of stress to the smallest area capable of meeting the requirements of the situation."[2]

Here's an important distinction. The ten-minute vent is not the same experience as working with a professional counselor or psychotherapist. Each serves a different purpose.

Your goal in a ten-minute vent is to relieve stress fast, clear the air, and get back to work. Your goal in professional therapy is to enhance your awareness of your feelings, to identify patterns and their origins, and to bring them under conscious control. This necessarily takes longer than ten minutes.

Consider a professional consultation if in your day-to-day living you feel caught in a nonproductive or counterproductive cycle. If the same unwanted feelings or behaviors repeat themselves over and over, it may be worthwhile to explore some personal issues in therapy. I'll discuss more about counseling for your family in Chapter 14.

BE PATIENT WITH YOURSELF

It takes time and practice to change a behavior. Some experts estimate that even a simple behavior change takes about three weeks.

Each of us has our own timetable. One mother of an Edison-trait child described her progress like this:

1. *I got mad as usual, but this time I heard what I said to him, and for the first time I realized it was mean. I was acting bossy and overbearing.*
2. *The next time it happened, I heard even more clearly how hurtful my words were, but I couldn't help myself. It was as though someone else were speaking, not me.*
3. *The next time I got mad, I was mad as ever at him, but this time I was mad at me too. I still said a few things that cut him down to size, but I stopped myself from going too far.*
4. *The next time, I tried to stay calm and remember how to be angry without attacking or insulting him. I tried the broken-record technique. It came out awkward and weak. We both felt uncomfortable and kind of strange. Afterward, I kept thinking about what I should have said and how I should have said it.*
5. *The next time I was better prepared. Some of the stuff came out okay. Mostly he just listened. I think he was confused. I think I was, too. Things were quieter than they've ever been. Later on I kept going over how I could have done things differently, especially the tone of my voice. I needed more conviction. And I needed to stop when I'd said enough.*
6. *I started to feel more comfortable about getting angry but not mean. The more I stuck to the incident at hand, the better things went. It started to come easier to me. It felt like part of my own personality.*
7. *One day I heard him get mad at his baby sister. But he didn't make her cry. He stopped himself from acting mean. "You have to stay out of my things," he said over and over in his own broken-record style. He didn't yell and he didn't hit her. I felt so happy. I'm the one who started to cry.*

STAY IN THE HERE AND NOW

One day my older daughter, Julia, and some of her friends were in the kitchen making popcorn. They started to talk about the most important moments in life. Being runners, they talked about moments when they'd won a race.

I walked in and said, "I know the most important moment in my life." I said it with so much confidence, it piqued their curiosity.

"Was it the day you got married?" they guessed at first.

"No," I replied.

"I know, Mom. It was really two moments—when Jeni and I were born." Julia thought she had it nailed.

"Nope," I replied with a smile.

"The day you got your doctorate?"

"The first time you drove a car?"

"Your first kiss?"

"Nope, nope, nope." I continued to smile.

"Okay, we give up." I had their attention.

"The most important moment in my life," I said in a deliberate way, "is this one, right now—the present moment. It's the one in which I have the most power. It is the only one I can do something about."

"Oh, Mom," Julia groaned. "You're always a psychologist."

I saw her smile, though. And I knew she liked my answer.

LAUGHTER IS GOOD FOR YOU

Cultivate your sense of humor. Cherish the wild ideas that are born of your Edison-trait child's mind. When he was two, did he ask you, "Who made God?" Did he unravel a paper-towel roll to make a path of paper through every room in the house? Did he wear a Superman cape to the supermarket unselfconsciously? Write these stories down to read and reread later. Tell them to your child as he gets older. Tell them to yourself and enjoy them.

There is a story about two kindergartners out in the playground at recess time. (See if they remind you of anyone you know.) They look up to the sky to see a military jet flying overhead. "Hey, that's a Grumman X-29," one observes. "Nope," his friend argues, "the wings are too thick. The X-29 has thin wings made out of graphite epoxy." The bell rings.

The two boys sigh. "Let's go inside and string those beads."

CHAPTER 11

∿

Step Eight: Take Care of Your Family

The family is one of nature's masterpieces.

—George Santayana,
The Life of Reason

KEEP UP WITH THE BASICS

No matter how focused you become on your Edison-trait child, keep your sights set on maintaining the basics for yourself and for your family: (1) eating nutritious food, (2) getting physical exercise, (3) getting enough sleep, and (4) protecting your children's impressionable young minds.

1. Eating Nutritious Food

As children get older, it gets harder for them to keep up good eating habits. The norm in most junior high and high schools is junk food. Keep up your family's awareness of the nutritional value of foods. Everyone feels better and stronger with good nutrition.

2. Getting Physical Exercise

What's the best kind of exercise? The one you will do. If the word *exercise* does not appeal to you, how about *sports, play, physical activity,* or *letting loose*? You and your child might choose to play or walk together during time-in. A brisk walk can work wonders. Physical activity produces endorphins. Endorphins are brain chemicals that make us happy.

3. Getting Enough Sleep

The surest way for you to appreciate the value of sleep is to have to do without it. Unfortunately, children seldom make the connection between lack of sleep and loss of cognitive abilities like judgment and self-control. Edison-trait children often go through stages where their sleep patterns are disrupted, and their daytime behavior suffers. This in turn disrupts sleep for others in the house, affecting everyone's daytime attitudes and behaviors. Keep as much stability as you can through these phases. Stay aware, and never underestimate the power of a good night's sleep.

4. Protecting Your Children's Impressionable Young Minds

It is every parent's job to encourage his child to explore his world while at the same time protecting him from experience he is not ready for. The Information Age makes this job an unprecedented challenge. Passive entertainment with graphic, distasteful, or violent content is readily available and hard to avoid.

As a parent, you model good decision making when you choose constructive activities for your family like reading, playing sports, and appreciating nature and the arts. Children do as we do, not as we say.

Nonetheless, children start early deciding for themselves how they want to spend their time. What kind of experience they give themselves rests on many factors. However, being children, they often make their decisions on the basis of expediency. This means they are likely to turn on the TV.

Edison-trait children are drawn to TV more than other children are. At the same time, TV can wreak more havoc with their brains than it can in children who are less imaginative and free-thinking. Siblings get drawn in. It is hard not to.

Assess the amount of TV watching your children do. Compare it to the amount of time they spend reading or playing games and doing puzzles. What ratio seems about right to you?

When I ask this question of parents at workshops, most say a ratio of about 2:1 in favor of reading, but they'd be happy with 1:1—they just don't think that it's possible. I ask them to consider adopting one basic rule.

Limit TV Watching

The rule is this: From now on, all TV watching is planned. No impulse watching. Get a Sunday paper and go through the TV listings with your children. Agree on what will be watched and when. No "vegging out" unless it's in the plan. Make sure everyone knows how to use the VCR, and keep an ample supply of videotapes, clearly labeled, near the set. The VCR is a useful tool to eliminate impulse watching, and can help you keep to your TV-watching plan.

If you want, you can give this analogy to your children: If a person spends more money than he earns, his spending is out of control. To stay within his budget, he must plan all his purchases. He needs to make a rule with himself: no impulse buying. Your brain has to have extra hours in its *active learning* account before you have enough savings to spend time passively in front of a TV. Tell your child: "I love you too much to let you go broke in your brain." Or, "It is my job as a parent to do this so that when you grow up, you aren't mad at me because you're not as smart as you could have been."

If your children like channel surfing, allow them to do this, but plan for it and count it as part of the total amount of TV watched. Follow up consistently. You may find more shows get videotaped than get seen. If this occurs, don't complain about wasted tape. Think instead of the number of hours you saved your child from wasting had he been watching, not recording, TV.

HANDLING SIBLING RIVALRY

Sibling rivalry gets complicated when one or more children in a family has the Edison trait. Your Edison-trait child is painfully aware of the successes of his more academically inclined brother or sister. He probably feels jealous and angry. Why do these things come so easy to his sibling, but require such effort for him?

Your non-Edison-trait children may be fed up with being provoked by their Edison-trait sibling who is constantly on a quest for stimulation. They are primed to feel jealous of the extra time and concern you give to your Edison-trait child.

Here are some guidelines to help you encourage peace among siblings in your home:

1. Stand Up for Safety

Each child in your family needs to feel safe and protected. Uphold basic rules such as no hitting and no invading bedrooms or bathrooms. Use your full authority to do so.

2. Respect Each Child's Individuality

When it comes to siblings, favoritism is wrong, and treating children identically is wrong too. Treat each of your children as the one-of-a-kind person he is. Each child is different, so you'll relate differently to each child. And each will relate in a different way to you, too. Practice time-in *alone* with each of your children. As you do, you will get to know each one better. You will see each child as a total person, not just in the role of son or daughter. This will help you decide how to keep attention and other family resources balanced to best meet everyone's needs.

3. Supply a Generous Flow of Attention

What do siblings compete for more than anything else in the universe? Your attention. (Somehow you knew that.) If there's enough to go around, there is less motivation to fight. No one argues when the pizza first arrives at the table. It's the last piece that starts the war.

It is no easy task for you as a parent to give each of your children ample attention. Raising your Edison-trait child is time-consuming. Where do you get the time?

Speak honestly and privately with each of your children. Explain to them: "Each of you needs me in your own way." Make no judgment of each child's individual needs.

Your children know they are not identical. Yet they may feel hurt when you give one child more one-on-one time than another. Encourage the child who gets less time to say how he feels. Validate his feelings without putting down his sibling. For example, say, "You're right. I did spend a lot of time with your brother tonight. I understand you feel slighted. Thank you for telling me how you feel." Don't say, "But you know your brother isn't as capable as you are. He can't do it without me."

Avoid being dismissive of the child who feels cheated. For example, don't say, "Oh, don't make such a big deal about it." Check to see that you *are* meeting his needs. Ask him directly: "Is there anything I can do to help you with your homework?" Set limits on how unevenly you allow yourself to distribute your time. Don't sacrifice time-in with any of your children.

4. Respect Each Child's Privacy

Privacy means just the two of you, with no siblings present. Talk about personal matters in private. Spend time-in in private. Correct your child in private. Except in dangerous situations where you must act immediately, take the time to say, "I'd like to talk to you alone." Even if you are upset, go the extra mile. Walk to his room or yours, close the door, and sit down together, in private.

5. Make No Comparisons

Resist the urge to compare, out loud or silently. You'll have tremendous temptation to compare your Edison-trait child with his non-Edison-trait sibling to feel better about yourself as a parent. When you and your spouse are alone you may be especially drawn to doing this. As parents, make a conscious decision not to. Redirect your conversation if it turns overly critical toward one child.

Train yourself so that when you talk about things one child has done, you do not automatically jump to thoughts of what his sibling would have done in the same situation. Say instead: "That's just like him!" And that's all.

SPECIAL SITUATIONS

Here are some guidelines for you to consider if your Edison-trait child is adopted, or if he currently resides in more than one household.

Adoption

Adopted children must face the realities of their adoption. A child who has the Edison trait has a hard enough time facing ordinary realities; he needs special consideration to accept the fact that he is adopted. In a recent study of eighty-five adopted children ages six to seventeen, younger children experienced intrusive thoughts about adoption. Older children had fewer intrusive thoughts, but greater feelings of ambivalence about it.[1]

Edison-trait children have difficulty inhibiting thoughts they don't want. This makes them particularly vulnerable to intrusive thoughts. If your Edison-trait child is adopted, be sensitive to his need to know more about his origins. Do what you can to provide a library of stories about his past. Explanations and assurances are important, but for an Edison-trait child, stories are better and pictures are best.

Two-Household Families

Single parents and two-household families face a special challenge. This challenge is *consistency*. Can rules, rewards, and consequences be consistent between two different households? This is a complex issue, since irreconcilable differences between father and mother are what caused the divorce to begin with.

THE STORY OF SEAN. Five-year-old Sean is a Dynamo. An only child when his parents divorced, he was the focus of a heated custody dispute.

A forensic psychologist was retained to conduct a comprehensive custody evaluation. Sean's teacher suggested that I be consulted. She knew Sean was an Edison-trait child. His behavior at school was deteriorating rapidly under the strains of the divorce.

Sean's father was an engaging, high-energy entrepreneur. He knew instinctively how to connect with his son. "His mother says he won't dress himself in the morning," he told us. "And now he won't even get out of bed." He sighed. "It's because she runs the house like boot camp.

"When he's at my place, and it's time to get him up, I go in there, tickle his toes, and tell him the circus is in town. I say the parade is coming right through the house and if he isn't dressed and downstairs in ten minutes, he's going to miss it. Then he rushes around, gets dressed, and runs downstairs. Then I say, 'Sean you just missed the parade. But the clown left something for you.' I say that every time. He expects it. Then he looks for what the clown left him. I make it different every time. It can be almost anything as long as it's silly. This morning I made him a tower out of paper cups. He knocked it down and built it up again till it was time to go to school.

"Now she'll go in there and say, 'Sean, this is your last chance. If you don't get up this minute, I'm going to put an X instead of a star on your chart. And there will be no dessert tonight after dinner.' Yeah, right. That's really gonna bring him to life. If I were the kid, I'd go back to sleep, too."

Sean's mother, an intent, soft-spoken managerial assistant, tells another side of the story. "He's a Disneyland Dad. Everything is fun, fun, fun. But was he there on Sean's birthday? No. When Sean got stitches? No. When the dog died? No. He was out of town, too busy to even pick up the phone and call.

"Has he ever been to a parent conference at school? There's a place on his desk where he just stacks notices from the teacher. It goes all the way back to September. Ask him if he knows if Sean has any allergies. He'll tell you to call me to find out."

Apparently, Sean's dad understands the Edison trait in his son better than he does in himself. This is not an isolated situation. An astute Edison-trait adult once asked me: "Are there times ADD really stands for Absent Dad Disorder? You know, where the kid is just like the old man, but the old man ain't around to teach him how to act?"

Sean's parents were awarded joint custody of their son. Sean will need to adapt to two completely different home lives. He'll relate to his dad, but he'll miss him a lot too. His mom will be there for him, but he'll fight her all the way. Sean will need every ounce of his Edison-trait resourcefulness to adjust to the lack of consistency between his two homes.

THE STORY OF JESSICA. Ten-year-old Jessica, an Edison-trait Dreamer, spends alternating weeks with each of her parents. They divorced one year ago. Jessica's mother remained single. Her father recently remarried.

Jessica was failing fifth grade. She attended a small private school, where the administrator recommended that she be tested professionally. Jessica's scores on the ADDES, a standardized questionnaire for symptoms of ADD, were extreme. She scored in the lowest two percentile for the symptom of inattentiveness. Other tests showed Jessica to be a reasonably intelligent child. Her scores did not indicate any specific learning problems.

Jessica's parents reported that she had always been a Dreamer. At school she had never been an honor student, but up until now she had gotten passing grades. In separate interviews, both parents said that while the divorce had its tense moments, things had settled into a routine now. They each reported that Jessica's study habits were poor and that they had been lenient with her, in view of the stress of the divorce.

After the testing, by their request, I held separate feedback sessions with each parent. I explained my findings and recommendations and suggested we discuss consistent guidelines to help Jessica structure her homework time. I said I would talk further with Jessica's teacher, but if we could not stop her steep rate of decline, we needed to consider an evaluation for medication.

When Jessica's father came to his session, he also brought his wife, Jessica's stepmother, but she did not say much. The next day she called and asked to schedule another meeting with me for herself and her husband.

At the meeting she spoke up. "I talked with Ed, so he knows what I'm about to say," she began. "I don't want Jessica to have to take Ritalin. When you talked about consistency, I kept thinking about how things must be for her right now. We don't talk to her mother. But I see the homework she does there, and knowing what I know, I bet it's the same deal there as at our house.

"Everyone is afraid to say no to Jessie, because when she is fourteen, she can decide who she wants to live with. She pretty much does as she pleases. No one wants to be the bad guy."

Jessica's stepmother continued. "And there's no reward we can use to help Jessie do her work. She's got everything she wants and more. You should see her room!"

Jessica's father agreed, and in a separate session, so did her mother. We then set up a joint session at Jessica's school with her mother, father, stepmother, and teacher. We wrote out guidelines for getting homework done and created a system for E-mail correspondence to keep continuity between the two households. The next day after school we met again, this time with Jessica. The plan was put in place.

After a few weeks of consistent follow-through, Jessica's schoolwork improved considerably. Interestingly, in English class that year, Jessica wrote a charming fairy tale about a spoiled princess whose greed almost caused the peasants in her kingdom to lose their land.

PART III

A Parent's Guide to Resources

As you practice the eight steps you learned in Part II, you'll get a better sense of your child's Edison-trait nature. You'll develop skills and discover new ways to nurture and encourage your child.

In Part III you will read about qualified professionals who can support you in your efforts. Some, like your child's teachers, you will meet along the way. Others, like private counselors, you will need to seek out.

Some chapters in Part III may not apply to you and your child. Feel free to skip ahead to Part IV at any point.

CHAPTER 12

—◊—

Your Edison-Trait Child at School

She probably wanted to learn to read very much. What she rightly resented was my taking it upon myself to teach her without being asked. When she learned to read, it was going to be by her own choosing, at her own time and in her own way. This spirit of independence in learning is one of the most valuable assets a learner can have, and we who want to help children's learning, at home or in school, must learn to respect and encourage it.

—John Holt,
How Children Learn

MASTERY STUDENTS

Columbia University psychologist Carol Dweck, Ph.D., has spent the last twenty years studying children's approaches to school. She has identified two patterns: mastery vs. helplessness.[1]

Mastery students have a pattern of learning based on what she calls an "incremental theory." They believe people have to do things in increments to become smart. They focus on learning and effort.

Helpless students act on the basis of an "entity theory." They believe people are entities who are either born smart or aren't. They focus on performance and on passing or failing.

When solving new problems, mastery students try harder and longer. Helpless students give up more easily, attributing failure to their own inability. Findings show that mastery students achieve throughout their academic years. Helpless students may do fine in grade school, but in junior high, their grades typically decline. The more they must rely on their own inner resources, the less they can keep up with their studies.

Dweck observed evidence of the two different styles as early as kindergarten. Mastery kindergartners assessed their own handmade work as "good" and continued to do so in the face of the teacher's criticism. Helpless kindergartners started out the same way. Initially, they assessed their handmade work as good. But after hearing a teacher's criticism, they reassessed their work as "bad." Then they attributed this "bad" work to a fixed trait inside themselves that would never change.

Mastery kindergartners held on to their own opinions and drive. Helpless kindergartners gave their authority away to the teacher. By doing so they created a need to protect themselves from the impact of criticism over which they had no control. To stay safe they could no longer risk making mistakes. When it came to schoolwork, they tried less.

FROM MASTERY TO HELPLESSNESS

Your Edison-trait child starts off as a natural-born mastery student. He likes to explore, take risks, do things his own way, and learn things for himself. He is his own thinker, has his own style, and takes off in his own directions.

When he gets to school, he learns that he must conform. He must do the things that the other students do, in the way that the teacher instructs him to do it. The Dreamer must give up his flights of fancy, so he can listen carefully and follow directions. The Discoverer must give up asking his questions, so he can answer the teacher's. The Dynamo must give up his impetus to action, so he can sit still and behave.

When we ask our children to give up their strengths, why are we surprised when they give up their ownership and motivation, too?

> *"Nothing matters to him. He doesn't care what his work looks like."*
> *"He'll lie and say he has no homework, or that he left it in his desk. If I don't check up on him, he won't do it."*

We get angry at their apathy and indifference. Yet it is we who take young mastery students and turn them into helpless ones.

We ask thinkers who are exquisitely divergent to confine themselves to convergent thinking. We force them to comply with models that belittle their natural tendencies. We criticize them for not knowing things they have no way of knowing. And then we wonder why they don't come back for more.

Writing on self-esteem, Gloria Steinem once said that no one should have to choose between "bettering oneself" or "being oneself."[2] Yet that is exactly the choice we force on Edison-trait students every day.

BETTERING ONESELF *AND* BEING ONESELF

"I haven't met a child incapable of thinking and participating to some degree in school if we let him know we value what he can contribute," says William Glasser, M.D., author of *Reality Therapy*. Glasser has worked extensively with children in the Los Angeles school system. He observes that our educational system works in opposition to the "diverse thinking, creative, artistic, emotional brain."[3]

What if we make school a place where we truly honor diversity, where we teach and we value both convergent *and* divergent thinking? The convergent thinker can go to school, knowing his orderly way of learning will be respected and exercised *and* that he will be challenged to open his mind and think imaginatively. And the divergent thinker can go to school confident that his active and creative style of experimenting with life will be nurtured and appreciated *and* that he will be taught ways to manage his time and organize his work efficiently.[4]

In a newsletter column a mother asked this question of psychologist and author Sydney Zentall, Ph.D.[5] First she explained that her eleven-year-old son pays attention to everything that goes on around him, every sound, every movement. At school he has trouble finishing his work. His teacher suggested that to do his "seatwork" he should sit at "an old library carrel which is enclosed on three sides."

"The school psychologist said this has been used in other schools and it might not hurt to try it," the mother related, "but my son thinks it would be a punishment." Then she asked: "Does this seem like an idea worth trying, or could it be harmful to my son?"

"I agree with your son," Dr. Zentall replied. "It would be punishment—not only punishment but exclusion from participation in classroom activities." Dr. Zentall noted that research has failed to document *any* performance gains from the use of cubicles.

Her suggestion is to "replace isolating the child away from movement and sound by *using* sound, movement and interest as a way to capture and focus his attention on important events and stimuli."

In other words, don't ignore the nature of his divergent-thinking style and force him to play the role of a wayward convergent thinker. Instead, see the richness of his style, and use it to attract him to practice and enhance his convergent-thinking skills.

Dr. Zentall also suggests that for this child's desk work, the teacher replace the goal of completing a long task with the goals of completing several shorter ones.

To sum up, her recommendations are twofold: First, present materials to the child in a novel and stimulating way; and second, adjust your expectations of him so he can successfully achieve his goals. Are her ideas well advised?

WAYS THAT YOU AND YOUR CHILD'S TEACHER CAN HELP

"Life isn't going to change to accommodate Steven. He may as well get used to it, while he's still young and can roll with the punches. You don't think his boss is going to color-code his assignments and modify his deadlines, do you?"

Sometimes a teacher feels this way and sometimes it is the opinion of a parent. It is a valid argument. It's not right to modify the environment too much to accommodate a child. The child must learn how to adapt to the environment.

The goal is a balance, a reciprocity of child and school *adapting to each other.* But to accomplish this state of balance, it may be necessary, at first, for us to adapt more to the child.

If we create conditions that ensure a child's academic success, the child will respond, take risks, and try to do what he is asked. The more the child tries, the more successfully he adapts to school, and the less we need to adapt to him. Eventually, balance is achieved.

Dr. Zentall's recommendations are sound. Divergent-thinking children need to have their strengths recognized.

Edison-trait children learn best by means of

1. The use of fantasy
2. Multisensorial experience
3. Visual cues
4. Learning through self-expression
5. An emphasis on quality, not quantity

STOP HERE. If you don't have a pen in your hand right now, please go and get one. As you read this chapter, clearly mark the principles you like and the methods you want to try. Highlight or underline. Make stars and notes.

As soon as you can, try these principles and methods with your child. Notice what works and what does not. Think up new ideas. Build on what works. Continue to make notes.

Your written notes will make it easier for you to share your ideas and findings with your child's teacher. Lend him your notes. Brainstorm with him.

The two of you are partners in your child's learning and growth. Working together, you can develop the best solutions to help your child.

1. THE USE OF FANTASY

John Holt, one of our country's most respected educators and reformers, was a dedicated advocate of young children's right to fantasize.[6] He saw play as a vital part of their learning process at school. Holt firmly believed that "children use fantasy not to get out of, but to get into, the real world."

Holt was careful to define "children's fantasy" as the imagery that originates in their own minds. He distinguished it from adult-imposed fantasy. He was all for games, especially those that introduced body movement into the classroom. But he made a careful distinction between a child's own fantasy and one that is directed by a teacher. For example, Holt observed that it is not the same thing for a child to spontaneously feel like a snowflake as it is for children at circle time to be asked to dance like snowflakes. He denounced high-tech, ready-made, sold-for-profit fantasies delivered through TV and other mass media.

Holt maintained that it is mostly through personal fantasy that children connect new experiences and ideas to the ones they already have. He offers the following example of a mother teaching her preschooler how to read.[7]

> The child draws a picture of one of his favorite subjects: pirates. The mother asks him to tell her about the picture. "Pirate Sam has a sword," the child replies. She asks his permission to print this sentence on the same paper as his picture. She has him choose whatever color felt marker he wishes. She prints it under his picture and then also on a separate sentence strip. Then she uses the same felt-tip pen to print each individual word on its own 3 × 5 card. She mixes up the words and he matches them to the appropriate sentence strip or to the sentence under his picture. They play this game over and over. The boy draws divers and composes the sentence: "Four divers are on a submarine." Again they play, this time the words are printed in a new color that goes with the new picture. The boy draws a hydrofoil. "This hydrofoil is one hundred feet long." Another game, another color.

The boy is good at the game. Ask him how he does it and he'll tell you: The cards are cars of a train. The period is always on the caboose and the capital letter is the front of the engine.

What is the role of fantasy and play here? John Holt maintains it is the expression of the child's current knowledge base. It is the foundation upon which he builds new learning.

In *Mindstorms,* Seymour Papert says that anything is easy to learn if we can assimilate it into our personal collection of models, our own way of seeing the world. In the example of the preschooler learning to read, Holt is showing how fantasy is a child's way to do this. The toddler who says "tent" for the word "triangle," or "snake" for the letter S, also demonstrates this principle.

It's how a child takes in the enormously complex new learning he has to do. In Holt's words, it's the child's way to "fill his word learning with reality, to hook it up more strongly and unforgettably with what he already knows and cares about, *to take possession of it.*" In Dr. Dweck's terms, this child is exercising his skill as a mastery student.

As Holt points out, *all* children benefit from teaching methods that honor their own imaginative powers. But Edison-trait children hunger for and thrive on these methods. They think and talk in visual images, metaphoric language, and action. For them, imagination is the wellspring of their strength.

Personalize Your Child's Learning

No one knows your child's dreams and delights better than you do. Is there a way for you to bridge some of his school assignments to his personal interests? Can you personalize the facts that he must commit to memory? Can you and his teacher modify project requirements to include the "free-thinking" component he needs, so he can claim ownership of new material?

Say, for example, that your child's class is studying weather. A Dreamer might learn best if he sketches the types of clouds and the precipitation each one brings. A Discoverer might E-mail students around the globe to get reports and chart air pressure changes in the atmosphere. A Dynamo might fly a kite or model glider next to a ridge, to directly experience and try to predict the invisible patterns of the wind.

Talk with your child's teacher about ways that you can translate the new things he must learn into models he knows already. Tell her more about your child's inclinations and interests, so she can bring up appropriate metaphors and illustrations and suggest topics of personal relevance for assignments. Let her know when your child has connected with a particular idea or assignment.

2. MULTISENSORIAL EXPERIENCE

A multisensorial approach stimulates many senses. In the classroom, this usually means visual, auditory, tactile, and kinesthetic.

The Edison-trait learner favors hands-on experience. Edison-trait students learn math best by using "manipulatives" such as cubes, rods, or an abacus. It literally gives them a feel for numeric concepts. Edison-trait students grasp social studies lessons best through activities like reenacting vignettes from history. They get stimulated by literature when they visualize or play out scenes from books.

Edison-trait children usually respond to rhythm and movement. This preference can be applied toward helping them through activities that are less intrinsically interesting. For example, memorizing times tables is often a tedious task for the Edison-trait child. An activity that can motivate practice is to combine a drill with a quick game of catch. In multiplication catch, as you throw the ball to your child, make up an example, like "eight times seven," and say it out loud. Your child answers as he catches the ball. If he gets it right, he gets to make up an example for you to answer as he throws the ball back to you. If he gets it wrong, you give him the answer and do the same example again. The pace of the game has to be fast (not boring). For best results, play spontaneously in the family room with a foam ball, Koosh, or beanbag. This game also serves as an example of multitasking, that is, doing more than one thing at a time. This is a special talent of Edison-trait children, who feel happy doing many things at once. After a few rounds, your child will probably come up with his own variation of the sport. Go for it.

Talk with your teacher about the kind of multisensorial experience your child needs to learn. Let her know when a hands-on lesson made a difference. With large class sizes, a teacher may need parent volunteers to prepare materials or supervise special events. Volunteer and help recruit volunteers for learning activities that sound as though they will appeal to your child's Edison-trait need for multisensorial stimulation.

Kelly was a four-year-old Discoverer who had a problem at her preschool. It had always been difficult for Kelly to settle down at quiet time after lunch. At Kelly's school, after lunch, four-year-olds got their choice of either nap time in one room or quiet time in another. (Quiet time meant sitting still and listening to stories and tapes.) For several weeks Kelly refused to go to either room. Sometimes she got so disruptive that the teacher called her mother to come pick her up. Kelly's mother tried talking to her, offering her rewards, and practicing sitting still with her. But the problem continued to worsen.

One day Kelly's mother asked to observe, starting at lunch. Her daughter was well behaved throughout lunchtime. Then, after cleanup, trouble began. Kelly's mother noticed that at the very moment the five-year-olds left to go inside, Kelly started her tantrum. Kelly's mother learned that the five-year-olds were headed for hands-on science choices, and that Kelly knew where they were going.

After that day, Kelly's mother set out to get permission for her daughter to go to the science center with the five-year-olds. By discussing the situation with all those involved, and volunteering to supervise her daughter personally for a trial period, Kelly's mother succeeded. Kelly went to the science center, where she soon became known as one of the most curious and origi-nal thinkers in the room.

3. VISUAL CUES

The Use of Color

The mother in Holt's example who used colored felt pens to print out her preschooler's sentences was employing a method that is par-ticularly effective with Edison-trait children: color coding.

Color coding can be adapted for use at any age. If your child is very young, you can introduce color into whatever he is now learn-ing. Is he trying to learn sounds? Have him use one color for con-sonants and another for vowels. (This is a Montessori-based technique.)

Older children can use another effective method called *color shock*. Color shock is the technique of using a vivid color against a mono-chromatic background to attract visual attention. Edison-trait stu-dents can use color shock to train themselves to follow directions and complete assignments. For example, a child can highlight or use a colored pen to underline or circle key words in written instruc-tions *before* beginning an assignment. Or, on a page of arithmetic examples, the child can circle each operational symbol before he begins to do the work. If a child has been turning in incomplete pa-pers, he can use color shock to correct himself by drawing a colored line in every space that requires an answer. Then he fills in the an-swers and when he's done, he'll find it easy to scan the page from colored line to colored line, to check for completion.

These colorful methods are effective tools for an Edison-trait child to give himself reminders and keep himself organized. But your child will not give any technique a fair chance unless it is pre-sented to him in the right spirit. When a teacher or parent intro-duces color coding or color shock, a child must not feel defeated, demeaned, or, as the child would say, "like a baby."

A teacher or parent needs to present a technique in a respectful and positive manner. For example: "Here's something new I want you to do starting today." A teacher needs to give a child extra time and extra credit to underline, circle, or highlight written directions or operational symbols in color. Whether or not a child gets the work itself correct, if he has made the extra effort to apply the technique, it is right to acknowledge and reward him for doing so.

Do not suggest to your child that he use colors to highlight mistakes. Invert the process to color-highlight your child's successes. For example, after he has written a page, he can circle in color all the new words he's never used before, or any new words he feels proud of because he thinks they were good word choices. After he learns for himself that color shock is a tool he can use, he might want to apply it to correct misspelled words. But that is his decision. If you use it as a way to call attention to his faults, it is likely to backfire and cause more problems than it solves.

Talk with your child's teacher about these ideas and guidelines. Your child's teacher may think of practical ways your child can benefit from color coding in the classroom. These methods work best when there is a high degree of consistency between school and home.

In middle school or junior high, color coding can help your child organize his notes, homework, projects, and deadlines. Have him choose a color for each subject. Everything in that subject gets labeled in that color: the file tabs in his loose-leaf binder, the sections of his assignment pad, the notes on his bulletin board, and the circles around calendar dates when projects are due. You may be able to help him with this, especially if you have a similar system in your own home office. Or your child may be more receptive to the suggestions of a tutor, older brother or sister, family friend, or well-organized peer.

Your goal is to support your child to become a mastery student. Helpful guidelines are: Be imaginative, stay flexible, honor his ownership of his schoolwork, and know when to back off.

Stay in contact with your child's teacher. Your goal and hers is to recognize your child's extra efforts without his feeling singled out or deficient.

Visual Models

Edison-trait children need visual models. These visual models need to be consistent but not boring. The preschooler who is learning to write his own name needs to see it in print many times. Post versions on the wall, the mirror, and the refrigerator door. The best models to post are the ones he has printed himself (with his permission, of course).

If your child needs to put a heading (for example, name, date, subject) on the top of his papers for school, make sure he has several samples to choose from, either full-size or mini. Volunteer to make a poster-size sample to go on his classroom wall.

Make sure your child has a clearly visible sample of the kind of problem he is expected to solve before he begins a work sheet. If the first problem was solved as a model, draw a box around it (in color) to set it off from the rest of the page. If no sample is provided, make up a sample and solve it for him on a separate sheet of paper.

In language arts, write out at least one answer in the exact form that is asked for in the directions. For example, if the directions say to answer in a complete sentence, clearly write out the answer to the first question in a complete sentence for your child.

In math, write out the first example with all the numbers lined up exactly. Use graph paper to show your child how to line up numbers. Encourage him to use graph paper all the time if it helps. Give him a generous supply. Draw heavy lines to divide each page into four or six large areas, one for each example on the page.

Doing math work on graph paper gives your child clear visual cues for lining up numbers to keep their place value. If you can't find graph paper with boxes big enough for your child's ease, make your own by enlarging and photocopying what you have.

Talk with your child's teacher about the use of visual models. Let her know what examples have helped your child understand concepts well enough to come home and complete his homework independently. Also let her know when he needs more sample problems or other visual aids to do his work.

Bob's mom decided to have Bob use graph paper to do his math homework. It greatly improved his accuracy. Bob did not want to use graph paper in class. He was afraid the other kids would make fun of him.

Bob's mom decided to talk to his teacher anyway. The teacher thought it was such a good idea, she decided to have the whole class do their classwork math on graph paper. She gave bonus points to everyone who stayed in the lines. At the end-of-the-term party, she told Bob's mom that the entire class had improved in neatness and accuracy in math. She believed that the graph paper had helped everyone.

Diagrams

Often, Edison-trait children are fond of comic books, magazines, and computer graphics. These media forms combine vivid graphics with printed words.

Pairing pictures with words is an Edison-trait strategy that can serve many purposes in school, particularly in language arts. To build his vocabulary, a child can link a new word to a familiar picture. To improve reading comprehension, a child can draw a series of scenes from a story. This practice improves his skill for orderly recall.

As your child matures, he can develop picture-plus-words methods further. He can make diagrams that include drawings, shapes, and symbols. He can use these diagrams to take class notes and to study for exams. He can also use his diagrams to make outlines before writing an essay or a story.

The simplest way to diagram thoughts is to use a cluster. You start with the main idea in a center circle and draw lines radiating out, like the rays of the sun. On each ray you write a word or draw a picture to express a related idea. You can extend rays to record more than one association, even a whole new line of thinking.

Author Tony Buzan has developed a system of diagrams that he calls mind-mapping.[8] When you mind-map, you draw lines that branch out and connect one thought to the next. It is a tool for you to see and remember your trains and circles of thought. It stimulates relational thinking, to help generate novel yet relevant associations and ideas. Other formal systems of diagrams are available too.

4. LEARNING THROUGH SELF-EXPRESSION

One way to identify an Edison-trait child is in the contrast between the following two kinds of classroom scenes:

> *Scene 1: A student raises his hand because he has a story to tell. The child who talks until Tuesday is the Edison-trait child.*
> *Scene 2: The teacher asks a question. This time, the Edison-trait child is the student who answers in one word or two.*

Your child's exuberant, expressive nature is a *strength*. The challenge is to get him to apply that strength to accomplish the work of learning. Holt observes:

The only way children can learn to get meaning out of symbols . . . is to learn first how to turn their own reality into symbols. They have to make the journey first from reality to
symbol many times before they can go the other way. We must
begin with what children see, do, and know, and have them
talk and write about such things, before trying to talk to them
much about things they don't know.[9]

Holt offers the following example, taken from the written account of a fifth-grade art teacher.[10] The teacher gives each student a
piece of construction paper and holds up a folded paper fan for
them to see. The students duplicate the fan easily. The teacher gives
everyone a new piece of paper. This time, slowly and carefully, he
reads written instructions on how to make a fan. This time the children cannot reproduce the fan. Clearly they are able to make the
fans. They just demonstrated this. They are not ready to accept the
symbolic meaning of the instructions.

Here is Holt's idea to give them what they need to be ready to
accept the instructions. Have the students make the fans. Now ask
them to tell someone else how to make a fan using words only, no
gestures. In pairs, each child takes a turn making a fan according to
the other child's instructions. The child who composed the instructions gets to watch as his partner follows his directions.

Next, students write out and read one another's written instructions. Older children can do this themselves. For younger children,
the teacher reassembles the class, then writes out one composite set
of instructions by recording what student volunteers say. The
teacher then reads the final version to the class.

After having done this, the children are now in a position to hear
and analyze the written instructions the teacher read before. Now,
with the use of their own inner model, they glean the meaning of
the same words they could *not* make sense of only an hour earlier.

Edison-trait children learn by doing and teaching others. They
have a strong drive to express themselves. This is why they learn by
writing, producing, and acting out dramatizations. This is why they
like creating their own science experiments or ingeniously varying
the ones so well prepared for them in their printed lab manuals.

When you are helping your child with his homework, try this.
Reverse roles. Ask your child to teach you. If you find this method
works for your child, talk to his teacher about it. There may be a

way she can give him a teaching role, possibly with younger students. Some schools have found this practice so helpful, they have formed student-to-student "buddy" programs.

Dictated Writing

The Edison-trait child is a natural-born storyteller. Ask this same young bard to *write* a story, and you are likely to get a few sentences with the same simple verbs and generic adjectives repeated over and over again. Why?

Handwriting, grammar, and spelling are weak points for the Edison-trait student. He has learned to anticipate that these mechanical aspects of writing will drag him down. The Dreamer would rather remain in the story. The Discoverer and the Dynamo just don't have the time.

If an Edison-trait writer does take the time and effort to try to self-correct these mechanics, he often still makes a number of mistakes. His natural aptitudes lie elsewhere. Consequently, he feels criticized and inadequate. He begins to avoid using complex sentences and words he can't spell. This severely limits his writing style. In written composition, he becomes, as Dweck says, a helpless student. He doubts that he can ever learn to write any better. He stops believing that he can.

To restore his sense of mastery, ask the Edison-trait child to dictate a story while someone else writes it out. You can use a tape recorder as an intermediary step. His imagination is free to soar, just as it does when he tells a story for fun. Then, when he sees his words in print, he feels ownership over an original story that he knows is good. His feelings about writing improve. He starts to believe in his abilities again.

In this state of increased motivation, he will be more open to learning about other techniques, like the use of diagrams. He might want to develop his own kind of shorthand, or learn the keyboard well enough to use a word processor with ease. These methods help him get his thoughts down on paper quickly. Chances are he will enjoy writing much better when he writes on a word processor that has a spell-check function. He may benefit from the use of a pocket electronic spell-check, too.

Talk to your child's teacher about dictated writing. More than one teacher I know does this as a regular class assignment. Every student then gets the chance to hear and see his own words as they are spoken and as they are written. For some students it is a useful exercise in exploring literary form. For Edison-trait students it is a revelation of their own literary power.

Journals

Some teachers have children write in a journal on a routine basis. Sometimes the teacher gives an open-ended assignment like "Write about something you did over the weekend." Sometimes the child may write about anything he wants.

A journal is a home for "free writing." The teacher does not edit or correct what the child has written. Many teachers allow their students the option of deciding which journal entries a teacher may read and which the teacher may not.

Journal-writing creates safety and freedom of expression. It can be an especially constructive method for the Edison-trait child who is losing his self-confidence because he makes technical mistakes when he writes. It is a way for him to reclaim ownership over his writing. In Dweck's words, he can become a mastery student once again.

Ask your child's teacher his views on student journals. Some teachers are reluctant to introduce a practice that could take up too much instructional time. To experiment with the idea, a teacher might want to try a time-limited practice like having a "journal week" or "journal Wednesdays."

5. AN EMPHASIS ON QUALITY, NOT QUANTITY

When faced with a work sheet filled with problems, the Edison-trait child can easily feel overwhelmed. If he gets overexcited and races through it, he'll probably make lots of mistakes. If he shuts down and won't do the work, it will be hard to get him to try again. Either way, he goes from being a mastery student to becoming a helpless one.

Often, the child can solve these same problems correctly if there are fewer of them on each page, and if they are presented in several parts, preferably in several sittings.

In the primary grades especially, most Edison-trait children require this kind of structure. The layout of their work sheets must be tailored to meet their needs. Along with this, they will benefit from simple, supportive reminders to slow down or to finish the job.

One effective third-grade teacher I know talks to her Edison-trait pupils like this: "If I was going to write a secret message to you, to help you get your work done, what would it be?" She will offer suggestions, if the student wants some.

To the Discoverer and the Dynamo she might say: "You are a quick thinker. Your mind wants to go faster than a locomotive. But to do this work, you have to slow it way down as though you were walking around the neighborhood, taking a stroll and noticing things along the way. So on top of each paper you work on, suppose I write the words 'Slow down!' " She writes this in a color the student chooses, on the top of his work sheet.

To a Dreamer she might say: "You are an expert at thinking of many different ideas and coming up with wonderful stories. You could write your own book of fairy tales! But to do this work, you really need to tell your mind to stay in one place until you are finished. So on top of each paper you work on, suppose I write the words 'Stay here!' " She does, in a scented colored marker chosen by the child.

You might try offering the child a list of ideas to choose from, from "Whoa!" to no words—just a drawing of a yellow traffic light—to "Please stay here." If a child doesn't want a reminder, don't give one. (You can try again another time.) If he takes to the idea, give him a colored pen and ask him to remind himself. Remember to reward him when he does.

If you feel that your child needs special consideration in this regard, talk to his teacher. Discuss your concern and ways that the teacher can modify assignments and provide encouragement, without your child feeling labeled or stigmatized.

KEEP MOTIVATION HIGH

Edison-trait children need a steady flow of new ideas and solutions. What worked today may not work tomorrow. And what did not work yesterday may work today. This is because novelty and stimulation play an important role.

Vary tasks, for example:

- Quiet or conversational
- Individual or group
- Hands-on or listening-only
- At the desk or away from it

Provide structure and rewards:

- Give simple, clear instructions and make them stand out.
- Divide goals into subgoals.
- Generously reward both creative and convergent thinking.
- Think and talk about progress, not performance.
- Point out efforts, not mistakes.

This last guideline may call up the question "How will the student learn if you don't point out his mistakes?"

Actually, every student needs a mix of recognition for efforts and feedback about mistakes. To get a sense for the right kind of mix for an Edison-trait child, try this: Think of the last time you were a new learner, trying to speak a foreign language or keep your balance on skis. What is the feeling? Now imagine the kinds of comments you want to hear from your instructor.

The Edison-trait child is an explorer at heart. In treating life as open territory, he has tremendous possibility available to him. At the same time, he lives with the uncertainties and vulnerability of feeling like a new learner much of the time.

As your Edison-trait child grows stronger as a mastery student, he will learn to accept his mistakes as a normal and expected part of learning in school. Eventually you'll hardly need to point them out to him. In his typical Edison-trait "I'll-do-it-my-way" style, he'll be pointing them out to himself.

Computers

Most Edison-trait children like working at computers. They like the visual stimulation of graphics, the immediacy of feedback, and the control they can exercise over the pace. Discoverers and Dynamos like the fact that they don't have to raise their hands and wait. Dreamers like the fact that they won't be called on unexpectedly. Usually the best kind of software for divergent thinkers is the type that lends itself to the discovery process. To learn more about this kind of software, read *The Connected Family* by Seymour Papert, which includes a resource guide.[11]

TO TELL THE TRUTH

"It's like there is a black hole somewhere between here and the classroom. If the teacher gives him papers for me, or if he has homework to hand in, that's where it goes—into the black hole."

This is how one mother describes the way things are with Sam, her eight-year-old Dynamo. She has tried all the "usual" methods. Her son's three-ring binder is full of brightly colored folders with slip-in pockets for loose papers.

"It's not just that he's in a hurry," Sam's mother adds. "It's like he's really someplace else. I'd say 'befuddlement' is a good way to describe Sam and school."

Sam's father has a different view. "Sam 'forgets' his work because he doesn't want to do his work," he says unemotionally. "He doesn't have any trouble remembering what day his roller hockey game is on."

Are Sam and children like him forgetting on purpose? That's a tough question, and the answer is different for every child, every time.

In Sam's case, the answer was sometimes yes, sometimes no, and most of the time somewhere in between. Sam's story goes on.

Sam's first report card of the year was not good. After several team conferences, Sam's parents and teacher decided to make some changes. They decided that their highest priority would be encouraging Sam to become a mastery student. They set realistic goals for him. Each of his assignments was divided into manageable portions. And each portion could be further divided, if that's what was needed. For example, if Sam "forgot" last night's assignment, then tonight's assignment would be revised to be shorter and more motivating for him. The theme of Sam's new learning program was "No punishment, just success."

If a problem arose, a parent or teacher spoke to Sam about it privately. If he needed directions repeated, he got them. If he needed more sample problems as models, he got them. Sam's parents and teacher made a pact to convey positive expectation and confidence to Sam. If he "forgot" his work they said things like "It's good to be able to talk about things like this."

Sam started to remember more of his assignments and papers. And of even greater significance, when Sam did forget, *he* was the first one to notice.

Why Children Lie

In *Schools Without Failure*, William Glasser, M.D., describes class meetings he held with students in Los Angeles schools. The children who participated were promised anonymity. Glasser wanted to know why children lie, so he asked them. Their answers all had one theme in common. From the children's point of view, all lying was a protection from punishment or feeling put down.

Glasser describes the emotional impact one of his meetings had on his colleagues and him. They decided to ask students to make a commitment "on their honor" to tell nothing but the truth for twenty-four hours. Not one student would agree. That's how strongly the children felt they needed self-protection.[12]

GRADES

A natural corollary to the issue of whether Edison-trait students feel punished or motivated is the question of grades. Does the child perceive grading as a threat or as an incentive? When he thinks about his grade, does he feel fear or desire? How does his teacher decide on his grade?

Criteria- vs. Norm-Based Grading

Criteria-based grading means that a child's grade is determined by whether or not he has met the requirements or criteria for a particular grade. In effect, it is a contract between teacher and student. If the student completes the work for a "B," the student gets a "B." If the student completes the work for an "A," the student receives an "A." Theoretically it is possible for every student who works up to a standard of excellence to get an "A."

Norm-based grading means that the teacher has an idea of about how many "A"'s and "B"'s and "C"'s should be given out. If there are going to be around ten "A"'s, then the top ten students will get "A"'s. If there are going to be around ten "B"'s, then the next ten students will get "B"'s. Theoretically, a student may be trying his hardest and doing excellent work but does not get an "A" because of factors beyond his control.

Many teachers avoid criteria-based grading because they fear it will lead to grade inflation. However, from the point of view of teaching mastery vs. helplessness, every student needs to be awarded an "A" if he completes an "A"'s worth of work.

In norm-based grading, getting an "A" depends on what someone else does. If this is true, the student is correct to feel helpless and disconnected from the outcome of his work at school. It is, in fact, beyond his control. In criteria-based grading, getting an "A" depends on self-reliance and achieving specific goals. When this is true, the student is correct to feel proficient and connected to his school success. He develops belief in his ability to learn and accomplish what he sets out to do.

The Edison-trait student in particular needs criteria-based grading, because he is at high risk for becoming a helpless student. His criteria need to include divergent- as well as convergent-thinking assignments. And he needs a clear explanation of exactly what criteria are required to get a grade.

Grading by Portfolio

Many school districts are now adopting policies for students to keep a portfolio of their work in a particular subject.[13] There are many variations on how this is done. The teacher may decide on what is to be included, the student may decide, or the two may decide together.

If an Edison-trait student is keeping a portfolio, he needs to have a major part in the decision about what to put in and what to leave out. This enhances his sense of ownership and mastery over his work.

If a portfolio is assembled correctly, it can demonstrate a child's progress. It shows how his skills have improved over time. This places emphasis on individual learning, rather than on competition for grades and approval from others.

TEACHER CONFERENCES

There is a Sufi story about two men and an elephant. The two men are aware that they are looking at the same beast, but one man can see only its head while the other can see only its tail. After each one says what he sees, the two break out in argument.

A parent sees an Edison-trait child at home, where there may not be many demands on him to think convergently. A teacher sees the same child in a classroom, where he is asked to think convergently in a room full of other children, some of whom may think even more divergently than he does.

A teacher conference is an opportunity for you and your child's teacher to share your different views of your child. Unlike the argumentative men in the Sufi story, understand that you are each looking from a different vantage point.

Listen, and be open to what the teacher is saying. Save time to tell your child's teacher what you know about your child, too. When you talk about your child's strengths and interests, you generate new ideas and new ways to open doors for him.

You may feel that modesty prohibits you from telling your child's teacher about his talents and abilities. This is understandable. A parent wants to be seen as objective and unbiased. But standing up for your child's strengths is not the same as bragging. Your child needs you as his advocate. You are the adult who knows what remarkable things he can do under other circumstances.

Be specific in telling your child's teacher about your child's abilities. Tell her your child knows the make and model of every car in the parking lot, or that he produced a neighborhood play with a cast of seven and an audience of eighteen. If your child choreographs dances in the backyard or if he keeps a sketchbook under his bed, share this. Give her a chance to see the full range of your child's abilities.

The influence of a teacher's expectations on a child's progress in school is well established. It is sometimes called the Pygmalion effect. In the field of psychology, the Pygmalion effect is sometimes referred to as the Rosenthal effect. Rosenthal was a researcher who gave teachers bogus IQ scores for their incoming students. He found out that over the course of the school year, the students' progress correlated to the bogus scores, not to their actual ones.

Help your child's teacher form accurate perceptions of your child. Give her the information she needs to see your child multidimensionally. This will prevent your child from getting overidentified with problems he has at school.

Actively listen to what your child's teacher says to you. Communicate respect and a team spirit. Accept, don't deny, her point of view. If necessary, reframe what she says into a strength-centered statement.

To get more information about your child's classroom behaviors, ask to observe. Better yet, volunteer to help. Of course, your child will not act exactly the same when you are present. Nonetheless you will learn more than you know right now.

If your child's teacher is not open to your ideas about how to help your child, continue to stay open to hers. You do not want to polarize positions. Keep communicating. Invite a third party, such as your principal or school counselor, to help mediate the situation.

SCHOOL PROGRAMS AND POLICIES

Private Schools

If your child attends a private school, it will probably be easier for you to get individual consideration for him. In small schools, especially Montessori-based ones, students can progress through different subjects at different paces. This is also true of selected programs in public schools, for example, charter schools, which have their own curriculum guides.

Typically, in these settings a child moves through each subject and takes proficiency exams at his own pace. Individualized, self-paced learning can be a boon to an Edison-trait child, just as it was to Thomas Edison himself.

GATE Programs

The acronym GATE stands for "Gifted and Talented Education." The intent of GATE programs is to provide enrichment work for students who are likely to be understimulated by the ordinary curriculum. Customarily, admission to GATE programs is by exam. Usually, a student must score in the upper 97th percentile on a standardized intelligence scale to qualify. This translates to an IQ score of approximately 130.

Usually your child's school will give a group intelligence test to students who want to enter its GATE program.[14] Because some children perform better in one-to-one settings than in groups, schools generally will accept the score of a child who gets tested individually by a licensed professional as an alternative to the group testing score.[15]

As a rule, Edison-trait children will perform better on intelligence tests given in a one-to-one setting than in a group setting. But Edison-trait children would do better yet if the GATE admission criteria included some measure of their forte, namely, divergent thinking.

In Chapter 14, you will learn more about standardized intelligence tests. They are heavily biased toward linguistic and logical-mathematical types of intelligence. There is no measure of creativity, imagination, or practical intelligence.[16] (Chapter 17 addresses the relationship between practical intelligence and success in the world. There is a section on "tacit knowledge," a term used by researchers to describe action-oriented know-how.) Ironically, creative abilities are what most people think of when they use the words "gifted" and "talented."

Intelligence tests reward convergent thinkers. They measure "school smarts," i.e., the ability to get high grades on structured exams. In this regard, it is more accurate to describe GATE programs as they currently exist as enrichment for the "academically oriented" rather than for the "gifted and talented."[17]

IEP Programs

If your child has problems at school and they are so serious that they "substantially limit his learning," then he is eligible for specialized help in the form of an Individualized Educational Program (IEP). Also, he is eligible for other "reasonable accommodations" if he needs them.[18]

Because the law guarantees a learning disabled child's right to an education, the school district pays for that child's IEP. This is true whether the child attends private or public school.[19] Your school district also pays for an evaluation to determine whether your child qualifies or not. It may designate your child as "learning disabled," mild, moderate, or severe.

This kind of labeling causes many parents to feel afraid. It is a legitimate matter of concern. Talk to your school officials about it.

Get more specific information about your child's records. Find out how evaluation reports are kept and used. Ask questions. Explore possibilities.

If you want, you can initiate a request for an IEP evaluation for your child. Your child does not need a diagnosis like Attention Deficit Disorder to get an IEP. If you have good reasons and the support of your child's teacher, the school district will probably agree to test. If you are refused, you have the right to "due process" to challenge the district's decision.[20]

An IEP evaluation is a comprehensive assessment carried out by a multidisciplinary team of professionals. This may include your school principal, one or more special education teachers, and a school psychologist. This evaluation routinely begins with a team meeting for gathering information where you, together with your child's teacher, are the main sources.

At the meeting, the IEP team decides what individualized tests to give your child. Usually these tests will include a standardized intelligence test and one or more standardized achievement tests.[21] (See Chapter 14, "Professional Diagnosis, Testing, and Counseling," for more information about testing.)

After test results have been analyzed, the team meets again to deliver and discuss recommendations. You are an active part of this meeting, too. Recommendations may include suggestions to your child's teacher, time with a resource specialist, small-group language therapy, and, in extreme cases, instruction in a specialized classroom.[22]

"Reasonable Accommodations"

The law says that if your child is found to have a disability, then the school must make "reasonable accommodations" for him. The IEP team can recommend or require a broad range of accommodations. Some examples are a tape recorder or printed assignment pages with outlines, so your child can get a thought down on paper before he forgets it; changes in the physical arrangement of the classroom; and special training or consultation for your child's teacher. The IEP team may forbid a teacher to lower your child's test grade because of illegible handwriting, if the purpose of the test is to assess the student's knowledge of a subject other than handwriting. An accommodation that is a cause of controversy today is the exemption of a student from time limits on examinations like the SATs.[23]

WHEN TEACHERS AND PARENTS
WORK TOGETHER

"Just wait till his body catches up with his mind. He is going to be something else," Josh's teacher repeatedly reassured his mom.

"He is something else," his mom kept thinking.

"Josh is exceptional. He's never going to be mediocre." Josh's teacher spoke with confidence and enthusiasm.

"I'd do anything for a 'mediocre' kid right now," Josh's mother thought anxiously.

Years later, when Josh's mother told me this story, she had completely different feelings about her son's independent thinking. "I'm glad he's *not* mediocre!" she said proudly, with conviction. She still felt gratitude toward the teacher who saw Josh's potential at a time when she could not.

At other times in Josh's school career his mother has been the one to persuade teachers to see a different side of her son. Teachers and parents seem to take turns feeling discouraged and hopeful, baffled or confident.

With honest, ongoing communication, you and your child's teacher can borrow each other's strength. You share a common and worthy goal: to bring out the best and believe in your Edison-trait child.

CHAPTER 13

---⁓---

What Is ADD?

From legislatures to classrooms, attention deficit disorder has become a topic of conversation and debate. What is it? Who has it? What do we do about it? . . . While there are differences of view, there remains the overriding reality that there are children and adults whose needs are not being met in our schools, homes and communities.

—George E. Ayers,
executive director,
Council for Exceptional Children

TWO DIFFERENT POINTS OF VIEW

I sat at a conference table in the director's office at a prestigious private school in San Diego. To my left was a concerned fourth-grade teacher. To my right was an exasperated school administrator. It was by her request that I was there as a consulting psychologist. Across from me sat two well-dressed, college-educated adults locked in heated dispute about their nine-year-old son.

"I can't believe you, Ron. Are you even listening?"

"Look, Trish, you want to stick a label on him, and I won't let you do that."

"Did you hear what his teacher just said? He needs help. We need to do something."

"Joel's not going to grow up thinking he has a defect, just because he doesn't do things a certain way."

Trish and Ron are both responsible parents who love their son, but their attitudes collide when it comes to deciding what's best for him.

Trish believes that Joel, who is bright and original but disorganized and easily distracted, might have a medical diagnosis called

Attention Deficit Disorder (ADD). Ron believes that Joel is a normal, healthy child who is creative and headstrong, though sometimes immature—hardly the makings of a psychiatric diagnosis. He isn't sure what ADD is and he doesn't like the sound of it.

WHY ADD IS CONTROVERSIAL

In the United States today, an estimated 1.8 million children qualify as having ADD.[1] The term was introduced in 1980 and has been a source of controversy ever since. Why?

ADD Is Invisible

Although it has a biological basis, there is no physical test to detect ADD. The neurological exam of a child who has it is normal. The process of diagnosis is imprecise and has a strong subjective component.

ADD Is Heterogeneous

For years ADD was equated with hyperactivity. Now several types of ADD, with or without hyperactivity, are recognized. The forever-in-motion boy who can't wait for his turn to talk in class has ADD. But so does the mesmerized little girl in the back row who misses directions while she dreams about rainbows, castles, and unicorns.

ADD Is Elusive

ADD symptoms appear under some conditions but not others. A child who can pay attention in a one-to-one setting at home loses his ability to concentrate in a classroom of thirty students.

ADD Is Perplexing

Children with ADD have strengths and talents all their own. The youngster who stares out the window all day could be a natural for the lead in the school play, or he might be someone who spends hours absorbed in sketching evocative scenes from science fiction stories.

ADD AND A HEALTHY SELF-CONCEPT

Trish and Ron have opposing views about their son. Who is right? *Both* of them.

Trish is correct in her conviction that Joel should be evaluated professionally. Whether or not it turns out that Joel has ADD, test results can guide his parents, teachers, and doctors to make good decisions on Joel's behalf. For example, Joel's teachers can change the way they instruct him. If Joel does have ADD, he may be a candidate for medication, which he can learn to use as an effective tool.

On the other hand, Ron is right too. It won't help Joel to hear adults wonder if, or decide that, he has a "deficit" or a "disorder." Children are impressionable and need to be protected. This is *their* time to feel secure and free to form the healthiest self-concept possible. They have the right to be themselves, the right to learn in their own unique ways, and the right to grow up without feeling limited as a result of the words we choose to describe them.

With or without ADD, Joel needs to be appreciated for his individual style. He needs to feel valued for his own ideas and choices, and be encouraged to develop his own personality. If he does think and act more impulsively than most of the other children his age, he needs to face this fact and learn to harness his unbridled energy.

Joel needs a self-image that keeps his dignity intact. He needs to feel happy and confident that he can make it in this world, and that this world has a place of respect and value for him.

UNDERSTAND, DON'T BLAME

"Who cares what they think? It wasn't such a big deal. Ryan said to do it, and he's not even in trouble."

Paul moves side to side in his chair as he speaks. Across from him his dad is seething. His mom is tearful, but also furious. Their eight-year-old son has been suspended from school for a day for having tampered with fire safety equipment. It is only the most recent in a long series of Paul's impulsive misbehaviors—hitting others, starting fights, disregarding teachers, saying the wrong things, and doing things that endanger himself and others. As Paul later described the moment he took the bright red extinguisher from the wall: "My hands did it quicker than my brain could say not to."

"What do we do?" Paul's mom asks. "All my life, I've believed, you can do the right thing if you try. But Paul's tried and we've tried and it doesn't get better. What are we doing wrong?"

This stormy session was part of a psychological evaluation that ultimately resulted in Paul's being diagnosed with Attention Deficit Disorder. When this took place, Paul and his parents started to see things in a new way. They began to take into account Paul's neurochemistry and innate tendency to be impetuous and excitable. They began to map out a path to get the help they needed for themselves and for their son.

Everyone felt intense relief. Paul's mom stopped blaming herself. She and his dad stopped blaming Paul. At school, Paul's teacher was supportive and soon Paul started to feel less angry and defensive.

WHY WE DIAGNOSE

On one hand, ADD sets limits on how we see a child. A diagnosis of ADD describes only convergent-thinking deficiencies with no mention of divergent-thinking strengths. On the other hand, diagnosing can open the door to getting help. A diagnosis of ADD can be a watershed event in the life of a child who is chronically failing.

Chronic failure in childhood is a serious inequity. It has painful, long-term effects. A diagnosis of ADD can help a child get proper treatment. This can reverse the course of failure.

For example, professional services cost money. Proper treatment may include individual and family counseling, continued evaluation, and medication. Health insurance may cover some of these expenses, but only if a medical diagnosis is provided.

DEFINING THE DIAGNOSIS

DSM-IV. The fourth edition of the *Diagnostic and Statistical Manual of Mental Disorders* (the *DSM-IV*), published by the American Psychiatric Association, is the authoritative source in the United States for legal and medical definitions of all mental disorders. It was published in June 1994 and serves as the official handbook for professional diagnosticians in all disciplines.

The *DSM-IV* gives a complete list of symptoms and qualifiers to define the diagnosis of ADD. The *DSM-IV* uses the term *Attention-Deficit/Hyperactivity Disorder* or ADHD as the technical name of the disorder.[2] According to the *DSM-IV,* 3 to 5 percent of all children qualify for the diagnosis.[3]

Significant Impairment

The *DSM-IV* states that before ADD can be considered as a diagnosis, there must be "clear evidence of clinically significant impairment in social, academic or occupational functioning." This is the hallmark feature of ADD. Significant impairment *must* be present for the diagnosis to apply.

In addition, a child must show some of the defining symptoms before the age of seven. Current impairment from the symptoms must show up regularly in at least two different settings (usually school and home). And for at least six consecutive months, the symptoms must persist at a frequency and intensity that is "mal-adaptive and inappropriate," given the child's age.[4]

These requirements are important criteria, since the list of symptoms taken alone is nothing more or less than a definition of childhood. ADD is *not* "normal childhood." It is a legally and medically recognized mental disorder.

TYPES OF ADD

The *DSM-IV* lists full criteria for three distinct types of attention deficit disorder:

1. Inattentive Type
2. Hyperactive-Impulsive Type
3. Combined Type

INATTENTIVE TYPE

If your child is an Edison-trait Dreamer and he is failing because of this, he may have the Inattentive Type of ADD. The following checklist can serve as a guide to see if your child's behaviors fit the pattern. However, please remember, no checklist can take the place of consulting a professional.

Every child displays some ADD criteria behaviors to a degree. A professional can estimate how extreme your child's behaviors are by comparing them to norms for children his own age. Also, there is a complex of reasons that can legitimately account for your child's actions. A proper diagnostic inquiry examines multiple causes and assigns relative weights to each.

Symptom Checklist for the Inattentive Type of ADD
Are six or more of the following statements true for your child?
1. Doesn't pay close attention to details or makes careless mistakes
2. Has difficulty sustaining attention in work or play
3. Doesn't seem to listen when someone talks to him
4. Doesn't follow through on instructions and doesn't finish schoolwork or chores
5. Has difficulty organizing tasks or activities
6. Avoids or strongly dislikes doing things like classwork or homework that require sustained mental effort
7. Loses things he needs, like school assignments, pencils, books, tools, or toys
8. Is easily distracted by the things around him
9. Is forgetful about day-to-day things

HYPERACTIVE-IMPULSIVE TYPE

If your child is an Edison-trait Discoverer or a Dynamo, and his behavior is dysfunctional because of this, he may have the Hyperactive-Impulsive Type of ADD. The following checklist may be helpful. However, please remember: There may be numerous ways to explain your child's actions. An actual diagnosis requires careful consideration and a competent professional consultation.

Symptom Checklist for the Hyperactive-Impulsive Type of ADD
Are six or more of the following statements true for your child?

Symptoms of Hyperactivity
1. Fidgets with hands or feet, or squirms in seat
2. Leaves seat when not allowed, for example, in the classroom

3. Runs and climbs when not allowed; if a teen or adult, has feelings of restlessness
4. Has difficulty playing quietly
5. Talks excessively
6. Acts as if "driven by a motor" and can't stay still

Symptoms of Impulsivity
7. Blurts out answers to questions before the questions are finished
8. Has difficulty waiting in line or waiting for a turn
9. Interrupts or intrudes on others

COMBINED TYPE

If your child meets the criteria for both the Inattentive Type and the Hyperactive-Impulsive Type, he may have what is called the Combined Type.

IS ADD THE SAME IN BOYS AND GIRLS?

According to the *DSM-IV,* four times as many boys are believed to have ADD as girls; nine times as many boys are treated professionally for it.

Boys are more apt to be diagnosed with the Hyperactive-Impulsive or the Combined types of ADD. Usually their symptoms include aggression, loss of control, and oppositional behaviors—the kinds of problems that are hard to ignore.

Girls are more likely to be diagnosed with the Inattentive Type of ADD. They suffer more language and cognitive deficits, depression, and social rejection. Their problems are easier to overlook.[5]

COMORBIDITY

Before making a diagnosis of ADD, the professional doing the evaluation must be sure that the child's symptoms cannot be better explained by another disorder, such as depression or dyslexia. This can be a difficult determination to make, since stress and learning-related problems so often coexist with ADD. Many times a dual diagnosis is the best explanation. In other words, both ADD and another disorder are present. The medical term for this is *comorbidity*.[6] When comorbidity occurs, it is important not to neglect the effective treatment of one disorder because of overemphasis on the other.

IS THE DIAGNOSIS DEFINITIVE?

Just what *is* a "significant impairment"? What is "maladaptive" or "dysfunctional"? How can the complexities of comorbidity be distinguished and defined? The fact is, with no medical test to establish a well-defined threshold, there is an unavoidable subjective aspect, or "fuzzy nature," to the process of diagnosing ADD.

For some children, diagnosis and treatment of ADD may mean salvation from chronic failure, but for others, things are less clear-cut. We risk harming these children if we are too quick to give them the diagnosis.

Diagnosis involves a judgment call. And this call may be influenced by factors as diverse as your diagnostician's orientation and experience, your insurance company's reimbursement schedule, and the effects of the most recent wave of media coverage of ADD.

IS ADD OVERDIAGNOSED?

Currently, there is evidence that ADD is overdiagnosed in clinical settings. This stems from a number of causes.[7] One major problem is that to achieve their goal of cost-effectiveness, managed health care companies question complicated diagnoses and expensive treatments, but reimburse for well-defined ones that are treatable with medication. This creates financial incentive to providers to diagnose ADD instead of less definable conditions.[8]

Another problem is our culture's ready acceptance of the diagnosis. In an article in *Time* magazine it was called "an almost messianic movement."[9] One recent investigative report in *The Wall Street Journal* concluded: "Promiscuous overdiagnosing and treatment of ADD is a serious problem."[10] According to a recent *Newsweek* cover story, school psychologists report feeling "pressed" to diagnose it.

One official from the National Institute of Mental Health called ADD "the disease of the month syndrome." Another noted how physicians have become "complacent" about diagnosing it. In a survey of pediatricians, doctors themselves acknowledged that their evaluation methods were too hasty. Typically, they diagnosed ADD after only a brief office visit.[11]

Physicians in other countries do not do this. Most of the world does not diagnose ADD as often as we do in the United States. Asian nations, like Japan, hardly recognize it at all. European nations, like France and England, report one tenth the U.S. rate.[12]

A DEFICIENT VOCABULARY TO DESCRIBE DIVERGENT THINKERS

The more we accept overdiagnosis without question, the more we casually bandy around the term ADD. Ann Landers says, "Attention Deficit Disorder has become a fashionable catchall for children with behavior problems."[13] Elsewhere in the media, ADD has been dubbed the "disease of the hour" and the "yuppie flu of the 90's."[14]

Many divergent thinkers *who function adequately* are mistakenly said to have ADD. This probably happens because ADD is the closest term we have in our current nomenclature to describe the Edison-trait profile. We call divergent thinkers deficient, when it's really our vocabulary that's deficient. We do this in public—for example, in the high profile of national news coverage.[15] And we do it in private—for example, in personal communications such as parent-teacher conferences.[16]

The rise in the number of divergent-thinking children is a comparatively new phenomenon. At the moment it outpaces our comprehension of its potential. We have names for the problems it causes, which serve as arrows to direct our attention to those problems.

For our children's sake, we need more words to describe their divergent-thinking strengths. It is time to update and expand our vocabulary, to speak freely about Edison-trait diversity. We need healthy terms—like the assets listed in Chapter 9—to see and name desirable Edisonian qualities. We need arrows that point us in the direction of our children's aptitudes and abilities.

THE DANGER OF OVERDIAGNOSIS

The diagnosis of ADD specifically denotes abnormality (statistical difference from the norm) and pathology (dysfunction). While diagnosticians unavoidably disagree on exactly what these terms mean, they must be able to justify a determination of debility and impairment. Deviant behavior, a bad temper, or a mediocre report card are not sufficient cause for a diagnosis of ADD.[17]

Overdiagnosis is unacceptable and dangerous. When we loosely apply the diagnosis of ADD, we become numbed and dismissive of children with impairment that truly qualifies them for the diagnosis. At the same time we harm those who get labeled but do not actually qualify. We inaccurately revise our expectations of them and become prone to medicating them unnecessarily.

Overdiagnosis of ADD also harms children who have other serious problems that get overlooked. Overdiagnosis creates the illusion that the problems themselves do not exist. This promotes denial and avoidance of taking corrective action, and leaves children feeling helpless and families feeling frustrated.

If your child has ADD, he should be properly diagnosed so the true extent of his problems can be recognized and addressed. (I'll talk about diagnostic procedures in the next chapter.) However, if your child has the Edison trait, a personality profile that is at risk for being diagnosed as ADD, and it is not extreme enough to cause dysfunction, or if conditions are optimal and he is coping satisfactorily, he does *not* have ADD, according to its legal and true meaning. For his sake, don't use the term, and don't let others use the term to describe him.

IS THERE A CURE FOR ADD?

The answer to this question is yes and no.

"Yes" because the treatment of choice, called *multimodal,* is an effective one. "Yes" because maturation alone reduces many ADD symptoms.

"No" because ADD is an impairment that results from the extremes and excesses of an inborn personality type; it is a long-term condition. The child who qualifies for a diagnosis of ADD will probably be at least somewhat at risk for it for the rest of his life.

Multimodal Treatment

Proper treatment of children with ADD requires the input of professionals from several disciplines, primarily those of psychology, education, and medicine.[18]

A multimodal treatment approach is likely to include

- Individual, parent, and/or family counseling
- A structured learning program in the classroom
- Medication when required
- Parent training and support

Maturation

Long-term studies indicate that approximately 50 percent of those who have ADD as children will not have ADD as adults.[19] Those who do have ADD as adults have fewer symptoms than they had in childhood. Hyperactivity usually decreases after puberty. The ability to inhibit impulsive actions also increases as the child grows.

IS ADD INHERITED OR LEARNED?

The answer is: both. Research findings suggest that a child's genetic makeup predisposes him to develop ADD *and* that his environment makes a difference in whether or not symptoms develop.

Evidence of Heredity

Studies show that there are higher rates of incidence of ADD in parents, offspring, siblings, and twins of children with ADD than there are in the general population.[20] For example, approximately 30 percent of the parents of children with ADD have ADD themselves. Also, by comparing the prevalence of ADD in identical twins (who have the same genetic makeup) with those of fraternal twins (who do not), researchers have demonstrated that the rate of ADD in identical twins is about sixteen times higher than the rate for fraternals.

Efforts to isolate a specific gene or to designate a "genetic marker" have yielded suggestive but not definitive results.[21] All in all, an overview of the current evidence argues strongly in favor of a genetic predisposition.[22]

A Developmental View

When a child grows up in an environment that is inhospitable to his inherited or natural-born traits, his development is adversely affected. In an environment more compatible with his innate tendencies, a child will mature in a healthier, more age-appropriate way. This interactional perspective is called the developmental view.

Recently, a developmental view of ADD was supported by significant research findings. Elizabeth Carlson, Ph.D., and her associates at the University of Minnesota tracked the effects of environment on children with ADD from their early childhood to their later elementary school years. This research is noteworthy because it was well designed. The study was longitudinal (long-term, conducted over the course of many years) and prospective (data were collected periodically as the children grew up). This gives it greater validity than a retrospective study (where data are collected years later, relying on people's memories, which may not be accurate). Findings showed that ADD symptoms were best predicted by a combination of inborn temperament and environmental influences, not by inborn temperament alone.[23]

IS ADD RELATED TO BRAIN DAMAGE?

For nearly a century, neuroscientists believed "minimal brain damage" would explain the syndrome we currently call ADD.[24] They searched vigorously for structural damage but found none. When no brain lesions were found, they looked for systemic rather than structural injury. Still, no operating system of the brain showed damage.[25] In other words, it appears that neither "hardware" nor "software" is substandard in the brain of a person who has ADD.

The brains of children with ADD work differently, but not "defectively." As Dr. Judith Rapoport, chief of child psychiatry at the National Institutes of Health, pointed out, referring to the results of MRI studies (to be discussed later in this chapter): "A radiologist would not read these scans as abnormal, but differences [between ADD and non-ADD brains] are there."[26]

Brain functions that correspond with ADD are best understood as individual differences. Individual differences are nonhierarchical qualities that vary from one person to the next, such as left- or right-hand dominance, hair color, or body type. Environmental favoritism of one particular trait (or individual difference) over another is largely a matter of chance. It is conceivable that in another place or time (quite possibly in our own future), an extreme preference for divergent thinking would be more adaptive than it is in our culture today.

THE NEUROCHEMISTRY OF ADD

Current research suggests that ADD is a cluster of specific behavior patterns that have a corresponding neurochemistry.[27] These findings are not surprising. Research on brain-behavior connections has revealed that all human thoughts, feelings, and actions correspond to neurochemical events. A human experience *and* its corresponding neurochemical event occur simultaneously.

With technological advances, more types of neurochemical patterns can now be detected, measured, and described. Some behavior patterns appear to correspond with distinctive neurochemical patterns. Some ADD behavior patterns appear to fall into this category. However, we need to respect the limits of what these findings mean.

It is a common mistake to assume that if we can identify a neurochemical pattern that accompanies a behavior pattern, it is the neurochemistry that *causes* the corresponding behavior to occur. All we know for sure is that the two exist together. Behavior patterns and their corresponding neurochemical patterns are actually a human biological version of the question: Which comes first, the chicken or the egg? Neither one is the exclusive cause of the other. Each appears to be *both* the cause *and* the expression of the other.

We say that the behavior pattern and its corresponding neurochemical pattern *coexist* or *correlate*. They appear to be interactive, or *mutually causative*. Each one influences the creation *and* response of the other.

This is an important understanding. It explains how learning and experience affect brain functioning while at the same time brain functioning affects learning and experience. Plainly stated, changes in behavior cause the brain to change, and a changing brain causes further behavior change.

This fits well with the developmental view of ADD. It also has significance for setting positive, realistic expectations about the rate at which a child who has ADD can change his behaviors. With the right approach and climate, behavior change will occur, but it proceeds at its own pace. This will be discussed further in the section "The Plasticity of the Brain."

THE NEUROCHEMISTRY OF THE EDISON TRAIT

In most cases, ADD behavior patterns are comparable to but more extreme than the typical patterns of an Edison-trait child who does not have ADD. In other words, by learning about the biology of ADD, we are also learning about the biology of the Edison trait, only to a lesser degree.

It is useful to understand both the behaviors and neurochemistry that distinguish the Edison-trait child. That way, when we guide our children, we can apply this knowledge wisely. We can set attainable goals in a reasonable time frame, and build on our children's natural strengths. We are more productive when we work with Mother Nature than when we work against her.

RESEARCH FINDINGS

Neuropsychological studies use various methods to measure the brain functions of persons who have ADD. These methods are expensive, intrusive (except for EEGs), and have not been shown to have diagnostic validity or reliability. That is why they are used only for research and not for diagnosis.

Current research methods include

1. Electroencephalograph (EEG) measurements
2. Magnetic resonance imaging (MRI)
3. Blood-flow studies
4. Positron emission tomography (PET) of cerebral glucose metabolism

1. EEG (Electroencephalograph)

An electroencephalograph measures the frequency and intensity of brain-wave activity. According to their EEG measurements, when children with ADD are engaged in certain types of attention-related tasks, they show patterns of brain-wave activity in their frontal regions that differ from typical non-ADD brain-wave patterns. Frontal regions are rich in catecholamines, the type of neurotransmitter affected by stimulants, which is the most common type of medication used to treat ADD. So these findings are consistent with the fact that stimulants alter the thinking of children who have ADD more than they alter the thinking of children who do not.[28] (For more about EEG findings, see the section on neurofeedback in Chapter 16.)

2. MRI (Magnetic Resonance Imaging)

An MRI scan produces computerized pictures of brain tissues. It can be seen from MRI scans that the brains of subjects with ADD tend to show a distinguishing pattern in the lobes of the frontal regions of the brain (the site of "executive" functions such as decision making) and in the caudate of the basal ganglia (the center for regulating motor activity and for inhibiting behavior). The normally seen pattern is one of "right-greater-than-left" asymmetry, which means that the right side of the brain has greater volume than the left. The MRI scan of a subject who does not have ADD typically shows this asymmetry. The distinguishing pattern of a subject with ADD is the absence of "right-greater-than-left" asymmetry. Stated another way, the ADD scan shows greater right-left brain symmetry. This is true in both the frontal regions and the basal ganglia.[29]

The reasons for this are speculative. One explanation has to do with the inverse relationship that may presumably exist between the structure of a brain region and its function. In other words, an underutilized part may "try harder" to keep up with its counterpart (or other half), because the brain is a self-regulating mechanism trying to achieve a state of equilibrium. (For more on this, see "Self-regulation and the Disinhibition Model," page 189.)

Since to a large degree convergent thinking corresponds to left-brain functioning and divergent thinking corresponds to right-brain functioning,[30] the non-ADD subject who has "right-greater-than-left" asymmetry can be viewed as having a stronger inner drive for left-brain convergent thinking than the ADD subject. The non-ADD brain would be trying harder to move in the direction of increased symmetry. Such a drive in a non-ADD subject might be expressed as a persistent inclination toward orderliness, sequencing, and correction of detail. It's as though the left side of the brain, trying harder, would cause a desire for orderliness; you'd *want* to put things in their right places.

The ADD subject with right-left symmetry has no need for this inner drive. Symmetry satisfies the need and there is no inner striving for further order, sequence, or correction of detail. It is enough for him to perceive stimuli as they happen, with a global acceptance and a nonchalance about incorrect detail.

MRI scans also suggest subtle differences in brain activity in the corpus callosum, which interconnects the brain hemispheres. The corpus callosum is central to the cooperative functioning of the two halves of the brain, in other words, where and how an individual coordinates different types of thinking.[31] This finding has important implications for understanding the kind of guidance children with ADD need. They are likely to benefit more from learning how to coordinate divergent and convergent styles of thinking than from trying to replace divergent styles of thinking with convergent ones.

3. Blood-Flow Studies

Blood flow through the brain can be detected by the study of computerized pictures of brain regions. Results of blood-flow studies are just about the same as MRI results. Subjects who have ADD tend to have more symmetry in blood flow between their two brain hemispheres than do non-ADD subjects. These findings, like MRI results, show up in both the frontal regions and the basal ganglia.[32]

4. PET (Positron Emission Tomography)

A PET scan produces computerized pictures that show levels of activity in different parts of the brain. PET scans can be used to demonstrate different levels of blood flow, as in the blood-flow experiments described above. Or they can be used to measure a function known as glucose metabolism, the rate at which the brain converts nutrients to energy.

In 1990, Alan Zametkin, M.D., used PET scans to measure cerebral glucose metabolism in adult subjects who had hyperactivity. His study attracted national attention. He found that subjects with hyperactivity had lower glucose metabolic rates than subjects without hyperactivity.[33] Measurements were taken while subjects performed an auditory-attention task. Adults with hyperactivity demonstrated a glucose metabolic rate 8.1 percent lower in key frontal regions of the brain than adults with no hyperactivity. (Adults were used as subjects so as not to expose the sensitive nervous systems of children to the radioactive tracers required to conduct a PET scan.)

In 1993 and again in 1994, Zametkin and his associates tried to replicate his 1990 findings. In these studies, teenagers served as subjects. The teens did *not* show the same effect. As Zametkin suggests, ". . . adolescence may be a time of increased variability in brain metabolism."[34]

Teens' brains are known to have higher average metabolic rates than adults'. In Zametkin's studies, teen glucose metabolic rates were 18 to 31 percent higher than adult norms. (As a basis for comparison, recall that the difference in rates between the two adult groups in the first study was 8.1 percent.) Younger children's cerebral rates are known to be higher still. Overall, the average rate of a child between nine and fifteen years old has been found to be 62 percent higher than that of an adult.[35] Apparently, childhood is a time of overall rapid brain metabolism—and great potential for mental development.

As research proceeds in this area, it becomes increasingly more difficult to know what Zametkin's 1990 findings in adults mean. It appears that metabolic rate is unrelated to the changes in symptoms brought about by stimulant medication. In a 1993 study, adults with hyperactivity performed a standardized auditory attention task and were PET scanned before they took their medication and then again after taking stimulants. The PET scans showed no change in their brain activity, although the stimulants had apparently produced one, since they performed better on the task after taking the medication.[36] Similarly, a 1994 PET scan study failed to show before-and-after brain differences in subjects who took stimulant medication for a minimum of six weeks.[37]

ADD AND THE BRAIN

A number of concepts have been advanced by leading experts to help explain the underlying biology of the ADD temperament. In the United States, there are professional journals and newsletters dedicated exclusively to the study of ADD.[38] (See the notes for a review of some of the theories found in these publications.)[39]

The hypothesis most widely accepted in the field today is the disinhibition model.[40] *Disinhibition* means that a person's ability to inhibit his response to stimulation is weaker than his ability to be aroused by it. In other words, it's easier for that person to respond to stimulation—bright lights, loud sounds, outrageous ideas—than it is for him to ignore it. According to the disinhibition model, stimulant medication is effective for people with ADD because it helps (or stimulates) the brain to dampen (or inhibit) its response to stimulation such as lights, sounds, and ideas. In other words, it stimulates inhibition.

SELF-REGULATION AND THE DISINHIBITION MODEL

To control a function, a self-regulating system receives feedback and automatically self-corrects. For example, when you're hungry your brain sends signals telling you to eat. As you eat, your brain sends signals replacing hunger pangs with feelings of satiety. The feedback results in self-correction: you stop eating.

The disinhibition model postulates that arousal and inhibition are controlled by a self-regulating system in the brain. Too much arousal tells the brain to start to inhibit; too much inhibition tells the brain to increase its response to arousal. The system seeks equilibrium at a "setting" that is the brain's target or ideal state of equilibrium between arousal and inhibition.

Sometimes the "setting" on a self-regulatory system can be extreme. The system experiences equilibrium at a point that is very far in one direction. We say that such a system is biased. In the disinhibition model, the brain of a person with ADD has a self-regulatory system that is biased. It is set at a point that permits too much arousal, as compared to the settings of most other people for self-regulation.

However, because of feedback and self-correction—the way self-regulation works—a setting for too much arousal creates a potential for greater inhibition. The overaroused state in turn gives the brain feedback to generate inhibition that is comparable in quality and strength to the overaroused state. In this way, the brain becomes capable of a wider range of response, a higher level of complexity in the regulation of arousal and inhibition.

To picture how this works, imagine you are at a house party. You're in the kitchen, where it is relatively quiet. You listen as your host tells a story. You don't need to do much to pay attention. You hear every word he says.

Now the two of you move into the living room. There are twenty-plus people talking and laughing. Music plays through the speakers. Glasses and dishes clink and clatter. Every few minutes a troop of children race through, in one door and out another.

In the midst of this noise, your host tries to finish his story. This time his words get lost in the fray. You move closer to hear what he is saying. You tune out other voices, watch his lips, and concentrate even harder. You strain to listen. You fight not to tire more quickly with the extra effort.

After a while you adapt and succeed at listening to him speak. You follow his story and at the same time you also pick up on several strands of conversation around you. In addition, you find yourself enjoying the music and the laughter of the children when they appear. You have to work harder to listen in the living room, but you accomplish more, too.

Your kitchen experience is akin to having a setting on your self-regulating system that is "average" for arousal and inhibition. Your living-room scene is like having a setting that is biased in the direction of overarousal. It challenges you more, and with sustained effort, you refine your ability to inhibit, so you achieve more too.

In their best-selling book, *Driven to Distraction,* Edward Hallowell, M.D., and John Ratey, M.D., say that ADD is not "an inability to concentrate" but rather "the ability to concentrate on everything." They argue cogently for a disinhibition model and the favorable view it affords:

> Instead of framing the syndrome as an inability to pay attention to cues, this definition [the disinhibition model] focuses on the ability of someone with ADD to pay attention to many more cues than the average person. . . . It stresses that the positive components of the syndrome will assist the problematic ones.[41]

THE PLASTICITY OF THE BRAIN

The human brain, an extraordinary three-pound universe of over one hundred billion neurons, each with over one hundred connections, can instantaneously form new interconnections as needed. This is what brain plasticity means. Learning, or new *information* to the brain, results in new *formation in* the brain. This is how human behavior and neurochemistry interact. Each causes change in the other. The brain forms and reforms itself continually.[42]

Plasticity of the brain, the neurological manifestation of learning, occurs throughout the life span, but during childhood it functions at its highest rates.[43]

Learning and new experience result in new connections (of the neurons, the basic functional units of nervous tissue). The brain is dynamic and alive; it constantly changes and grows. Given optimal conditions, new neuronal connections can respond to a bias in self-regulation. However, these changes may require long periods of time while a state of disequilibrium in the direction of overarousal must be tolerated. This is analogous to having to be in the noisy living room for a long time, having to tolerate the chaos, until you can master listening.

These states of disequilibrium are necessary to the learning process. This is how Edison-trait children develop skills like multitasking (doing more than one thing at a time) and hyperfocus (the extreme inhibition of irrelevant responses).

Brain plasticity permits a child to "rise to the occasion," so to speak. The brain continues to receive voluminous incoming messages, but the child develops an enhanced ability to handle them in his own way.

A GOOD BRAIN—ADD OR NOT

Sara is a seven-year-old daydreamer. She likes baby animals, picture books, and dances that she makes up herself. She spends much of her school day staring out the window. She dislikes most class assignments and flatly refuses to read out loud. Because she has problems following directions and completing projects, her classmates don't want her at their table or in their group. On her teacher's recommendation, her parents brought her to her pediatri-

cian, who diagnosed her as having ADD. Sara's parents are considering a trial course of medication for their daughter, but they want to try some other approaches first.

Today Sara is in my office because she came home crying, insisting that she was "dumb" and "stupid," and that she hated herself.

"And this is Charlene," she tells me, looking up sad-eyed from her drawing. "She's a pony nobody wants because her brain is no good. Even the other ponies don't want her around."

"I wonder what's wrong with Charlene's brain?" I ask.

"Oh, I think it's got holes in it. That's why she doesn't know what to do, even when she's told."

"Could it be that Charlene has a good brain, and that there are no holes in it at all?" I reply. "Maybe Charlene just has her own way of thinking . . . her very own, one-of-a-kind way of thinking."

Sara has heard me say this before, but I sense she wants me to say it again. Luckily, she's tuned in to what I am saying at this moment. "You mean nobody really knows how smart Charlene is?"

"Yeah," I reply. "Different ponies are smart in different ways."

Sara smiles. "Charlene can belly-dance. Watch!" Sara ripples the paper back and forth. We laugh.

Sara, my young client, leaves. I fill out the paperwork for this therapy session. The form for Sara's insurance company requires a diagnosis. I fill in the code for Attention Deficit Disorder. It is an accurate diagnosis: Sara's functioning at school is significantly impaired.

However, this terminology says nothing of factors like Sara's intelligence, perceptiveness, sensitivity, creativity, and wit. It ignores the fact that Sara's pain is the result of a mismatch between her porous imagination and the requirements for succeeding at school. Her insurance company's form doesn't list a choice like "good brain, but owing to its atypical neurochemistry, it is being misjudged, passed over, and not educated optimally to realize its potential." Yet that also states Sara's problem accurately.

It takes extra effort for Edison-trait children to think convergently, to inhibit extraneous thought. When we diagnose, we tend to see what they *lack* and not what they *have*. We become obsessed with their shortcomings and overlook their strengths. We have popularized the name of their disorder (ADD), ignoring the potential in their overall personality (the Edison trait). We've named the disorder for their weakness (attention deficit), ignoring their gift (abundance of imagination). Perhaps an acceptable middle ground would be something like "Imagination Mismanagement Syndrome."

A MISMATCH OF CHILD AND SETTING

As in Sara's story, ADD symptoms are best explained as a *mismatch* between a child's neurochemistry (the Edison trait: widely divergent) and the demands of a situation (the school setting: highly convergent). The greater the mismatch, the worse the symptoms. Having to listen to a teacher's lecture, do a timed class assignment, read lengthy reference materials, or perform repetitive tasks will aggravate your child's symptoms. On the other hand, his symptoms will lessen when he is being tutored one-on-one (forced convergence); he is getting extra rewards for his efforts (highly reinforced and therefore more highly motivated convergence); he is in a novel setting (divergence); or he is doing intrinsically interesting activities (divergence).

As ADD specialist Ron Reeve, Ph.D., states: "ADD is not just a disorder within the child. Its expression depends on the match between the child and the environment."[44]

DID THOMAS EDISON HAVE ADD?

Now that you know what ADD means, let's look again at the life of young Thomas Edison. We know his characteristic style of thinking was divergent. At school, did a mismatch between his style and his environment result in the dysfunction we now call ADD?[45]

Right from the start, Al, as young Edison was known, did things on impulse, out of the blue. As a toddler he turned up missing one day. He was found that night in a neighbor's barn, asleep on a nest of eggs. Someone had told him that geese squat on eggs to make them hatch, and Al had to see this for himself.

Another time, Al became interested in how a grain elevator worked. Totally absorbed, he got a little too close, fell in, and almost suffocated in the wheat.

In September of 1855, Al entered the Reverend G. B. Engle's school. His restless and fidgety seven-year-old mind often wandered. He could not sit still in his seat, even when the reverend struck him with a cane to get him to pay attention. Consequently, Al was at the bottom of his class. He hated school and lasted only until the first frost. He could not conform to his teacher's expectations, a disability that today sounds a lot like ADD.

At that point, Al's mother, Nancy, a former schoolteacher, decided to teach her son at home. She knew he needed special consideration. Following his lead, she encouraged his interest in science. When he was nine, she got him a copy of R. G. Parker's *School of Natural Philosophy,* a book of one hundred experiments that demonstrated the scientific knowledge of the day. Al did every one of the experiments on his own.

At home, with his passion for inquiry encouraged, Al thrived. He built a basement laboratory with more than two hundred jars and bottles of chemicals. He cleverly labeled each one POISON to prevent intruders from tampering with them. He experimented with model steam engines and built a simple transmitter and receiver from scrap metal and the necks of old bottles.

Luckily for Al and for modern civilization, his mother helped create a prodigious match between his nature and his environment. She was never able to teach him to spell properly or to write grammatical English, but this impairment was not significant. In twentieth-century terms, she took the "deficit" out of ADD.

Al progressed academically and was no longer dysfunctional. Nonetheless, he continued to demonstrate widely divergent thinking, often without regard for possible negative consequences. For example, at age ten, he tried an experiment that was not in Parker's book. He wanted to see if a boy could rise in the air, the way a lighter-than-air balloon did. To test his theory he gave his friend Michael Oates huge doses of Seidlitz powders that, when mixed with water, bubbled up and gave off carbon dioxide. Of course Michael did not float like a balloon. He fell like a rock and suffered unbearable stomach pain. On another occasion, Al tried to generate static electricity by attaching wires to the tails of two cats and vigorously stroking their fur. What he generated instead were two maniacal cats.

In September of 1857, Al returned to a formal classroom. He liked his new school better than Engle's, but once again he began getting into trouble. Al became known for playing practical jokes, and neither teachers nor students liked him very much. This time

Al lasted a little over a year. In the language of today, we can say his dysfunction or "ADD" resumed. In the winter of 1859, at age twelve, Al was withdrawn from school for the last time. He continued to learn at home and on his jobs, in his own nonconforming way.

As he grew into adulthood, Thomas Alva Edison developed his style and realized his dreams. A doer and man of many talents, he was far from impaired in occupational functioning. He learned to capitalize on the strengths of his personality and make them work for him. In addition to inventing the lightbulb and the phonograph, he invented a vote recorder, electric pen, dictating machine, speaking doll, and a way of preserving fruit. He improved the telephone, typewriter, stock ticker, electric generator, and motion picture. He was extraordinary in his ingenuity and resourcefulness, generously endowed with the trait that today bears his name: the Edison trait, the gift of intensely divergent thinking.

CHAPTER 14

Professional Diagnosis, Testing, and Counseling

> There is a high degree of dynamic relativity in living Nature, and what may be regarded as healthy under one set of circumstances may be unhealthy under another.
>
> —Jonas Salk

WHAT IS THE PURPOSE OF A PSYCHOLOGICAL EVALUATION?

The first question I ask a child who has come in for an assessment is "Why are you here?" These are some of the reasons children give:

"To find out what's wrong with me."
"Because my mom said I have to."
"Because I'm not so good at math."
"To see if I have that attention disease."
"So you'll know if I'm smart or dumb."

The reason I give is: "I would like to know more about you, especially about the way you think. If grown-ups, like your parents and teachers and me, understand you better, then we'll be able to do a better job of helping you."

Usually it is counterproductive for children to hear the medical terminology that grown-ups use to organize and report the findings of a professional psychological evaluation. Often it is counterproductive for the grown-ups to use the terminology to begin with. In the midst of words like *deficit, impairment,* and *disability,* we tend to lose sight of concepts like *strengths, solutions,* and *accountability.*

The act of diagnosing is a model rooted in the practice of Western medicine. Medical insurance plans—and managed health plans in particular—subscribe to this model. In managed care, the purpose of a professional evaluation is to establish a psychiatric diagnosis. If a formal diagnosis exists, the costs of services are covered; if there is no diagnosis, there is no coverage.

Diagnosing is a reasonable and understandable practice. There is a drive within each of us to get a name for a problem if it affects our life. It is comforting to agree on a label. But this should not be the main purpose of a professional evaluation.

A professional evaluation is meant to serve a broader, more useful function: A professional evaluation is a way to get an overview of your child's strengths and weaknesses, so you can navigate a course of action to meet her needs. In a sense, a diagnosis is a means to an end, not an end unto itself.

When a parent comes in to have his child tested, I sometimes ask the question, What difference would it make to you if your child had ADD? Often a parent answers, "Well, then I would know why she acts the way she does." Sometimes he says, "At least I would know it's not something I'm doing wrong."

It's hard to accept the fact that ADD is a diagnosis that has "fuzzy" boundaries. With no biological test to detect ADD, it is not a well-defined disorder. What one doctor calls childhood another calls ADD. An "active learner" in one classroom is an "impaired learner" in the classroom next door.

More important than applying or not applying a particular label is doing all we can to identify and meet your child's needs. The purpose of a professional evaluation is to define a set of goals, get a direction, create a plan. A professional evaluation is not the end of your search. It is a new beginning.

If you anticipate getting a professional evaluation for your child, read this chapter, then ask yourself what you want from the testing. To educate yourself even further, follow up on some of the more detailed information contained in the notes.

Be a knowledgeable consumer. Talk with your psychologist before the evaluation. Know what questions you want to ask. Find out whether you and your psychologist share the same vision of the purpose of your child's evaluation. If you find that you are not at ease, ask questions until you are. Or get more than one professional opinion. Do this *before* you agree and begin.

Should I Get My Child Evaluated?

This is a question that can cause a parent uneasiness, concern, and thoughts like these:

> *"He doesn't do what every other kid does."*
> *"If we go looking for problems, I'm sure we'll find them."*
> *"He's just a normal kid who knows how to push people's buttons."*
> *"If I knew he had ADD, at least I'd know it's not his fault or mine."*
> *"You hear so much about it. Suppose he's got it and we don't know."*

You want a professional evaluation for your child if . . .

- you have a sense she behaves differently in some important ways from many of the other children her same age
- you need to know more about your child, especially how she compares with others, to make better decisions on her behalf
- your child is making acceptable progress in school but you feel she could be achieving much more than she is
- the ways you have been trying to help her don't work, and you want some new approaches
- your child is failing, acting out, emotionally distraught, or chronically unhappy

If your child is an Edison-trait Discoverer or Dynamo, chances are you've had an intuition about her nature practically since birth:

> *"He was an escape artist, right out of the crib."*
> *"She emptied everything out of every cabinet."*
> *"I could see the expressions on parents' faces change when we took him to a birthday party. And it wasn't my imagination."*

You've known she has a temperament that distinguishes her. She thinks and acts in her own high-spirited and strong-willed way.

However, if your child is an Edison-trait Dreamer, you may not pick up on her natural style until she starts school. Before then, no one ever asks her to trade in her magic wand for a pencil and ruler.

This is why it is often a Dreamer's teacher who is the first to notice she is a mind wanderer. You may notice her struggle when she starts to get homework assignments, or if you spend time observing in her classroom.

If you feel uncertain about whether or not to seek a professional evaluation, your child's teacher can help you decide. Teachers see many students your child's age. Most have learned what to expect and what is unusual.

Also, your child's teacher can recommend an assessment at school to see if your child qualifies for an IEP or Individualized Educational Program. An IEP assessment is a battery of psycho-educational tests conducted by a team of professionals from your local school district. Its main purpose is to identify learning disorders in children and recommend specific instructional methods to teach them. (See Chapter 12, page 169, for more information on IEPs.)

A psychological evaluation differs from an IEP assessment in that a psychological evaluation can address any referral question dealing with any aspect of a child's psychological functioning—intellectual, emotional, behavioral—and psycho-educational. An IEP assessment is solely psycho-educational.

There are many approaches to the diagnosis of ADD but no objective, definitive test. These approaches vary and some are more subjective than others. The advantage of a psychological evaluation is that at least some of the assessment methods yield quantitative results, that is, results expressed in numbers. For example, instead of a finding that states "Your child is inattentive," the finding states "According to one measure, your child is more inattentive than 90 percent of the other girls her age."

Who Should Do the Evaluation?

A properly credentialed psychologist is qualified to conduct a psychological evaluation. A major advantage of a psychological evaluation is that results are quantified and compared to norms. (I'll discuss the value of this in the upcoming section on standardized rating scales.) Another benefit of a psychological evaluation is that recommendations are usually multimodal: In other words, they include a range of possible suggestions, for example, tutoring, therapy, or an evaluation for medication. You can usually obtain a referral to a psychologist from your child's pediatrician, from a teacher or counselor at school, or from another parent.

If you have substantial reason to believe that your child has ADD—for example, as a result of a psychological evaluation—you will want to consult a medical doctor such as a pediatrician who understands and treats ADD.

Most pediatricians now practice behavioral medicine to the extent that they can and will prescribe drugs for a child with ADD. Others pediatricians refer to specialists, usually child psychiatrists, who have more expertise in the field. Typically, a physician asks about symptoms and then prescribes a drug on a trial basis. The physician then monitors the results by asking about symptoms and adjusting dosage accordingly.

What a Professional Evaluation Can and Cannot Do

A professional evaluation can give you an estimate of how extreme your child's Edison-trait behaviors are, as compared with the behaviors of other children of her gender and age. If your child shows symptoms of inattention, impulsivity, or hyperactivity that are in the most extreme 5 percent for children her age, *and* they interfere with her functioning, *and* there are no other causes that explain them better, she *may* qualify for the diagnosis of Attention Deficit Disorder.[1]

A professional evaluation cannot tell you with certitude *why* your child's behaviors are so extreme. Over 50 percent of children who are diagnosed with ADD also meet the criteria for one or more other disorders, such as depression or learning disabilities. (See Chapter 13 for an explanation of comorbidity.)

This figure is even higher if a child is under emotional stress. An irate father once called me long-distance from Hong Kong. Was this the office who had diagnosed his daughter as having ADD? Was I aware of how much his child had been shuffled around while her mother, his ex-wife, was trying to "find herself"? His voice boomed through the receiver: "Kate's got ADD all right. ABANDONED DAUGHTER DISORDER!"

No single test or measure can be used by itself. A professional evaluation consists of a range of tests and measures. It gathers information from a number of sources.

Also, a professional evaluation can test for other causes, like specific learning differences, and estimate how much of a role each cause plays in the current picture of symptoms. ADD is a diagnosis by default. This means that whatever dysfunction is left over after other causes have been ruled out is assumed to be Attention Deficit Disorder.

Most important, a professional evaluation can give you specific ideas and recommendations that you can check out for your child. It can tell you how well your child's profile matches the profiles of other children who have been helped by special education methods, therapy, or medication. It is a way to generate a things-to-do list of strategies and approaches to better serve your child's needs.

In this chapter you will learn about how psychologists measure attention. This includes traditional tests, as well as computerized CPTs (Continuous Performance Tests), a method you may have heard about, as it is currently rising in popularity. You will also learn how psychologists assess multiple causes of attentional problems such as anxiety, depression, and learning disabilities. Measures of stress, emotional factors, and learning will be described.

MEASURES OF ATTENTION

Parent and Teacher Interviews

Typically, an Edison-trait child encounters attentional problems only in demanding or overstimulating settings. In the nondemanding, one-to-one setting of a psychologist's office, she is likely to be charming, creative, and problem-free. That is why it is vital for a psychologist to get information from parents and teachers. Their observations are the psychologist's window on the child's day-to-day functioning.

A psychologist usually begins a professional evaluation by conducting a structured interview with you, the parent. You will be asked to give a "developmental history," to recount events in your child's life chronologically. The psychologist is looking to identify behaviors that fit typical patterns, and to identify the most likely causes of those behaviors.

A developmental history will include information about medical problems such as hearing and visual impairments. A growing child's physical problems interact with her cognitive development. For example, auditory learning is sometimes delayed as a result of chronic ear infections at ages when brain development is optimal for the acquisition of language skills. Visual learning is sometimes delayed as a result of a condition in which a child's left and right eyes focus in different ways.

A psychologist might give you a questionnaire to complete prior to coming in for an interview. A questionnaire can help you organize your memories and observations.

A psychologist needs information about your child at school. You may be asked to authorize your psychologist to obtain records, speak with your child's teacher, or observe in your child's classroom. You may be asked to bring in report cards and samples of her work.

Standardized Rating Scales

In addition to giving your child's developmental history, you will be asked to rate your child's current behaviors. Usually the psychologist will give you and your spouse each a rating scale and ask you to fill it out independently. The psychologist will also give you a school version of a rating scale for your child's teacher to complete.

Most rating scales list problem behaviors that indicate inattentiveness, impulsivity, and hyperactivity. These categories correspond to the diagnostic criteria for Attention Deficit Disorder listed in the *DSM-IV.* (See Chapter 13.) You are asked to check off how frequently, per hour, day, week, or month, your child engages in each behavior.

Examples of behaviors from rating scales that indicate inattentiveness are if your child . . .

- needs directions repeated
- loses place or leaves out words when reading
- is unable to copy letters or numbers accurately from a textbook or chalkboard

Examples of impulsivity are if your child . . .

- interrupts when others are talking or trying to work
- does not wait for, or follow, directions
- makes unnecessary physical contact with others

Examples of hyperactivity are if your child . . .

- hops, skips, and jumps to get from one place to another
- cannot settle down after recess
- becomes loud and unruly during group activities

The answers that you, your spouse, and your child's teacher give are scored and then compared to norms, the average scores of children who are your child's gender and age. Each rating scale has its own set of norms, which were established when the answers of a large number of parents and teachers were analyzed. This is what makes the rating scale standardized. A scale that is standardized well has been generated by a large number of respondents who represent a cross section of the population. Some of the rating scales currently used and the range of norms that have been established for each are listed in the notes.[2]

The psychologist compares your child's score to the norm on each scale and translates it into a standardized score for each category of symptom. Each rating scale has its own cutoff scores for categories such as "indicates a serious level of concern," or "at risk." In general, if your child's scores fall in the most extreme 5 percent, her symptoms are in the range of consideration for a diagnosis of Attention Deficit Disorder.[3] Of course, it is still necessary to examine what reasons best account for those symptoms before a diagnosis is made. Stress, emotional factors, and learning differences usually play a part.

Symptom Checklists

As an expedient way to decide whether or not to recommend a professional evaluation, a teacher, a pediatrician, or a school nurse might use a symptom checklist as a screening tool. (Chapter 13 includes a symptom checklist.)

The difference between a standardized rating scale and a symptom checklist is the existence of established norms. Because a standardized rating scale has norms—a point of reference, a basis for comparison—it is considered to be an objective measure. Because a symptom checklist has no norms, it is said to be subjective. There is no way a symptom checklist can distinguish between behaviors you can expect from most children and behaviors that are extreme for your child's gender and age.

Self-Rating

Some rating forms are designed to be completed by the child herself, if she is nine years of age or older. The intended purpose is (1) to get direct information from the child, and (2) to empower the child, so she feels she is an active part of her own evaluation.

The downside of self-rating is that it can slip into an experience of self-berating. Consider the experience through your child's eyes. To complete the form, your child reads sentence after sentence describing shortcomings and failures she is likely to have: "Most of the time my handwriting is messy." . . . "I make lots of careless mistakes." . . . "When the teacher gives directions, I get mixed up more times than the other kids do." There is even the possibility of a "negative halo effect," where your child becomes vulnerable to suggestions of symptoms that were not a problem for her before.

There are alternative ways to get information directly from your child without the use of a self-rating scale. This can be done formally with tests like CPTs (Continuous Performance Tests—see below) or other performance tasks. And it can be done informally, using art, play, or conversation.

CPTS (CONTINUOUS PERFORMANCE TESTS)

Take a pencil and cross out every *t* on this page. When you're finished, you will have completed a continuous performance task.

Now, suppose I standardize this task—give it to many other people, record their scores and times, average the scores by gender and age range, and construct a table of norms. Now I can compare your score and time on this task with the appropriate norm and tell you how you did, compared to your gender and age peers.

If you missed a lot of *t*'s compared to your fellow test takers, you committed errors of omission. This is presumed to be a measure of inattention.

Perhaps you crossed out many letters that were not *t*'s, such as *l*'s or *f*'s. Then you committed errors of commission. This is presumed to be a measure of impulsivity.

Did you finish the page? That's a measure of your "sustained attention." How long did it take you? Your time is an indicator of "compensation" or how much you needed to slow down to be accurate. Would you do better if the page had more *t*'s or fewer? This is a measure of performance sensitivity to high or low stimulation.

Psychologists have used paper-and-pencil CPTs for years. Now, computerized CPTs are gaining in popularity. On one, the Connors test, one letter of the alphabet at a time is flashed on a screen at a variable rate of speed. You are required to press the space bar every time the letter you see is an X. On another, the IVA (Intermediate Visual and Auditory), you see either a 1 or a 2. You click for 1 and don't click for 2. The IVA is both visual (on-screen) and auditory (through a speaker). On the Gordon, you press for a "9" when it is preceded by a "1." On the TOVA (Tests of Variables of Attention), you press for a rectangle in one position but not in another. Because it uses a geometric shape and not a letter or number, the TOVA is called a "non-language-based" CPT. These CPTs and their norms are listed in the Notes.[4]

Major advantages of a computerized CPT are efficiency, precision, and standardization. A CPT takes about twenty minutes to administer. Responses are scored and analyzed automatically. CPTs are easy to use and give discrete, objective measurements. This invites researchers to use them, so we can build and share a store of scientific knowledge about human attention. CPTs make a good attempt to define specific functions or activities of human attention, which makes more sense than generic, vague terms like *attention deficit*.

The major disadvantages are a potential for faulty assumptions, overgeneralized applications, and prejudicial conclusions. For example, if an Edison-trait child loses interest and does not complete the CPT, or if she completes it but with less than full effort, is it right to assume she has a deficit in "sustained attention," or is it an example of "off-task behavior"—the act of doing something else, mentally or physically? She could be expressing her unwillingness to engage in a meaningless activity. Several studies have shown that children with ADD achieve significantly higher scores on CPTs if someone was standing over them watching—which reduces off-task behavior.[5] When a child engages in off-task behavior in the face of a boring activity, is it a "symptom"? Or is it a pretty decent decision on her part about what to invest herself in? (Did *you* actually cross out all the *t*'s on page 204?)

A computerized CPT can flash symbols at a slow rate or at a fast one. When symbols are flashed at a slow rate, some children with ADD, when left alone, do not keep up their scores for as long as children who do not have ADD. This measure—whether a subject prefers and performs longer when symbols are flashed quickly or slowly—holds promise for the study of how convergent and divergent thinkers differ. Divergent thinkers tend to like it better and perform longer when symbols are flashed quickly. Research of this measure might even reveal ways for both kinds of thinkers to increase their skills at variable rates of speed.

However, it is unwarranted to conclude that a child's response preference on this measure is a "symptom."[6] It is also unwarranted to conclude that this measure can be used as the sole rationale for a child to be given medication.[7] Some children with ADD who score below average on this measure when unmedicated show improved scores when given psychostimulants.[8] But this finding raises more questions than it answers: How do psychostimulants affect the scores of all subjects on this measure, regardless of whether or not they have ADD? What other effects (for example, on creative problem solving) does taking psychostimulants have? What training methods or other drug-free strategies can children use to learn to improve their scores?

There are additional concerns about reading too much into a child's scores on any of the measures of a CPT. Response time is measured in milliseconds. This is useful to researchers who want to analyze the process of human attention, but it has no real-world application for children. For example, on one CPT, over the course of the entire test, a subject varied her rate of responding in only fractions of a second. On the basis of this finding, the computerized report concluded that "there is evidence [she] has an attentional problem."

CPTs hold promise as research tools. At this time, however, as leading expert C. Keith Connors, Ph.D., notes in his review of the current literature, "Results are inconsistent with respect to diagnostic relevance and sensitivity to medication."[9] To sum up, exercise caution when reading a CPT report, and don't use it as the sole basis for a judgment about diagnosis or medication.

MEASURES OF STRESS AND
EMOTIONAL FACTORS

The psychologist uses your child's developmental history to identify stress and emotional factors. When children are depressed, anxious, or overwhelmed by stress, they are more easily distracted, preoccupied, and disorganized in their thinking.

In addition to reviewing your child's developmental history, the psychologist needs to observe and communicate directly with your child. The psychologist will choose a method to do this, depending on your child's age and personality.

The Use of Play

For younger children, most psychologists have a repertoire of methods like playing with puppets, telephones, or miniatures (for example, using a dollhouse or schoolroom). For older children, a psychologist might solicit memories and stories by asking open-ended questions or by using a "you-finish-the-sentence" format.

Imaginative methods are usually necessary to connect with Dreamers. Usually Dreamers respond best when gently invited to talk through drawing, painting, or storytelling. Discoverers and Dynamos, on the other hand, are often quite outspoken. They usually have clear, unambiguous opinions about the causes of their problems.

When it comes to talking about their feelings, all Edison-trait children prefer to speak in language rich in metaphors and dramatic scenes. A Discoverer whose parents got divorced will tell you about an earthquake that split the world in two. A Dynamo who is mad at his sister wants to plant a bomb under her bed tonight. A Dreamer who feels small will draw an amazing picture of a redwood forest. In it she is a speck, an ant afraid of getting squished.

Projective Drawing Tests

In a projective drawing test, your child is asked to draw a specific picture, for example, a picture of herself or a member of her family. Your child is then asked a set of questions about what she has drawn. These drawings are called projectives because it is assumed that your child projects herself and her feelings into her drawings. Her answers about her pictures tell the psychologist how she sees herself and give her a chance to say how she feels. Since the same basic picture and questions are asked of many different children time and again, the psychologist can compare your child's response to the responses of others who have taken the same projective.[10]

MEASURES OF LEARNING

Intelligence Tests

A psychologist will usually administer one well-standardized, individual intelligence test to assess your child's cognitive strengths and weaknesses. The test most often given is the Wechsler Intelligence Scale for Children, third edition, called the WISC-III.[11] The WISC-III is normed for children ages six to seventeen. Other intelligence scales and their norms are listed in the Notes.[12]

A standardized individual intelligence test takes about ninety minutes to two hours to administer. Then the examiner needs to score and analyze it properly. Although intelligence tests were originally designed to compute a child's IQ, this is not their main purpose today. The main purpose of giving an intelligence test today is to get a profile of your child's different intellectual abilities. Is she more visual than auditory? Will she guess if she doesn't know something? Does she answer more quickly on some types of tests, but wait before she answers on others?

The psychologist is looking for large differences in your child's scores between different categories of thinking. For example, half of the WISC-III is called "Verbal." It requires a child to use word skills and has subtests with names like "Vocabulary" and "Similarities." The other half is called "Performance." It requires the child to use nonverbal skills, for example, eye-and-hand coordination. It has subtests with names like "Block Design" and "Mazes." If your child scores much higher on the "Performance" tests than she does on the "Verbal" tests, her nonverbal skills are outpacing her verbal ones. She is smarter than she can say in words. This may explain many of her problems at school. It also means she may benefit from seeing a language specialist.[13]

Because intelligence tests are so widely given, their norms are well established. There are clear cutoff scores, the scores that separate levels in each category. A psychologist can compare your child's score between categories, and express the degree of her confidence about conclusions. This analysis helps to point out your child's underdeveloped skills. It also helps to identify your child's intellectual strengths.

Intelligence tests like the WISC-III do not measure creativity and therefore underestimate the intelligence of a divergent-thinking child. Any IQ score derived from an intelligence test should take this into account.

Currently, there is a growing movement to adopt assessment tools that measure multiple kinds of intelligence. It is becoming more widely recognized that standardized tests are biased in favor of linguistic and logical-mathematical aptitudes. They do not test for other kinds of intelligence, like spatial knowledge; "tacit," or practical, knowledge; ingenuity; or intuition. The Edison-trait child's strengths would be detected best by an instrument that measures skills and potentials to visualize, see possibilities, and generate a broad range of solutions.[14]

The WISC-III includes a number of different scales that help the psychologist piece together your child's profile of cognitive abilities. Some scales have names like "freedom from distractibility." However, despite what the names of these scales may imply, there is no measurement on the WISC-III, or on any other intelligence scale, that has discriminant ability to diagnose ADD.[15] Research has demonstrated this unequivocally. This is true of neuropsychological tests as well.[16]

Achievement Tests

If there is reason to believe that your child may have what is viewed as a learning disability, the psychologist will also want to see the results of a standardized achievement test. An achievement test measures the fund of information that your child has already learned. The results are expressed in "age equivalents" or "grade levels." These scores indicate your child's academic achievement in major subjects like phonetic reading (sometimes called "decoding"), reading comprehension, and arithmetic. The psychologist looks for gaps between your child's level of intellectual ability (her scores on an "intelligence test") and what she knows (her scores on an "achievement test"). The names of commonly used individual achievement tests are listed in the Notes.[17]

The psychologist may administer an achievement test or use the results of a school-administered achievement test. Usually, schools give group-administered achievement tests to students in the classroom at regular intervals. The results of these tests serve as a screening tool to identify children at risk for "learning disabilities." Those children might then be referred for an IEP evaluation, which generally includes a standardized intelligence test as well as a battery of individually administered standardized achievement tests.

WHAT IS A LEARNING DISABILITY?

This question probably has as many answers as there are teachers, psychologists, and parents struggling with the concept, and students struggling to learn. The term is defined by law, because the law requires schools to accommodate students who are *learning disabled*. (LD).

The law says a learning disability exists when there is (1) an impairment and (2) a severe discrepancy between a student's level of ability and her level of achievement. The discrepancy is measured by subtracting the student's scores on an achievement test from her scores on a test of ability.

Each state has its own specific criteria. California law says that to be learning disabled a pupil must have (1) a disorder in a basic psychological process and (2) a severe discrepancy between intellectual ability and achievement. It defines "basic psychological processes" as including attention, visual processing, auditory processing, sensory-motor skills, and cognitive abilities. It defines a "severe discrepancy" as a statistically significant difference between a child's score on an individually administered standardized intelligence test and her score on an individually administered standardized achievement test. The decision as to whether or not a pupil meets the criteria for LD rests with the school IEP (Individualized Educational Program) team.[18]

Recently, many professionals have been reexamining the basic assumptions that underlie the entire concept of learning *disability*.[19] Some say that the deficit approach to describing learning problems maintains the status quo of educational structures and methods at the cost of individualism and diversity.[20] They advocate restructuring schools to accommodate new modes of learning without deficit approaches. The *Journal of Learning Disabilities* published a special issue exploring this question.[21] Experts suggested changes in teacher education and instructional practices such as the recognition and encouragement of divergent-thinking strategies, alternatives to regurgitational test taking, and fostering cooperative work in diverse groups.[22]

Auditory Processing Problems

Edison-trait children tend to be visual. Their ability to imagine mental pictures is a major strength. The inverse of this strength is a relatively less strong aptitude for listening. Their auditory abilities are not as strong as their visual capacities.

In addition, Edison-trait children are opinionated. In psycho-educational terms, they are more "expressive" than "receptive." They prefer forming their own thoughts to hearing about the thoughts of others. Discoverers and Dynamos do this out loud. Dreamers do it in their heads. They talk more than they listen.

As a result of these factors, many Edison-trait children are diagnosed as having "auditory processing problems."[23] This diagnosis can be useful if it leads a child to a helpful resource, for example, a qualified language specialist. However, keep in mind that your child has gifts for visualization and talking, not just "auditory problems." Let her know she has a talent for seeing and speaking, not just a "need for improved listening skills."

Letter Reversals

All children reverse some letters and numbers when they first learn how to use these symbols. If reversals persist and interfere with a child's ability to read, they are seen as symptoms of a learning disability called *dyslexia*.

Few Edison-trait children actually qualify as dyslexic, but many continue to reverse letters much longer than their classmates do. Some will stop reversing letters when they learn to write in cursive. Some may continue to reverse the printed letters *b* and *d* occasionally all their lives.

If letter reversal is inconsequential, there is no reason to regard it as an impairment. In fact, another way to understand letter reversal is as the natural expression of a fluid-thinking mind. Edison-trait children conceptualize imaginatively and pictorially. Their minds are an animated motion picture of thought. Letter reversal is, in effect, your child's mental act of resistance to giving up some of her fluidity. There is a strong relationship between visual ability and spatial intelligence. Your child's spatial intelligence tells her *not* to limit the meaning of a given symbol to one direction only. Functionally, this limits future possibility.

Research in the field of creativity and spatial intelligence demonstrates that there is an advantage to maintaining flexibility in visual perception. The most creative architects are those who can instantly reverse mental representations of forms left to right, up or down. Consider the mental agility of an inventive genius like Leonardo da Vinci, who wrote his scientific notes backward.

It is interesting that astronauts observe how the state of weightlessness requires them to alter their spatial thinking. There is no "up" or "down." Like elite gymnasts, they must create a mentality in which fluid reversal of direction is an essential skill. They "unlearn" the kind of thinking that gives *b* and *d* separate meanings. They develop their ability to recognize that the integrity of a form persists in three-dimensional space regardless of its variable position. They train themselves to perceive that rotation does not alter the identity of a form.[24]

A MULTIMODAL APPROACH

Testing usually marks the beginning of a multimodal approach. Recommendations give you leads on how you can seek help for your child from a number of resources. A full range of recommendations might include further evaluation by another specialist, for example, a language specialist for language therapy or a physician for medication. You may get some new guidelines for yourself as a parent, or suggestions for your child's teacher or therapist. The psychologist may recommend one or more types of professional counseling for you and your family.

PROFESSIONAL COUNSELING

Parent Education

You and your spouse may want to work together with a professional, without your child being present. In this format, you come to the office prepared with specific examples of the problem behaviors you want to remedy. The therapist acts as a consultant. You use a "personal scientist" model, meaning that you take a humanistic yet scientific approach: Between sessions you try out new methods and observe the results. During sessions you pool your knowledge and improve on these methods.

Often a mother and a father hold two different points of view. One parent is more strict, the other is more lenient:

"He doesn't pull this kind of stuff with me, only you. You let him walk all over you."

"He's afraid of you. He's not learning anything, except how to hide the way he really feels."

Most of the time, when this occurs, it turns out that each parent speaks the truth. Their viewpoints are actually complementary, not oppositional. An objective third party who understands their situation can help them communicate and unite.

Family Therapy

In family therapy, the goal is improved communications among family members. There is no "identified patient," no one person who is "the reason" why the family is there. Improving the way the family functions is the reason for therapy. The family therapist encourages active listening skills and disrupts dysfunctional patterns. A therapist who has experience with Edison-trait children will employ methods such as using metaphor and Socratic questioning.

Edison-trait children are fiercely independent thinkers. They and their parents often get into control issues:

"They're always trying to run my life."

"Getting her to do things is such a battle."

Sometimes opposition has become part of the atmosphere, like the water a fish swims through in a bowl. A skilled family therapist can observe when this is happening during the session. With new awareness, a family can give up "adversarial" positions and become allies to solve common problems.

Individual Counseling

Edison-trait children have vivid imaginations that fuel their emotions to an extreme. Many have nighttime fears when they are alone. If fearful thoughts become unmanageable, they develop fear of their own fear. Some, especially Dynamos, express frustration more intensely than most.[25] As they mature, Edison-trait children become better equipped to use therapy to manage fear and anger and improve self-control. An experienced therapist can help a child develop strategies to deal with her emotions.

Individual counseling also can help if your child is building self-doubt. If she has been struggling recently at school or with her friends, her confidence in herself may be shaken. Robert Brooks, Ph.D., the director of child and adolescent psychology at Maclean Hospital in Massachusetts, has collected hundreds of stories written by children in this situation. He reads them at conferences to promote empathy for their fear and loss of self-esteem.[26]

He tells the story of Stephanie the Koala, written by a girl with ADD and learning disabilities. Stephanie and "a friend like her," a bunny named Candy, get "F"'s on their report cards. Together they say, "We were born dumb and stupid and *we will always be stupid*."

The story of Speedy Jaguar, always in trouble, was written by a hyperactive boy: "Speedy thought that *things would never change*."

An impulsive eight-year-old wrote the story of John and the monster who lives inside him. "John sometimes worried about *how he would be when he got older*."

"This comes across in every story I get," Dr. Brooks observes. These young writers feel pessimistic. They worry and wonder. How will they fit in?

Counseling can be a safe place for Edison-trait children to air their fears. They can use it to build self-confidence and a hopeful vision of themselves and their future.

Parent Support Groups

If your child has been diagnosed with ADD, you may be interested in an organization called CH.A.D.D. (Children and Adults with Attention Deficit Disorder). It is a parent network that has over six hundred local chapters, holds a yearly national conference, and sponsors local support group meetings. At a typical meeting, during the first hour there is a guest speaker and a question–and–answer period. After a break, parents socialize and share problems and solutions. Parents feel less isolated and benefit from one another's experience. They trade names and stories about schools, therapists, medications, books, and programs.

Parents also network in cyberspace. No other psychological condition draws on-line interest like the topic of ADD. There are special interest groups on the Internet and on all of the major information services.

Many Edison-trait adults communicate electronically to try to understand their own Edison-trait qualities. They post questions, download files, and chat on-line about the processes of human attention and imagination.

Late last night I sat at my computer screen reading messages from the ADD Forum on CompuServe. One contributor was reflecting on what ADD means: "I still think, as time passes, we'll come to view this 'affliction' as a 'side-effect' (if you will) of creative, abstract thought."[27]

I saved it to a file and logged off. Time will tell.

~~

CHAPTER 15

Medicating a Child Who Has ADD: A Personal Decision

The strongest element of growth lies in the human choice.

—George Eliot

A PRIVATE AND COMPLEX ISSUE

"If his grandfather knew we were giving him Ritalin, he'd try to have him taken away from us."

"We're getting a lot of pressure from the school. Some of it's subtle, some of it's not so subtle. They want us to get him on Ritalin."

"Talk about a guilt trip. I'd like to see one of these holier-than-thou parents spend just one night doing homework with my son when he's not on medication."

"I wanted to cry. I was backstage helping when I heard one of the other mothers refer to Chris as 'one of those Ritalin kids.'"

No parent likes the idea of giving her child drugs, especially a drug that is getting a lot of attention from the media. At the same time, every parent wants what's best for her child, what will give her child the best chance to succeed in school and social situations.

If your Edison-trait child has been diagnosed with ADD, and she is failing in some important ways, she may be a candidate for medication. The right drug treatment can cause a dramatic improvement. Medication is the fastest single treatment approach to ADD.[1] It can be a valuable tool for your child to learn how to calm herself and be more receptive to the tasks of convergent thinking.

The problem is that there is much we do not know about these drugs.[2] The effects of a stimulant medication like Ritalin are "nonspecific," meaning that the drug affects many aspects of brain function, not just those related to ADD.[3] The decision to medicate requires careful thought.

Cost-to-Benefit Ratio

Every treatment approach has its costs and its benefits. The two must be weighed against each other. Cost-to-benefit ratios apply to all treatment decisions: individual counseling, family therapy, special education programs, specific training like biofeedback, etc., as well as medication.

Treatment costs may be financial, emotional, biological, or psychological. They may be clearly defined, like doctor's fees, or estimated, like risk factors. They may be long term or short term, visible or hidden, probable or improbable. All of the same is true of benefits.

Cost-to-benefit ratio takes on a more serious tone when the treatment decision involves medication and especially when it involves a child. Children are more dose-sensitive than adults; they have less body weight and their metabolism is faster and less predictable.

Ritalin is known to increase a child's compliance, enhance self-control, decrease off-task behaviors, and reduce aggression. While it has not been shown to increase learning, Ritalin appears to make a child more available for learning to occur. Known benefits occur in about 70 percent of the children with ADD who take it.[4] Known side effects for most children are considered to be minimal: decreased appetite, trouble getting to sleep. (More information about side effects is provided in the Notes.)[5] However, when it comes to Ritalin, parents are usually more concerned with the unknown than the known.

Sometimes the cost-to-benefit ratio points to a clear-cut decision. If a child is chronically failing to perform, medication needs to be considered. Often, however, the decision whether or not to medicate is a judgment call.

In making this decision, it is important to consult the professionals who know your child. Talk with your child's pediatrician or child psychiatrist. Discuss the matter with your child's teacher and her school counselor. Educate yourself. Consult your pharmacist. Take the time you need to consider the overall cost-to-benefit ratio of medicating your child. Remember that medication is but one aspect of a child's treatment program.

If you and your child's physician agree to proceed, you may begin to give your child a trial course of medication. You will start with a small dose and increase it until you have obtained the best effects you can. You will monitor and record the changes you see in your child. You will ask for and consider the feedback you get from your child's teacher.[6] Your physician will recommend adjustments until you both agree you have the right drug at the right dose. After you have established a routine, you will still need to decide about "drug holidays" (specified periods of time when your child takes a break from medication), adapting to schedule changes, trying out new drugs, and responding to your child's varying needs as she matures.

THE DRUGS OF CHOICE

Psychostimulants

In 1995, approximately 90 percent of children who took medicine for ADD took the stimulant Ritalin (methylphenidate). Ritalin is known to decrease hyperactivity, impulsivity, and inattention.[7] As explained in Chapter 13, stimulants are believed to stimulate the brain's ability to inhibit these unwanted behaviors.

Ritalin starts to work right away. You can see positive results in about forty-five minutes. Its effects usually last about four hours. There is a time-release or longer-acting form, but many find these sustained pills to be less effective.[8]

Individual reactions to Ritalin vary from child to child. For one child one 10-milligram tablet three times a day may be the proper dose to decrease symptoms. For another child, a single 5-milligram tablet in the morning might suffice. Response depends on many factors: a child's age, weight, metabolism, severity of symptoms, level of stress, environmental support, etc. The CIBA Pharmaceutical Company, which manufactures Ritalin, recommends that Ritalin not be used in children under six years of age.[9]

A doctor may prescribe a stimulant other than Ritalin.[10] Dexedrine (dextroamphetamine) is currently gaining in popularity because it comes in a long-acting form that lasts six to eight hours.[11]

Cylert (pemoline), another stimulant, is also long-acting, six to eight hours, but is less popular because side effects related to liver functioning are a concern. Dosage must be increased gradually, so it can take up to several weeks to achieve a full effect.[12]

Common side effects of psychostimulants include loss of appetite and trouble sleeping. Other side effects include weight loss, irritability, nausea, dizziness, and headaches. There is a significant concern about the development of motor tics or Tourette's disorder. One study found that approximately 9 percent of the children treated with stimulants developed tics, although in the majority of cases the tics later subsided with or without discontinuation of the medicine.[13] Another study found a statistically significant increase in the frequency of motor tics when medicated children were observed in the classroom.[14] It is believed that stimulants may bring out tics, particularly facial tics, in those who are predisposed to them.[15]

Antidepressants (Serotonin-uptake Inhibitors)

It is becoming increasingly popular for doctors to prescribe Prozac (fluoxetine), Wellbutrin (bupropion hydrochloride), and Paxil (paroxetine) to children who have ADD. These drugs are called *serotonin-uptake inhibitors* because they work by interrupting the existing uptake cycle of the neurotransmitter serotonin, to increase its presence in the brain. Serotonin, like other neurotransmitters, enhances brain activity. Serotonin-uptake inhibitors may be prescribed alone, specifically to reduce symptoms of inattention, or they may be prescribed in addition to a psychostimulant, usually Ritalin, to reduce symptoms of co-morbid depression.

Doctors who prescribe Prozac and other serotonin-uptake inhibitors for children with ADD generally do so at much lower doses than they prescribe for adults to treat depression—it's called *low dosing*. Therapeutic effects should be noticeable right away, although it may take about four weeks for a full effect.

Side effects of serotonin-uptake inhibitors include anxiety, nervousness, difficulty sleeping, drowsiness, fatigue, tremor, sweating, nausea, and dizziness.[16] Most doctors are willing to accept the risk factors of prescribing the drug at low doses. However, the use of serotonin-uptake inhibitors for children who have ADD is relatively new, and according to Eli Lilly, the company that manufactures Prozac, its safety and effectiveness for children have not been demonstrated.[17]

The Eli Lilly company also issues a precaution about using Prozac in combination with other drugs that activate the central nervous system (CNS). Psychostimulants like Ritalin are CNS active drugs. The company states: "The risk of using Prozac in combination with other CNS active drugs has not been systematically evaluated. Consequently, caution is advised if the concomitant administration of Prozac and such drugs is required."[18]

Antidepressants (Tricyclics)

Tofranil (imipramine), Elavil (amitriptyline), Pamelor (nortriptyline), and Norpramin (desipramine) are tricyclic antidepressants that doctors sometimes prescribe for children with ADD. Tricyclic antidepressants work the same way serotonin-uptake inhibitors do, except that they are less specific. They interrupt the existing uptake cycle of a mix of neurotransmitters, not just serotonin, to increase their presence in the brain. Like serotonin-uptake inhibitors, they are prescribed at low doses, with noticeable effects right away, and full effect in about four weeks.

Because tricyclics affect more than just serotonin, more "binding sites" in the brain are affected. This results in a wider range of side effects, including sedation, drowsiness, and dizziness. They also include the range of side effects that occur when the neurotransmitter norepinephrine is involved: rapid heartbeat, dry mouth, and blurred vision.[19] There is growing concern about using tricyclics, particularly Norpramin (desipramine), in children, because they can pose some risk to the heart.[20]

Although tricyclic antidepressants have been on the market longer than serotonin-uptake inhibitors, their use with children who have ADD is relatively recent. As with serotonin-uptake inhibitors, caution is recommended regarding safety, efficacy, and use with other CNS active drugs. There is some precedent for the use of Tofranil (imipramine) with children, ages six to twelve, since imipramine is an approved treatment for bed-wetting.[21]

Clonidine

Doctors sometimes prescribe Catapres (clonidine) for children with ADD who also have symptoms of excess aggression or who are having trouble sleeping. Clonidine is taken once in the morning and its effects last most of the day (six to eight hours). It takes from one to three months to see the drug's benefits. Clonidine is known to decrease impulsivity and hyperactivity, but not inattention. It is possible to administer clonidine through the use of a patch. The principal side effects of clonidine are decreased blood pressure and sedation.[22]

Some doctors prescribe Tenex (guanfacine hydrochloride) instead of Catapres (clonidine). Tenex is similar to clonidine, but is thought to be longer-lasting and possibly less sedating.[23] Both drugs can cause dry mouth, weakness, and dizziness.

Other Medicines

A doctor might prescribe other medicines for a child with comorbidity, that is, a child who has both ADD and another disorder. These medicines might be prescribed alone or in addition to a stimulant or antidepressant.

A doctor might also prescribe a different kind of medicine if a side effect develops when a child is given a stimulant or antidepressant. For example, to reduce the jitters or anxiety that are sometimes associated with stimulants, particularly Ritalin, some doctors prescribe Corgard (nadolol), which is in a class of drugs known as beta-blockers. The safety of Corgard for children and the drug's effectiveness have not been demonstrated.[24]

THE RISE OF RITALIN

In 1937, Dr. Charles Bradley was using Benzedrine, a type of amphetamine, to treat headache pain in children. A serendipitous result was that overactive children showed behavioral improvement. Bradley reported his results but no one applied his findings to their practices. He lived in an era in which behavioral problems were not treated with drugs.[25]

In the 1950s, psychotropic medications, tricyclic antidepressants, and tranquilizers entered the pharmaceutical market. The age of taking drugs to treat psychiatric disorders had begun. In 1955 Ritalin came on the market. In 1964, early studies of its therapeutic effects on hyperactivity were published. Increasingly, doctors started to prescribe stimulants to treat overactive children, primarily in economically advantaged areas.

In 1970, an Omaha newspaper ran a story about the extent to which Ritalin was being used in the local area to treat children who were thought to be hyperactive. This story evoked national concern and a congressional inquiry. The Food and Drug Administration (FDA) made its first attempt to restrict the use of amphetamines with children. In 1971, amphetamine production in this country was still estimated at eight billion tablets annually.

The federal government then moved to reclassify amphetamines. The FDA placed them on the Schedule II list of controlled substances, making Ritalin subject to regulation by yearly quota by the Drug Enforcement Agency (DEA). Each year, the DEA estimates proper, current usage, and specifies the limit of pills that the manufacturer may produce. In 1972, the FDA sliced Ritalin production in half. But as this was happening, two other amphetamines entered the market: Dexedrine (dextroamphetamine) and Cylert (pemoline).

By the 1980s, doctors prescribed Ritalin for ADD in 90 percent of cases. They prescribed sedatives or tranquilizers for ADD in only 3 percent of cases. Dexedrine and Cylert split most of the remaining 7 percent of the market share.

Another trend at this time was the increased practice of prescribing medication for children who had symptoms of inattention, but not hyperactivity or impulsiveness. In the 1970s, only 7 percent of those treated were not hyperactive. By the late '80s that percentage had tripled.

In 1986 Ritalin received a considerable amount of criticism in the press, in conjunction with a number of lawsuits. Some of it was associated with the stand of the Church of Scientology against Ritalin's use with children. In the 1990s this anti-Ritalin campaign subsided, and stimulant treatment of ADD resumed its steady expansion.

Between 1990 and 1995, the DEA increased production quotas for Ritalin by 600 percent. It has been suggested that this figure may be misleading because of the way yearly quotas fluctuate, and that a more realistic estimate, based on other databases, is a 250 percent increase.[26] On July 18, 1994, *Time* magazine reported that "the use of Ritalin (or its generic equivalent, methylphenidate), the drug of choice for ADHD, has surged: prescriptions are up more than 390 percent in just four years."

Stimulants are infrequently prescribed outside of North America. Most other governments limit their availability. Amphetamines have been banned in Japan for some time now. Sweden categorized them as narcotics in 1944.[27]

In 1968, England restricted their usage to hospital pharmacies. During the same span of time that the production of psychostimulants increased 250 percent in the United States, their rate of use remained stable in England. According to Dr. Paul R. McHugh, the department chair and director of psychiatry at the Johns Hopkins School of Medicine, "British psychiatrists require a very severe form of hyperactivity before they'll see it as a problem. Unless a child is so clearly disturbed that he goes at it until he falls asleep in an inappropriate place like a wastebasket or a drawer, and then wakes up and starts it all over again, he won't be put on medication."[28]

In a recent *Newsweek* article it is noted that reliance on amphetamines "is, beyond question, an American phenomenon. The rate of Ritalin use in the United States is at least five times higher than in the rest of the world, according to federal studies."[29]

From 1994 to 1996, a group of Washington lobbyists campaigned to ease restrictions on Ritalin distribution. The DEA sought help from the International Narcotics Control Board to oppose these lobbying efforts.[30]

RITALIN AND THE PARADOXICAL EFFECT

Ritalin is a stimulant drug. It stimulates the central nervous system. Because of this, the fact that it reduces hyperactivity has sometimes been called its *paradoxical effect*. A popular myth has grown from this, the myth that if a child does not have ADD he will be "stimulated" by Ritalin, in other words, Ritalin will produce more activity in the child; and conversely, if Ritalin decreases activity, then indeed the child has ADD.

This is false. *All* children become more attentive and focused when given stimulants. Ritalin works the same way in every child. It has a so-called paradoxical effect on everyone.[31]

The reason for this paradoxical effect appears to be that when Ritalin stimulates brain activity, what it actually stimulates is the brain's inhibitory system. Stimulated or enhanced inhibition means fewer distracting thoughts to interrupt concentration and incite activity. Effects are more visible in children with ADD because there is more contrast between their medicated and nonmedicated states.[32] (For more about this, see "Self-regulation and the Disinhibition Model," page 189, in Chapter 13.)

DOES TAKING RITALIN NOW PROMOTE OR LESSEN SUBSTANCE ABUSE LATER?

The substance abuse issue is a two-sided coin: (1) If she takes Ritalin now, will my child be prone to substance abuse later in life, because I am teaching her to rely on drugs? (2) If she does not take Ritalin now, will my child be prone to substance abuse later in life, because not having gotten what she needed as a child, she is more inclined to self-medicate as a teen or adult?

There is no scientific evidence that suggests that children with ADD who take Ritalin are at any greater or lesser risk for future substance abuse than children with ADD who do not. There is a great deal of confusion about this matter because there is scientific evidence that suggests that children with ADD are at greater risk for substance abuse later in life. However, this is a separate issue from whether or not those children *who take Ritalin* are at greater or lesser risk.

Research shows elevated rates of substance abuse in adults with ADD as compared with the general population. One long-term study shows that among children with ADD, 20–30 percent have problems with substance abuse later in life.[33]

Research also shows that among substance abusers, an unusually high percentage also have ADD. One study reported that 25 percent of the adolescents in a substance-abuse treatment program had ADD.[34]

Researchers who study the link between ADD and substance abuse face a major problem. Abusers must undergo a prolonged period of abstinence for researchers to assess whether symptoms such as impaired concentration are caused primarily by ADD or by the substance abuse itself.[35]

The link between ADD and substance abuse, particularly alcoholism, appears to run in families. So does the concurrence of ADD with the diagnosis of "conduct disorder," a constellation of symptoms that may include cruelty, theft, or truancy, and increases the probability of drug abuse.[36]

It appears, then, that while children with ADD are at greater risk for substance abuse than children without ADD, there are mediating factors to consider, the primary one being family history. Children with ADD who have a family history of alcoholism and conduct disorder are at greater risk for substance abuse than children with ADD who do not.

Diversion

As use of Ritalin increases, so does the concern that Ritalin itself is becoming a drug of abuse. The most common type of abuse is diversion, when drugs that are prescribed for one person end up in the hands of another. Ritalin, an amphetamine, is a controlled substance, so the government exercises some regulation over its distribution. Physicians and pharmacists must follow legal directives when prescribing or filling prescriptions for a controlled substance. In most states, physicians have special procedures they must follow, for example, having to file a copy of the written prescription with the state narcotics board.[37] Pharmacists must take reasonable precautions to prevent diversion and abuse. In 1995, one nationally recognized continuing education program for registered pharmacists instructed them that it is their role to make sure that patients "understand that Schedule II psychostimulants have a high abuse potential, so access to them by friends and other family members should be controlled."[38]

In 1995, street use of Ritalin was brought up as a concern on several network television shows and in national magazines.[39] A 1996 *Newsweek* article reported that "a mini black market has emerged in a handful of playgrounds and campuses. 'Vitamin R'—one of its [Ritalin's] recreational names—sells for $3 to $15 per pill, to be crushed and snorted for a cheap and relatively modest buzz."[40]

The issue of diversion of Ritalin to unauthorized users is a reality that parents of children who take the drug, particularly parents of adolescents, need to address.[41] If your teenager takes Ritalin, you need to talk with her about what to do if one of her friends wants to try one of her pills. You and your child need to speak openly about why it is okay for her to take it, but not someone else. The two of you need to discuss exactly what she will say and do if she is approached.

Keep in mind that you are talking to someone who must figure things out for herself and who is strongly opinionated. It is not necessary to come to a philosophical agreement with her about why she may not share. It *is* necessary to communicate that it is against the law and that drug abuse is a serious violation with serious consequences for her and her friend.

Coach her and at the same time put yourself in her shoes. Help her decide what she can say to her friend.

She may be fine with a sturdy one-liner: "Nope. My doctor prescribed them for me."

She may want to offer her friend an alternative: "If you think it can help you, ask *your* doctor."

Or she may feel that she needs to explain her decision in terms of the negative consequences: "No. You won't get a high from it and it's not worth the risk. Suppose something happens, you know, something medical or something, and we have to tell them you took it. Or something else we can't predict happens and you have to take a drug test. No. It's not worth the risk if we get busted."

If necessary, encourage your teen to talk to her physician, pharmacist, or school counselor to help her make a firm decision about the right way to handle this situation.

Self-Medicating

In its July 18, 1994, cover story on ADD, *Time* magazine told the story of a man diagnosed with ADD at age fifty-one. He recalled how earlier in his life he unwittingly began medicating himself. "In my mid-30s, I would drink 30 to 40 cups of coffee a day. The caffeine helped."[42]

It appears that people with ADD are in fact inclined to self-medicate. This has led some people to believe that research exists to support the fact that if a child is treated with Ritalin, she is less likely to self-medicate with nonprescribed drugs when she gets older.

Considerable controversy, some of it well publicized, has arisen about this issue. In October 1995, PBS affiliates broadcast an episode of *The Merrow Report* that looked at this question. *The Merrow Report* challenged the validity of a statement that appears in educational materials published and distributed by CH.A.D.D. that "emotional difficulties, including substance abuse, are more likely to occur when a child with ADD is *not* treated." *The Merrow Report* maintained that current research does not support this contention.[43]

As previously mentioned, research does show that persons who have ADD are known to engage in substance abuse more than persons who do not have ADD. Persons who have ADD who are treated with Ritalin are known to have fewer symptoms. Some believe that it follows logically, then, that persons with ADD who are treated with Ritalin should be less likely to engage in substance abuse. Some physicians who prescribe Ritalin have publicly espoused this theory. But there is no direct evidence at this time for a causal relationship between Ritalin intake and reduced substance abuse. In other words, there are no known studies that show that if a child with ADD is treated with Ritalin, that particular child is less likely to engage in substance abuse than if she had not taken Ritalin.

DOES TAKING RITALIN STIFLE CREATIVITY?

"In our clinic we saw an adult poet who couldn't write poetry when she was on Ritalin," commented Russell Barkley, Ph.D., an ADD expert.[44] Hearing this, I was reminded of a high-profile attorney I saw in my practice. On days when he worked in his office he took Ritalin, but on days when he planned legal strategy or was in court and had to think on his feet, he would not take any.

Research demonstrates that Ritalin improves children's performance on selected measures of structured "vigilance" tasks such as CPTs (Continuous Performance Tests; see page 204, Chapter 14).[45] But the question remains: How does it achieve this effect? As the drug acts to narrow a child's wide range of thinking, does the child overfocus and lose some of her creativity?

There is no systematic research on Ritalin's effects on creativity that is comparable to the research on vigilance tasks such as the CPT, because creativity, by definition, has no norm. It defies systematic study. There is no standardization, no basis for comparison. Most researchers consider paper-and-pencil tests to be trivial and inadequate measures of creativity. These scores cannot predict the beauty of a poem or the elegance of a legal defense.[46]

Research has demonstrated that while Ritalin results in improved performance on vigilance tasks during the time that a child is medicated, it does not result in enhanced learning. Some researchers theorize that Ritalin achieves its specific results by effecting a trade-off or an even exchange, with no actual net gain of cognitive functions. In this model, Ritalin works the same way that a zoom lens changes the focal point of a camera. You can make closer things appear clearer, but you lose some of the clarity of things that are farther away. You get greater convergence, but less divergence.[47]

In *ADD: A Different Perception,* Thom Hartmann observes: "I've spoken with numerous ADD-diagnosed writers, artists, and public speakers about their experience with Ritalin and other anti-ADD drugs. Many report that, while their lives become more organized and their workdays easier when taking drugs, their creativity seems to dry up."[48]

A reporter for *60 Minutes* noted how parents had told her, "Once on Ritalin some kids lose their spark and creativity." She interviewed a group of teenagers who were taking it. In one boy's words: "I do feel that it dulls you and I don't like the way that it does that."[49]

TEACHING CHILDREN SELF-CONTROL

On the same *60 Minutes* program, Dr. Barkley noted that "the studies that have been published in the last year, my own included, indicate that nothing comes close to what this medication does for children.

"The downside," he went on to say, "is that sometimes people are too quick to turn to the medication when other things may be necessary or would have been helpful for that child."

James Swanson, Ph.D., another leading expert who appeared on the program, pointed out that it is the success of Ritalin itself that is a problem: "My concern about medication is that it *will* have an effect of making a child less disruptive and less active," Dr. Swanson said. "The parent and the teacher need to do behavioral interventions in the classroom and at home to teach the child to deal with their own behavior, be responsible for it. . . . That *needs* to be done. . . . And oftentimes when you give medications, you don't do the other things. . . . That's a problem. I'm alarmed about that."

Dr. Swanson is referring to the simple truth that we are motivated to solve problems that demand our attention more than we are motivated to solve problems that do not. If a child's problems are quieted by medication, it is a normal human response for us to become less motivated to solve them in other ways, especially ways that do not produce immediately visible results.

Dr. Swanson, who is a professor of pediatrics and the director of a U.S. Department of Education center, has created an experimental elementary school in Irvine, California, where children with ADD are "relentlessly cheered on for good behavior." Their efforts can earn points all day, and high scorers get desirable rewards. They start fresh every day, getting noticed and awarded all day for acts of sharing, being a good sport, and ignoring annoyances. Only 35 percent of the students at the school take medication, less than half the national rate for children with ADD.[50]

WHAT TO TELL YOUR CHILD
ABOUT MEDICATION

Respect your child's confidentiality about taking medication. Do not talk to others about it without her permission, except for professionals and trusted friends whose opinions can help.

If your child gets an after-lunch dose of medication, visit her school and see exactly how she gets it. When children have to line up and wait, they may feel self-conscious. The more conspicuous the procedure, the more your child is subjected to embarrassment, and possibly ridicule. This is sometimes a thorny issue at schools where many children need to get medicine at about the same time. Busy schools routinely use methods like public address systems to summon children. You and other parents who share your concerns might want to pool together and volunteer to help during this time of day.

Think through what you want to say to your child about the reason she takes medication. In Chapter 3 I described several metaphors to explain different types of attention to your Edison-trait child. The one I use the most to introduce Ritalin is the one behavioral pediatrician Dr. Dorothy Johnson uses in her practice.

You may recall that Dr. Johnson explains to the child that most of the time she has "photographer's attention," but in school she needs "student's attention." Dr. Johnson then goes on to explain that Ritalin can help her keep her "student's attention" better and longer. Most children easily understand and accept this explanation.

Edison-trait children, especially Dynamos, also like Thom Hartmann's metaphor of being a Hunter in a Farmer's world (also described in Chapter 3). Telling your child she has "Hunter's attention," but in school she needs "Farmer's attention," is another good way to present the rationale for taking Ritalin.

These metaphors have two main advantages: (1) They are neutral, and (2) they do not infer dependency on medication; in other words, they do not imply that your child is inadequate without it. This is important, so that a child on medication continues to perceive herself as accountable for her actions. It troubleshoots the situation in which the child feels she can excuse herself from responsibility for her actions:

> *"I hit my sister because I forgot to take my pill."*
> *"I couldn't pass that test because my medication was wearing off."*

Also, it gives your child room to grow out of or reduce her reliance on the medicine.

Some professionals like to introduce the use of Ritalin to a child by comparing a child who takes Ritalin to a child who needs eyeglasses. It is a neutral example in that it "normalizes" the need, and that is a benefit. Many children and adults need glasses.

However, this analogy implies that the child has a constitutional inadequacy that cannot be corrected except by external means. It invites excuse making. (Every child has heard someone say: "I can't read that without my glasses.") And since none of us can predict the future, it might convey more negative expectancy than the situation warrants. (People generally do not grow out of or reduce their need to wear glasses.)

One time at a lecture I gave to parents, a mother who had heard about the eyeglass analogy asked me my opinion on it. I gave her my views. Then another mother added her thoughts: "I get what you're trying to say about the eyeglass thing. You've spent some time thinking about this, haven't you?" I glowed, feeling recognized for my careful thinking. "Well, it seems to me there's a much simpler reason not to bring up eyeglasses," she continued. "My son hates wearing glasses. It would be a terrible example for him."

My careful thinking and I bowed to her greater wisdom. I thanked her for her observation.

A WINDOW OF OPPORTUNITY

When does a child stop taking Ritalin? The decision to stop taking medication is as personal and individual as the decision to take it.

Research suggests that 30 percent of the children who take medication stop within two years and 60 percent within three years. *CH.A.D.D. Educators Manual* notes: "Reasons for the discontinuance are speculative. Nonetheless, the implications of over-reliance are clear. Perhaps the use of medication is best viewed as a window of opportunity wherein educators focus on teaching organizational and learning strategies."[51]

MEDICATION AS A TOOL

ADD expert Larry Silver, M.D., has noted that "children with ADD are not unable to learn, but their difficulties with inattention and impulsivity often make them *unavailable* for learning."[52] Ritalin can make the child *available* for learning. This is how it creates "a window of opportunity." When medicated, your child gets experience she can use to improve her functioning when she is not medicated.

Ritalin can show a child what kinds of things are possible. This is beneficial in two important ways: (1) Your child gets external recognition for her success. She gets a taste of the rewards that come when she stops her impulses on time. One small but solid success can be a kernel from which future successes germinate. (2) Your child gets an inner experience of success. She gets to know what it *feels* like to be available and receptive to learning. She learns what it sounds like when she's "quiet in the brain." She gets a multisensorial memory of the experience of being calm—seeing, hearing, and feeling what it's like to be in a more reflective mode.

Troy, a twelve-year-old Dynamo I saw in my practice, told me what it was like the first time he played basketball on Ritalin. "For the first time everyone stayed quiet, even when I got to the basket." This was his perception of what it felt like to be able to concentrate. Interestingly, it felt to him as if the spectators behaved differently.

Before he took Ritalin, the noise from the crowd used to overwhelm Troy as soon as he got down to the end of the court. He did not know it could be any other way. On Ritalin, for the first time Troy discovered what it was like to shoot a basket without feeling overwhelmed by noise. His game improved considerably.

Aware of the benefit he could reap, Troy became more motivated to learn how to concentrate. On Ritalin, he tried to notice all he could about the experience he was having. He practiced repeating how it felt, especially at the moment he felt the greatest contrast, the moment when the Ritalin started to kick in. Troy made it his goal to learn how to use what he began to call "the volume control" in his head.

After taking Ritalin for the first time, Georgia, an eight-year-old Dreamer, told me: "I can stop a jingle. I don't have to finish it." She was referring to commercials she had heard on TV and the radio that would turn on in her head at various times.

"You didn't know that you could do that before?" I inquired.

Georgia shook her head. "I'd just finish them up. You know, they were there."

I imagined all the times this child missed what was being said to her because she was silently singing about a soft drink or car manufacturer or humming the call letters of a radio station. Would she be able to stop the jingles on her own, now that she'd experienced the possibility?

Georgia had begun taking medication because she could no longer keep up with her assignments in the third grade. She was an exceptionally bright child, but had fallen behind and was becoming depressed. She dreaded and resisted going to school.

Ritalin interrupted her cycle of failure. In addition it gave her a model. After taking Ritalin, Georgia understood what it meant to stop a distracting line of thought, even a song-in-progress.

Georgia discontinued Ritalin in the fourth grade. Today she gets "A"'s and "B"'s. Friday is still her favorite day of the week, but overall, she has a good attitude toward school.

CHAPTER 16

—〰—

*Controversial Theories
and Methods*

There is a better way to do it; find it.

—sign on Thomas Edison's
office wall

APPROACHES THAT ARE NOT
IN THE MAINSTREAM

Professionals from multiple disciplines who have addressed the problems of hyperactivity and inattention in children have developed various alternative approaches. You may be considering trying one. The *New England Journal of Medicine* reports that in 1990, 34 percent of Americans used one or more alternative therapies.[1]

As a parent, you must estimate the cost-to-benefit ratio of new or unconventional methods. Often, there is a core of useful information in a new hypothesis. But is the overall benefit enough to justify its cost? Cost must take into account the fact that when you invest your resources in one approach, you divert them away from another.

This chapter reviews what is known and unknown about two popular but controversial methods: diet and neurofeedback. Also, it briefly covers computerized training in temporal processing, a new approach for which only preliminary results have been reported. I could not include every nonmainstream approach. Probably even as I write this chapter new programs are in the making or about to be introduced.

My goal is twofold: (1) to give you the latest and most accurate information available about the specific treatments I cover, and (2) to give you some models to help you evaluate the cost-to-benefit ratios of other treatment methods you may be considering. I strongly recommend you discuss these approaches with your pediatrician before involving your child.

DIET

Some professionals claim that the right diet can decrease hyperactivity. No diet claims to be a method to decrease inattention.

Haptens, Food Additives, and Aggression

Ben Feingold, M.D., a pediatric allergist, created "the elimination diet" for hyperactive children. In 1974 he unveiled it in his book, *Why Your Child Is Hyperactive*. This book is still in print today.[2] Its original publication sparked a nationwide movement, in which "Feingold parents" spoke up on the radio and in newspapers and magazines while scientists published papers for and against the diet.

Feingold had begun his research twenty years earlier when as chief of the Department of Allergy at Kaiser-Permanente in northern California, he developed a special interest in the study of haptens. Feingold described haptens as low-molecular-weight chemicals so tiny they can induce neither an immune nor an allergic response in the human body. Haptens can, however, attach to proteins, which are larger-molecular-weight chemicals. A hapten attached to a protein can trigger a significant response in the body.

Finegold studied people's allergic responses to haptens they got from flea bites. He developed an interest in the role of small-size chemicals in provoking the defenses of the body. He concluded that chemicals used as food additives, which are of low molecular weight, behaved in the same ways haptens did. When patients came to him suffering from allergic responses such as hives, but tested negative for known allergies, Feingold suspected food additives. He began to suggest diets that eliminated artificial colors and flavors. At the same time Feingold noticed that when people began these "elimination diets," they experienced behavioral changes. Patients with excess aggression reported improvements in their attitude and actions.

Feingold had practiced as a pediatrician before he became an allergist, and he became particularly interested in the behavioral changes that occurred in children on the diet. He focused his attention on children he called *hyperkinesis-learning disabled* (H-LD). At that time the official diagnosis for them was "minimal brain dysfunction" (MBD), which turned out to be a misnomer. The term MBD preceded the diagnosis "Attention Deficit Disorder with Hyperactivity," which was formulated in 1980.[3] The most troublesome symptom of H-LD children was their excess aggression. Could they be helped by an elimination diet?

Feingold prescribed the diet for more than one hundred children, "plus others who have responded under the guidance of their own pediatricians." He concluded that there exists "a genetically predisposed group of H-LDs" who "suffer adverse reactions triggered by one or more chemicals contained in synthetic flavorings and colorings."

In June 1973, Feingold presented what he called his "preliminary findings" at the annual meeting of the American Medical Association in New York City. His report was picked up by the national media and he began to receive several hundred inquiries per week from parents. The following year he published his book, giving the details of his diet to the public.

The Feingold Diet

In his book Feingold stresses the necessity of keeping a diet diary. A parent has to record everything her child eats and keep detailed records of the child's behavior. Whenever the child's behavior changes, the parent must consult the diary to see what the child just ate.

The diet eliminates two groups of foods. Group I are the foods that contain natural salicylates, an aspirinlike compound. These foods include almonds, apples, apricots, berries, cherries, currants, grapes, nectarines, oranges, peaches, plums, tomatoes, and cucumbers. Group II consists of all the foods that contain artificial color and artificial flavor, as well as the food preservative butylated hydroxytoluene (BHT).

After four to six weeks, if the child shows a positive response from eliminating all Group I and II foods, Group I foods can be restored slowly. This is because a child may react poorly to food additives but still tolerate foods containing natural salicylates. As for Group II chemicals, if a child shows an individual sensitivity to artificial colors and flavors and BHTs, he must avoid them for the rest of his life.

Feingold stressed the importance of reading labels carefully. If a label contains a nonspecific word such as "flavor," he advised against using the item. He said that the diet must be adhered to 100 percent to be effective. "Compliance of 80 percent or 90 percent can lead to failure. It is important to remember that often a single bite or a single drink can cause an undesired response which may persist for seventy-two hours or more."

The diet places no restriction on "reasonable quantities of sweets, which are important to most children." However, to avoid artificial flavors and colors, parents must prepare baked goods, candy, and ice cream at home. The same is true for condiments, such as mayonnaise and ketchup. They must be made from scratch with only natural ingredients. Feingold's wife, Helene, kitchen-tested the recipes that appear in his book.

Feingold called his program the K-P diet, after Kaiser-Permanente, the health maintenance organization where he was employed. But parents who used it dubbed it "Kitchen Police," the diet that ruled the house. The necessary record keeping and food preparation are extremely time-consuming.[4]

For several years the Feingold diet captured the interest of parents and professionals. Parents formed "Feingold Associations" to exchange recipes and tips for keeping children on their diets. Testimonials by some parents kept other parents motivated. In the field, several practitioners conducted small-scale demonstration programs, but no controlled studies were conducted at that time.[5]

When effects of the elimination diet were looked at scientifically, results provided very limited support to justify Feingold's hypothesis.[6] In 1982, the National Institutes of Health held a three-day conference to review research findings on the effects of an additive-free diet on symptoms of hyperactivity. They concluded that there might be a relatively small subgroup of children who respond to this approach.[7]

Subsequent research findings continued to support their conclusion. The results of several studies in England suggested that children in this small subgroup who responded to the diet tended to be quite young and to suffer from allergies as well as hyperactivity.[8]

Today, American pediatric allergist Doris Rapp, M.D., argues that allergic responses are actually exceedingly prevalent and damaging. In her books and television appearances she maintains that unrecognized allergies cause a wide range of human ailments, including hyperactivity. She suggests that parents look carefully at behavior changes in their children and see if they occur at the same time that a particular food is ingested, a certain type of pollen is in season, or there is exposure to chemical fumes, dust, mold, or other toxins. Rapp diagnoses and treats "environmental illness," which she says often originates with pollutants children inhale from the air every day at school.[9]

Before he died in 1982, Dr. Feingold speculated that there were probably several categories of disorders that were being lumped together as "hyperactivity-learning disorders."[10] That would explain why confirmation of the effects of the diet are so sporadic. It appears that he was right.

How can you know if your child's hyperactivity is due to an overreaction to food additives? Statistically it is improbable. But if your child appears to have other allergies, particularly if he is aspirin-sensitive, you may want to consider a consultation with a pediatric allergist who specializes in this area.

Pharmacological Individuality

Through his work, Dr. Feingold raised people's awareness about the potential harm of the chemicals that we ingest. He also did much to change society's attitudes toward children who are hyperactive. He helped move us away from the prevailing view of "minimal brain dysfunction" and toward an approach in which we see our children as having problems that we can solve through our efforts.

He promoted the thesis of a colleague, Bert N. LaDu, M.D., that each "person has his own biological individuality that determines a pharmacological individuality." He called the human body "a remarkable, skin-draped, biochemical machine."[11] He believed that each person, each child, has "a unique body structure which will determine how she or he will react to many types of chemicals—in drugs and foods, even those that pollute the air."[12]

Many parents believe, as Dr. Feingold did, that variations in what their children consume can cause fluctuations in their behaviors. Most parents monitor their children's sugar and caffeine intake.

Children with hyperactivity may have a characteristic pharmacological individuality when it comes to these substances. In other words, they may have a heightened sensitivity as compared with other children. Pediatric specialist Lendon Smith, M.D., has written several books about the links between exacerbation of hyperactivity and the consumption of junk foods and refined sugar.[13]

Some parents who have explored these options believe that vitamins and food supplements, such as choline, can have a positive effect.[14] At this time there are no scientific findings that conclusively verify the therapeutic benefits of these dietary approaches but there is a considerable amount of anecdotal evidence to support them.[15] Moreover, it is hard to come up with a downside for cutting out junk food, reducing food additives, and boosting nutritional intake.

Homeopathic Medicine

Currently, the field of homeopathic medicine is gaining in popularity. It is being used to treat a wide range of body-mind problems. Homeopathic medicine is based on the "principle of similars." According to this tenet, whatever problem a particular kind of substance causes in overdose, it can cure in small doses. Homeopathic compounds are microdosages of substances that in larger doses would stimulate the body to produce the problem response. Theoretically, these tiny potencies activate the body's natural defenses.[16]

Many parents now experiment with herbs and homeopathic compounds that are intended to have relaxing and calming effects. For example, some have used colocynth and chamomile in an effort to decrease temper tantrums in their children.[17] At this time, these remedies have not been studied scientifically.

Homeopathic medicines can usually be purchased over the counter in health food stores and pharmacies. However, just because a product does not require a prescription, do *not* assume it is harmless. *Natural* cannot and should not be equated with *harmless.* If you are interested in trying some of these natural remedies, consult a medical doctor first. Some physicians specialize in dietary, holistic, and other alternative medical practices. Make sure you know the exact names and strengths of each ingredient in the products you are considering. Keep a written record you can refer to so you'll have an idea if a product was effective. Report the results to your physician.

NEUROFEEDBACK

Neurofeedback is biofeedback training for the brain. Biofeedback is a method in which a person gets immediate information, or feedback, on the biological functions in his body. In biofeedback, you use a machine to get information that would otherwise be imperceptible to you. You connect yourself to an electrophysiological mechanism, such as an electromyograph (EMG) or an electroencephalograph (EEG). The machine measures something that is happening inside your body. For example, an EMG measures how tense or how relaxed a particular muscle group is. An EEG measures different sizes and rates of brain waves. The underlying philosophy is that if you can detect it, you can learn to control it.

In biofeedback, you have a learning goal, for example, to relax your muscles, or to generate or suppress a fast or a slow brain wave. You see and hear results instantly and continuously. On most machines, you'll see a moving graph or some other kind of visual representation on a screen and you'll hear a tone that changes pitch, up or down. This is your feedback. It tells you when you are succeeding at your goal and when you are not. Then you know whether to do more of what you are already doing, or to try something new. For example, in learning to relax, you might change the way you're breathing, the focus of your eyes, the content of your thoughts, or the expression on your face. In learning to generate one particular kind of brain wave, you might change the content or pace of your thinking, or broaden or narrow the range of your thoughts.

Usually, the change you make is so subtle, you cannot verbalize exactly what you've done. But as you keep doing it, your feedback tells you that you are on the right track: You learn to self-regulate an internal body function through repeated practice using feedback in order to reach your goal. This is called *entraining*. Everyone can entrain to some degree, but some people have more of a talent for it than others.

Different Kinds of Brain Waves

At any given moment, each of us generates multiple brain waves. In neurofeedback, a person uses an EEG to entrain himself to generate or suppress one particular kind of brain wave. His goal is to bring this behavior under voluntary control.

Neuroscientists have categorized brain waves according to their frequencies, which are measured in terms of hertz, or cycles per second. Each category is associated with a different state of consciousness. From slowest (low-frequency) to fastest (high-frequency), the types of brain waves are:

Type of brain wave	Frequency (cycles per second)	Mental state
Delta	0–4 Hz	Sleep, drowsiness
Theta	4–7 Hz	Daydreaming, "twilight learning"
Alpha	7–14 Hz	Relaxed state of attention
Beta	14–35 Hz	Working state of attention

Delta and theta are called *slow-wave* activity. Beta is called *fast-wave* activity. Each person has an individual or "signature" resting EEG pattern,[18] when they are in a wakeful but disengaged state. This pattern changes in somewhat predictable ways when you change what you are doing mentally. For example, if someone starts to talk to you, you begin to receive new information. If you are like most people, when you begin to listen you decrease your theta, or slow-wave, activity and increase beta, or fast-wave, activity.

Preliminary findings suggest this is not the case for many children who exhibit symptoms of inattention. When they start to receive information, they do not show the same amount of decreased slow-wave activity as other children in their age range. In two controlled studies, children who were diagnosed as having ADD without hyperactivity showed more theta in their EEG readings than children who did not have ADD who were within three years in age.[19]

It is important to keep in mind that these are experimental findings and cannot be used to diagnose ADD, or even to infer that a disorder exists. EEGs are not used to identify ADD because there is no known EEG pattern that truly differentiates the syndrome.[20]

EEG readings document an individual difference, a response that varies from person to person. They show that a detectable pattern exists when a single brain function, namely brain-wave activity, is measured under well-defined conditions. Very little is actually known about the significance of brain-wave activity. We know how to measure it; we know it changes with age; we know it varies from one state of consciousness to another; and we know that information about brain-wave activity can be helpful in diagnosing seizure disorders. Other ideas about it are mostly speculative.[21]

The fact that brain-wave activity varies with age is important to keep in mind. As newborns, we generate mostly delta and theta waves (slow-wave activity). As we grow up, we generate more alpha and beta waves (faster brain waves). Throughout childhood we continue to develop in this direction. As we mature, increasingly we suppress more theta waves and generate more beta waves at the moment we begin to take in something new.

To sum up, the increased theta suppression that a child demonstrates when he starts to listen and get new information is a developmental process that occurs naturally. It happens on its own as a child gets older.[22]

Each child has his own inner timetable for maturation. Children don't learn to walk or talk at the same time. Children are individual in their readiness to give up their daydreaming and flights of imagination—to suppress their theta: They do this too at different ages.

We can help children learn how to think maturely, just as we can help them through any developmental process. Neurofeedback might best be viewed as a potentially useful tool to help some children through this process.

Neurofeedback Assessment

Procedures will vary from one neurofeedback facility to the next, depending on the physical space, equipment, software, trainers, and overall philosophy and orientation of the center. Usually, an initial evaluation consists of gathering intake information from you and conducting a neurofeedback data analysis for your child. Sometimes a continuous performance test (CPT) is given.[23]

To get neurofeedback data on your child, the neurofeedback trainer will place one sensor (electrode) on the top of your child's head. This sensor measures brain-wave activity. The trainer will place another sensor near the first, probably on your child's earlobe, to measure baseline activity. This is called a reference sensor.[24] These sensors connect to an EEG. A good way to explain this to your child is that the sensor is like the stethoscope his doctor uses to hear his heartbeat. It is a device placed on the outside to know more about something taking place on the inside.

Usually, initial neurofeedback data is collected in several phases or conditions. The first phase is a resting, or baseline, reading. Your child might be asked to stare at a spot on the wall and daydream. During a second phase, your child may be asked to read. This is a visual information–processing condition. During a third phase, your child may be read to by someone else. This is an auditory processing condition.

In the baseline "daydreaming" phase, your child is expected to have more slow-wave than fast-wave activity. In the second and third phases, when he is processing information, he is expected to suppress slow-wave activity and increase fast waves. If he continues to produce a high level of slow waves or he does not step up his production of fast waves, he is considered to be a candidate for neurofeedback training.

Sometimes, instead of having different phases of data collection, initial neurofeedback data is collected in the form of a sample session. After about five minutes of training, brain-wave activity is recorded and a goal for the session is set. The trainer continues to record data throughout the session and then estimates your child's potential to benefit from neurofeedback.

Unfortunately, there are no established norms for what children's theta and beta rates should be.[25] Evaluation is highly subjective. This means that the results are highly dependent on the trainer's judgment and experience.

Treatment goals are expressed as a specific percent decrease in theta and an accompanying increase in beta. (Actually the most recent findings suggest that for children with symptoms of inattention, suppression of theta is a relevant variable, but increased beta is not.)[26] Treatment is deemed to be successful if your child learns how to suppress slow waves and increase fast waves when he is processing visual or auditory information (i.e., while looking and listening).

A Training Session

Procedures vary from one facility to another. An average training session goes like this:

Your child walks in. He is seated in front of a personal computer. The trainer attaches sensors to his head. He then begins a training period. On screen a computer game begins.

Your child knows what his learning goal is, for example, to suppress theta. His goal at the computer is to keep the game going and earn points.

To keep the game going, he must sit still and maintain a minimum threshold of theta suppression. If he moves around or "spaces out," the game will stop. A light might flash and a high-pitched tone blares until he sits still and resumes paying attention to the game.

To earn points, he must make progress toward his goal: Suppress more theta. There is no joystick or other manual control. He makes things happen by the way he thinks.

On screen, the game has attractive graphics and sounds. Several different software packages are available. One is a series of action games, like Pac-man, that run about three minutes each. Another is a moving graph or figure that you must keep above a horizontal line—for example, flying a plane above the horizon—for about twelve minutes.

Periodically the trainer talks to the child about how he is doing. The trainer rewards the child with acknowledgment and chips for the points he has earned. The child may cash in his chips for prizes. The average total length of a treatment session is forty-five minutes.

A Course of Treatment

Sessions are usually held twice a week. A usual course of treatment is twenty to forty sessions.[27] At the conclusion of treatment, a final assessment is conducted. The final assessment is a retest of the initial assessment. Pretreatment and posttreatment data are compared.

Most facilities require that a child be at least six years of age to participate. Fees range from about fifty to eighty dollars per session, depending on your geographic location. Sometimes medical insurance covers part of the cost.

Effectiveness

In neurofeedback training, many children can and do learn to self-regulate brain-wave activity, specifically to decrease theta. The question is: What impact, if any, does this have on a child's ability to pay attention in school? Is it a valid tool for treating symptoms of ADD? What research has been done in this area?

Neurofeedback training to treat children with ADD was pioneered by Joel Lubar, Ph.D., a professor of psychology at the University of Tennessee. In 1976 he published a case study on the use of neurofeedback with a hyperactive child.[28] Over the next fifteen years about a half dozen more case studies appeared in scientific journals.

Then, in the September 2, 1991, issue of *Woman's Day* magazine, an enthusiastic parent put the spotlight on neurofeedback.[29] She wrote an article about her son's treatment success with Dr. Lubar. She said that as a result of the program, her son's ADD symptoms had decreased and that his school performance and social acceptance had improved. Parents from all over the country began asking their doctors and therapists about neurofeedback.

Six months later, in response to this surge of interest, Russell Barkley, Ph.D., an adviser for several nationwide parent and professional groups, wrote an article entitled "Is EEG Biofeedback Treatment Effective for ADHD Children? . . . Proceed with Much Caution." Dr. Barkley reviewed the relevant published research findings to date, and concluded: "There is not enough evidence from well-controlled scientific studies at this time to support the effectiveness of EEG biofeedback for ADHD children."[30] More well-conducted research is needed.

Since then, the number of neurofeedback centers has increased and additional findings have appeared in the scientific journals.[31] For example, in one study, children who successfully decreased theta activity showed significant improvement on several pre- and posttreatment measures, namely, a continuous performance test, a standardized parent rating scale, and a standardized intelligence test. There are several serious methodological problems with this study.[32] Nonetheless, results do suggest that neurofeedback helps some children improve the range of control they exercise over their attention to incoming information.

Dr. Barkley's caveat is still well advised, however. Marketing materials for neurofeedback centers may sometimes overstate research findings. For example, one brochure says that in a study reported in *Pediatric Neurology* an EEG was used "solely, to diagnose individuals with ADHD/ADD with an extremely high level of accuracy." The study it cites does not say this. The study used subjects who had already been diagnosed with ADD and who were then measured with an EEG and found also to have low theta suppression.[33] Another brochure states that neurofeedback is known to raise children's IQ scores. This conclusion is not supported by the existing data.[34]

Neurofeedback at School

In Yonkers, New York, an experimental program at the Enrico Fermi School for the Performing Arts promises to yield useful information. Neurofeedback is being offered to students at this urban public school. With parental consent, twenty-one students ages eight to ten have been selected by their teachers to receive a full course of treatment. A diagnosis (like ADD) was not required. Before training began, the children were evaluated for school behavior and given standardized tests. They will be reevaluated at the end of the study.

There are two groups of eight students each: a study group, which receives the training, and a control group, which will not receive training until the study is complete. In addition, five children will have their progress evaluated individually.

The program is made possible by grants and donations obtained by Fermi's assistant principal. She was impressed with the improvement she saw in her six-year-old son after neurofeedback treatment.[35]

COMPUTERIZED TRAINING IN
TEMPORAL PROCESSING

Information Processing and Temporal Processing

Information processing is an umbrella term used to describe the way that the brain senses, perceives, sorts, integrates, retains, and expresses information. There are different types and attributes of information processing, named for the specific brain functions involved. Temporal processing is the speed at which information processing occurs.

Visual processing, which is the information processing of visual input, is a strength of Edison-trait children. By comparison, their auditory processing is usually somewhat weaker. Sometimes it is so much weaker that a child actually misses a syllable in a word that he hears. If auditory processing is so weak that it impairs the development of a child's language skills, the child may be said to have an auditory processing deficit.

The Effect of Temporal Processing on Auditory Processing

The January 5, 1996, issue of *Science* reported two studies that strongly influence the way specialists now think of auditory processing problems. This groundbreaking research—and the method it introduces—is the result of a collaborative effort by a University of California at San Francisco neuroscientist and a Rutgers University psychologist.[36]

More than twenty years ago, Rutgers psychologist Paula Tallal began to study children who had normal IQs but who scored below the 16th percentile on oral language tests. She found that they had trouble distinguishing between syllables such as "ba" and "da." These syllables begin with a consonant sound that lasts only tens of milliseconds. She found that these children had "fast element" recognition problems in other areas of their cognitive functioning as well.[37]

Phonological Awareness

Tallal's subjects lacked "phonological awareness." Children with phonological awareness spell correctly, use proper syntax fluidly, read out loud with confidence, and learn rapidly to read phonologically at an early age. Conversely, those without it—like many Edison-trait children—struggle at these tasks.

Children with poor phonological awareness are "inattentive" listeners—and for a good reason. They are not distinguishing the very short-duration sounds of the spoken word, so what they hear has less information value for them, plus it is more difficult to decipher. It is analogous to listening to a lecture over a public address system that obscures some of the sounds. According to Tallal, approximately 15 to 20 percent of all children have poor phonological awareness.[38]

How to Teach a Fast Mind to Listen

In 1993, Tallal teamed up with neuroscientist Michael Merzenich to design a series of computer games to teach five- to ten-year-old children who had poor phonological awareness to distinguish fast sounds. Tallal's early results showed that children with this problem could distinguish "ba" and "da" when the consonant sounds that begin these syllables were stretched out by 50 percent and made louder.

Merzenich's lab created a computer program with colorful animation, animals that fly, silly characters, and contests that reward success. For example, a child using the program may have to catch a flying cow. He will hear a series of sounds that change unexpectedly: "pack, pack, pack, pat." He releases a button when he hears a change. If he's quick enough, the cow lands and he gets a point. If not, the cow keeps flying. Every time he gets three right in a row at one level of difficulty (of speed and loudness of the embedded sound), the program presents him with sounds that are one step harder to distinguish. An error causes the program to go back one level.[39]

Children Who Knew But Couldn't Say

Tallal and Merzenich tested the program. After a four-week period, subjects who trained showed significantly more improvement on a battery of language tests than control subjects did. The experimental group showed a gain of one to two years' worth of language ability during the four-week period. The children maintained most of their improvement when they were tested again six weeks after training.[40]

How could this happen? Can children learn two years' worth of language skills in one month? Tallal explains, "It appears that they had already developed considerably more language competence than they were able to demonstrate or use . . . under [their previous] listening and speaking conditions."[41] Think of having a message that you have prepared on your computer, and then finally getting the opportunity to go on-line, so you can send it. These children finally got the chance to communicate what they knew.

A Lesson in Learning

Tallal notes that originally she herself had feared that "these kids were 'broken' and there was nothing you could do" to fix their "primary defect": their poor temporal processing.[42] Common wisdom said a child could learn how to cope with a deficit like this, but the bottom line was, he would have to learn to live with it.

Tallal and Merzenich's research has reversed that kind of thinking. It is an innovative application of Gagne's Hierarchy of Learning (see page 119, Chapter 9) and an inspiring demonstration of how breaking a task into its component parts makes learning possible where it was not possible before.

OTHER APPROACHES

Nonmainstream approaches to treat attentional difficulties and learning disabilities are numerous. They include optometric vision training, sensory integration training, osteopathic treatment, chiropractic treatment, orthomolecular approaches, and more. How can you tell which approaches are effective, and which are right for your child?

In their book, *Attention Deficit Disorder and Learning Disabilities: Realities, Myths and Controversial Treatments,* psychologists Barbara Ingersoll, Ph.D., and Sam Goldstein, Ph.D., recommend that parents ask themselves the following four questions when evaluating a new treatment approach:

1. How does this approach fit with current knowledge in related fields like anatomy, medicine, psychiatry, psychology, and education?
2. How does this approach fit with what is currently known about human attention and learning?
3. What is the quality of the scientific evidence to support the effectiveness of this treatment?
4. What are the costs and the dangers, if any?[43]

As a parent, you will have to weigh the answers to these questions with your pediatrician's advice and the results of studies as they are released.

YOUR UNIQUE CHILD

Some treatment methods earn strong testimonials from parents but fail to demonstrate positive effects in scientific studies. One reason for this may be the placebo effect. The treatment itself is not the "potent ingredient," so to speak. The improvement has a different cause, such as dedicated attention from an adult, the infusion of optimism, a change in the way the child sees his own behavior, the use of a healthier vocabulary to describe that behavior, or coincidence. For example, some critics of neurofeedback say that in cases where therapeutic results are achieved, these results can be attributed to the fact that the child is in a situation where he is getting rewards for sitting still and paying attention for a sustained period of time, not to the impact of increased "suppressed theta."

This may be true, but it is also true that one ought not discount a result because, technically, it may be a placebo.

Jon, a nine-year-old Dreamer, went through a course of neurofeedback treatments. He turned out to have a talent for self-regulating his brain waves, and his self-esteem soared. At school, his attitude changed from "helpless" to "mastery" and his grades improved. At home, Jon knew his parents respected him for what he had achieved. They are avant-garde professionals who place a high value on the act of using your mind.

Were his improvements attributable to the suppression of theta or to his newfound pride and change of attitude? This is a question without an answer and will remain so. Jon and his family don't need one. I called Jon's mother, two years posttreatment, and she told me that he maintained the gains he had made in neurofeedback.

Each child is an individual and no one can predict the future. Leading psychologist Keith Connors, Ph.D., referring to findings in which only a small number of children responded to a treatment, said, "If one of these children is your child, you won't care very much about statistics."[44]

Examine the scientific evidence. Think about your own child and his Edison-trait profile. Take the time and get the information you need to decide if the benefits of a method are likely or unlikely to outweigh the costs.

PART IV

~ஒ~

Your Child's Future

CHAPTER 17

~~~

Edisonian Leaders of the
Information Age

The new hero is no longer a blue-collar worker, a financier, or a manager, but the innovator (whether inside or outside a large organization) who combines imaginative knowledge with action.

—Alvin Toffler,
Power Shift

DOES SCHOOL SUCCESS PREDICT
CAREER SUCCESS?

"He's just like I was," Matt's dad observed. Matt's dad is a self-made millionaire, a commercial real estate developer who has put together some of the most important deals in Southern California. "I hated school. And I barely made it through."

Matt attends a private school. He also attends a state-of-the-art learning center. He dislikes both. Matt says that when he grows up he doesn't care what he does for a living, as long as he doesn't have to sit at a desk.

His father completely understands.

According to the principal of the private school Matt attends, Matt's is not an isolated case. Many of her Edison-trait students who struggle in school have at least one Edison-trait parent who thrives in the world of business.

Tacit Knowledge

Research findings suggest that success in the workplace does not correlate significantly with academic potential. It does, however, correlate with *tacit knowledge,* which covers a range of nonverbal, intuitive abilities and practical intelligence.[1] Psychologist Joseph A. Horvath defines tacit knowledge as "action-oriented knowledge, acquired without direct help from others, that allows individuals to achieve goals they personally value."[2] Resourcefulness, the hallmark quality of Edisonian thinking, is the key feature of tacit knowledge.

Because they are rich in tacit knowledge, Edison-trait children, when they grow up, may do considerably better at earning a living than they did at achieving grades in school. Their classroom world may not reward their independent style of thinking, but the business world often will.

After graduation, new horizons open to many young Edison-trait adults. If their motivation and self-esteem have remained intact, they can become astoundingly successful.

THE THINK-FAST GENERATION

What kind of working climate does your child face? Your child confronts tasks in his generation that you and I did not. He must sift through mountains of data every day. From junk mail to E-mail, from telecommunications to cable TV, he must instantly select what is important and discard what is not.

Your Edison-trait child and others in his generation must develop a society that will not be overcome by technology. He must be master of his personal computer terminal, manage his time and communications, protect his privacy, and set and reset priorities rapidly. His natural abilities to scan, instantaneously change course, hold his ground, and see past detail give him the tools he needs to do this. His aptitudes suit him well to lead the way through his fast-paced, data-rich, twenty-first-century Information Age.

THE EVOLVING WORKPLACE

The September 1994 issue of *Fortune* magazine ran an article entitled "The End of the Job."[3] Articles like it appear regularly in business sections of newspapers and newsmagazines. It is a major topic of business books and discussions among managers at all levels.

There is a gradual, unmistakable movement currently under way in the workplace. Management guru Tom Peters calls it a revolution. Predictability is vanishing. Change, flexibility, and instantaneous responsiveness are replacing it. According to Peters, "No company is safe. IBM is declared dead in 1979, the best of the best in 1982, and dead again in 1986." Inside company walls, nontraditional roles are replacing traditional ones, as companies adapt to the new climate of unpredictability.[4]

"Human skills are subject to obsolescence at a rate perhaps unprecedented in American history," declared Federal Reserve chair Alan Greenspan.[5] This is due to automation and the computerization of business and industry.

Downsizing means more than just the dismissal of employees; it's the erasure of their jobs and job descriptions. It means a reduction in the number of customary workplace roles—namely, full-time salaried positions. At the same time we can expect an increase in innovative roles like office temps, part-timers, consultants, and independent contractors. Employers hire help by the hour, or pay to have a particular task done by an outsider who has the specific skills or technology to do it. That way they can fill temporary needs, or be immediately responsive to emerging needs in a volatile marketplace.

Peters observes that in the current climate, "Nothing is predictable. . . . The prices of the major currencies, once stable within 1% over decades, now swing 5% a week, and 50% a year." The prices of energy, agricultural products, and metals swing widely. From day to day, we don't know who will be partners, who will be competitors, who will be bought out, or who will go bankrupt.[6]

The acceleration of change is unstoppable. The key to survival is to learn how to ride change and enjoy it, to see it as a source of market advantage. Successful freelancers capitalize on market anomalies. Small startup businesses capture emerging markets. Current trends include working at home and in satellite offices, irregular work schedules, and rewards for being skillful with new technology. Business analyst Peter Drucker defines our present state as "an entrepreneurial economy" based on "converting innovation from a 'bright idea' into organized activity."[7]

Who is most likely to succeed in our new entrepreneurial economy? Resourceful workers who do more than *adapt* to change—

those who *thrive* on it. Edison-trait qualities are the assets of the day: originality, versatility, and diversity of thought, the ability to sustain bursts of high-paced effort, and a facility with computer-age power and speed.

Edison-trait people are action-oriented. They multitask easily. They do many different things with ease. Divergent thinking is a definite plus in today's unpredictable, accelerating workplace.

Six years ago Robbie, a Discoverer, was hired by a computer consulting firm. He was trained to offer telephone support to companies who had purchased customized management software. Three years ago, the firm that employed Robbie downsized. They let Robbie go. Within six months Robbie was hired by one of the companies to whom he'd given telephone support, as a result of a proposal he submitted in which he created a part-time consulting position for himself. His new employer was also a high-tech firm. With his foot in the door of a growing company, Robbie found out that he liked sales better than debugging programs. He also found out he had a talent for selling. He is now on salary plus commission, making more than twice as much money as he did as a consultant.

At one time the word *job* meant a long-term position of employment. Today a "job" more often means a "project" or mission to be accomplished. *Fortune* calls the changing workplace a transformation from a "structure built out of jobs" to a "field of work needing to be done."[8] Edison-trait minds have the range to cover this field and mine it for golden opportunities.

THE RISE OF THE ENTREPRENEUR

Those who scan the "field of work needing to be done," and who see profitable opportunities and act on them, are the pioneers of our economy. We call them entrepreneurs. They seize the moment, tap their inner resourcefulness, and create a growth business, at the right time, in the right place.

There is a rising trend for large companies to capitalize entrepreneurs who want to form venture companies that ultimately will benefit the larger company. For example, a large company might finance a supplier with a new idea to improve a product that the larger company needs. In 1982, large companies financed 32 start-up businesses. Five years later, they backed 477 of them.[9]

The names of some of today's entrepreneurs have become household words. We track their dazzling careers on the front pages of newspapers and magazines.

Bill Gates

The prototypic twenty-first-century entrepreneur is Bill Gates, co-founder and chair of Microsoft. In 1992, at the age of thirty-seven, Bill Gates became the richest man in America.[10]

Gates is notoriously eclectic. Besides his extensive knowledge of computer programming, he has a penchant for sports cars, puzzles, and art. In his home he has designed a computer screen for his living room that selects a new piece of artwork for screen display at designated time intervals. For example, he can command "French sculpture" to appear every minute. Or, as he told a *20/20* reporter, "I can say 'Give me something interesting.' " And it will.

In addition to knowing how to develop new software, Gates knows how to sell his products. He is a persuasive communicator. He gives imaginative, daring presentations. Once he dressed up as Mr. Spock, in full Starfleet uniform and pointy Vulcan ears, to give an important and well-attended speech.

Gates's coworkers note that his breadth of knowledge is vast and that it distinguishes him from many others in the field of technology. He is an inventive computer programmer, and he is knowledgeable about royalties and marketing. The Gates style is well known at Microsoft. When new ideas are presented, he immediately builds an encyclopedic checklist of all possibilities. The question "What if . . . ?" is classic Gates.

Mary Gates, Bill's mother, says that when Bill was a boy, "We would lose him for hours at a time. And when I would say, 'What are you doing?' he would say, 'I am thinking, Mother.' "

Bill Gates is a person who thrives on new ideas, exciting concepts, a changing market, and a fast-paced world. An interviewer once asked Gates: "Do you ever wake up in the morning and say, 'Hey, I can do anything I want, go anywhere I want!' "

Bill Gates, the youngest self-made billionaire in history, smiled broadly and replied: "Yeah. And I go to work."

Ted Turner

On June 1, 1980, Ted Turner did what media critics at the time said could not be done, and should not even be attempted. He boldly created a twenty-four-hour TV news station.[11] Critics dubbed Cable News Network, CNN, the "Chicken Noodle Network." Wall Street predicted financial doom. Media pundits declared it was lunacy. They pointed out how network news had to spice up a half-hour broadcast with folksy anchor persons and highly edited clips just to get viewership. They maintained that, satellite or no satellite, TV audiences wanted entertainment, not news.

Today CNN is considered by many to be the most influential broadcast news source in the United States. The channel is on constantly in the White House and the Pentagon, at foreign embassies and brokerage firms, and in millions of homes in America. It is the most global of all television networks, operating in eighty-six nations. Turner's business sense and competitive instincts made CNN more profitable than any of the three major networks. His vision and innovative ideas about broadcasting via satellite revolutionized TV news. News was redefined from something that *has happened* to something that *is happening*.

A hard-driving entrepreneur, Turner has a reputation as a maverick billionaire. His interests are varied. He likes to exercise his competitive skills in a number of diverse venues. He has set ocean-racing records, including an America's Cup victory. After purchasing the Atlanta Braves, he transformed them from a losing team into National League pennant champs.

His mother, Florence Turner, remembers how Ted felt about grade school: "He was not really too interested in schoolwork. It didn't move fast enough for him." She also recalls his days at boarding school: "Ted hated McCallie [his prep school]. He was a devil there."

His teachers recall that he was "a determined youngster" who would "sail in weather where no sane human being would." His classmates recall he won a five-dollar bet that he could fill a pillowcase with squirrels. He did it by smoking them out of a tree with a tin of shoe polish he set on fire to smolder.

Turner explains, "I did everything I could to rebel against the system. I had more demerits than anyone in the history of the school."

With CNN, Turner sensed opportunity, then did everything he could to rebel against the critics who said it couldn't be done.

Maya Angelou

On May 20, 1996, *Forbes* featured a story on the biggest earners outside corporate America. On its cover was the radiant smile of Maya Angelou, a celebrated poet who earned $4.3 million that year.[12]

While Angelou is older than most "new" entrepreneurs, her profile is archetypal. She is innovative, diverse, and amalgamated. She operates out of her home, directing three assistants and "a small army of professionals" who manage her public appearances, book contracts, and media deals.

Angelou describes her childhood in these poetic words: "I was a loose kite in a gentle wind floating with only my will for an anchor." Her biography gives ample evidence of her versatility:

Angelou had jobs ranging from being a Calypso dancer at the Purple Onion in San Francisco to becoming an author whose first book spent 149 weeks on the *New York Times* bestseller list. She toured America and Europe as a professional singer and dancer. She lived in Africa, where she worked as a reporter and as an actress. She has been a Creole cook, entertainer, journalist, activist, teacher, and writer.

Angelou's free-thinking shines through her songs, poems, and stories. She won a Grammy for her audio recording of the poem she wrote for Bill Clinton's inauguration.

"You may encounter defeat, but you must not be defeated." Angelou attributes these words to her mother. They express the kind of determination Maya Angelou has lived. She won her first victory in the workplace when she was sixteen years old, after weeks of tenacious application: Refusing to take no for an answer, she became the first black conductor of a San Francisco cable car.

Angelou describes the quintessential Edison-trait mind in *Won't Take Nothing for My Journey Now:* "We are created creative. And we can create new scenarios as we need to."

THE RISE OF EDISONIAN THINKING

You may recall that the neuroscientist Robert Ornstein views divergent thinking as a successful adaptation of the human mind to the zooming growth rate of the human species. In *The Evolution of Consciousness,* he points out:

> It took, roughly speaking, from the time of the first humans until about the time of my birth in 1942 to produce the first 2.65 billion human beings living on the planet at one time. It has taken only my lifetime to add the same number.[13]

This is a mind-boggling statistic. And it marks our generation as distinctively different from others who have preceded us.

Throughout history, for all previous generations, environments changed, but always at a pace that allowed the older generation to inform the younger one. Parents and teachers used rote learning to pass a collected store of knowledge down to a child.

Now, for the first time, the environment is changing faster than knowledge can be collected, communicated, and utilized. Specific knowledge gets outdated quickly. Now, when a person faces a new situation, he cannot rely solely on the content of what he already knows. He needs to be able to assess a situation, get the newest and best information available, and act.

It is futile to try to teach stores of factual information to our children. The world now changes faster than generation-to-generation adaptation time. We need a kind of adaptation that is unprecedented. We need minds that are ready to adapt at every moment.

Ornstein believes unprecedented adaptation is already under way. He describes the adaptive mind as one that is actually many minds. To adapt, you decide which mind to put in charge at the moment. You can develop your minds, but essentially, it is the flexibility afforded by having them all that is your twenty-first-century advantage.

The new adaptive mind is divergent-thinking–dominant. It is inventive, spontaneous, and global. It is the profile of the Edison-trait child.

When Ornstein describes a mind of many minds, he is describing the Edisonian thinker. The unprecedented adaptation under way at this time is the rise of Edisonian thinking.

CHILDREN OF TOMORROW

The Edison-trait child, all grown up, has a distinct advantage in this era of change. He has the natural ability to change minds without hesitation. His Edisonian mind is, by definition, essentially inventive. He can literally *reinvent himself* as needed.

Dreamers

A dreamer has a Zen, or "learner's," mind. He is open to the mysteries and possibilities of the universe. Every golfer wishes he were as free from tension and internal criticism as the child who is a Dreamer.

As the amount of information increases at exponential rates, we find ourselves in the midst of vast quantities and varieties of ideas and facts. We collect data that is bigger, smaller, older, newer, slower, faster, deeper, and further by orders of magnitude that boggle the mind. We examine phenomena that are as tiny as 1/1,000,000,000,000,000,000th of a centimeter in an explorable universe whose edge lies at least 100,000,000,000,000,000,000,000,000 miles away. We study events so short-lived that they occur in 1/10,000,000,000,000,000,000,000,000th of a second and evidence that dates our universe back 20,000,000,000 years.[14]

The Dreamer is someone who synthesizes this vast array of phenomena in unique and uncensored ways. The Dreamer draws elements of art and science together. He combines concepts from different cultures, different worlds, different times, and different species. He plays in a field that has no fences. He looks where others see chaos and instead sees possibilities.

I remember the first time I heard about the "butterfly effect," a concept in chaos theory named by meteorologist Edward Lorenz in 1961. Conducting computer simulations of weather patterns, Lorenz found that the tiniest change in the position of his variables completely threw off his calculations. This caused him to remark that "a butterfly flapping its wings in the Amazon could spawn a hurricane in Texas."[15]

The butterfly effect, as preternatural as it seems, *is* a physical reality. I decided it was something for me to keep in mind the next time I felt the urge to persuade a Dreamer to be more realistic.

Discoverers

When a Discoverer is set on an idea or plan, he is relentless. It's as though it has been burned into his brain. He will not give it up easily. Most times, he will not give it up at all.

The Discoverer has a strong intuition that points him in the right direction. It's his instinct to hold his course when the odds are against him. Explorers throughout time have had to face adversity. It comes with the territory.

To be successful in the new workplace, it is necessary for a person to face failure and try again immediately. The sheer volume of ideas and opportunities means that only some will lead to success. Many roads will lead to nowhere.

Small businesses are exciting new ventures, but start-up success rates are low. According to the Small Business Administration, 39.8 percent of new companies survive a minimum of six years. (In other words, six out of ten fail.)[16] Entrepreneurs who eventually succeed are the ones who can begin anew, as needed.

The Discoverer has the inner drive to keep going at the moment of failure. Since he does not depend on external sources for motivation, he does not lose his drive when external factors let him down. He continues to pursue his goals, even in his darkest hours.

In the new workplace, Discoverers will also have to face the psychological challenge of sustaining themselves through uncertain times. When you propose an idea that is truly innovative, you must be prepared to face a horde of disbelievers. You need a Ted Turner type of determination to stand up to critics. The Discoverer's strong will and persistence prepare him to do this. He has the courage to stand up to naysayers, the perseverance to proceed when others doubt him, and the salesmanship to persuade those he needs to back him.

Dynamos

The Dynamo is constantly on the move. He has the gift of tireless energy. He has stamina, a critical requirement in the new, accelerated workplace. He has the ability to move fast, and to sustain outbursts of hard-driving speed.

Fortune magazine quoted a high-level advertising executive as forecasting: "Time will be the currency of the nineties." The authors of *Workplace 2000,* Joseph Boyett and Henry Conn, note three reasons why an increased demand for speed is now a firm reality in the marketplace: (1) consumers prefer those who can meet their needs the fastest; (2) the company that gets a new or redesigned product to market first captures the market niche; and (3) the stakes are higher around the globe.[17] "Time leaders" in every line of work have quicker "best times" than before, and companies must match or better the leader's performance. In other words, "time standards" are higher and consumers are now conditioned to expect fast delivery.

The Dynamo is a natural-born "time leader." He is a racer. He thrives on racing with competitors, with himself, and with the clock. If he has a deadline and a good reason to meet it, he will do what it takes to make his goal. He will board a plane, get in a car, jump up from his seat and run down the hallway. He will travel halfway around the world to inspect a factory or a prototype. Or he will dash across town to see a supplier and decide on materials. He will work odd hours or set his alarm for three A.M. to call someone in a foreign time zone. He will find a way to finish the project on time.

The Dynamo was born to set the pace, to lead the way. He mystifies others with his ability to rejuvenate himself. He has the energy and drive to cross the finish line first.

INFORMATION-AGE SKILLS

Creativity and Innovation

The Edison-trait child specializes in creating and inventing. It is fundamental to his nature. If these qualities are nurtured and allowed to flourish, when he becomes an adult, he will be a leader in the emerging markets of the Information Age. He will become an inventor of economic reality.

According to the futurist Alvin Toffler, the new work regimen is governed by the "innovation imperative":

> No existing market share is safe today, no product life indefinite. Not only in computers and clothing, but in everything from insurance policies to medical care to travel packages, competition tears away niches and whole chunks of established business with the weapon of innovation. Companies shrivel and die unless they can create an endless stream of new products.[18]

In *Workplace 2000,* Boyett and Conn note that "workers of tomorrow need the skills to 'break mental sets,' 'think creatively,' analyze problems, and find innovative approaches to problem resolution." They note that "the real opportunities for professional and financial gains will lie in the ability to creatively identify small

business opportunities that can be exploited either within the organization (via a new 'business unit') or outside (as an entrepreneurial
business start-up)."[19]

Our basic raw material is now information. Our basic inner resource is now imagination.

Flexibility and Diversity

The Edison-trait child is an intensely divergent thinker. His interests
are broad. His ideas range far and wide. He has a strong inclination
to remain open and questioning.

If he develops his varied interests and adopts a multidisciplinary
approach, the working world he enters will reward him handsomely. His curiosity, versatility, and breadth of knowledge are desirable qualities in the new workplace.

Boyett and Conn predict that by the year 2000 most Americans
will find themselves working in a "small company environment"—
either an "intrepreneureal" group (i.e., a decentralized branch of a
large company) or an entrepreneurial small business. In a small company environment, there is a do-it-yourself mentality that requires a
worker to be able to perform many varied tasks—operate a computer, sift through data, make a presentation, conduct a survey,
write a report, travel, create a budget, confer with a tax expert, hire
a consultant, decide on health benefits, purchase supplies, contract
for recycling services. According to Boyett and Conn:

> Breadth of knowledge concerning business operations and
> customer needs is likely to be more highly valued than depth
> of knowledge in a narrowly defined specialty. Broad knowl-
> edge and experience in performing a wide range of tasks will
> not only increase an employee's value, . . . it will also increase
> his or her chance of identifying a market need and developing
> a spin-off business within or outside the organization.[20]

Remember that Bill Gates's coworkers said what distinguished
him from other computer programmers was his breadth of knowledge about a full range of business considerations.

Up to now, Americans were more likely to be successful in a
company if they began working there when they were young and
stayed on for many years. Advancement was a function of longevity.

That age is past. From now on, as Boyett and Conn note, "Flexibility and creativity will be more important for success than endurance and loyalty. . . . *The most valued employees will be those who are flexible and can perform a wide range of functions* [emphasis added]."[21]

Change Seeking

The Edison-trait child is attracted to novelty. He pursues stimulation. He likes newness and discovery, exploration and adventure. The Dynamo is a risk taker. He enjoys a challenge, a dare, and a thrill. These qualities are highly valued in the new marketplace.

When Tom Peters wrote *Thriving on Chaos,* at first he considered the title *Thriving Amidst Chaos.* But that title implied mere coping, to succeed in spite of chaos, not *because* of it. "The true winners of tomorrow," says Peters, "will deal proactively with chaos."[22]

The Edison-trait child is a "true winner of tomorrow." When he grows up and takes his love of change to the workplace, he will be a perfect match for the workplace he'll enter. It is driven by change. And it will reward his love of change.

Although the new workplace has less job security, it offers more job mobility. Workers need to expect and prepare themselves for periods of unemployment. However, they can also expect and prepare themselves for unprecedented opportunities to achieve profit and growth.[23]

Workers who are facile with the power and speed of advanced technology will be well compensated. Those who are capable, resourceful, and *enjoy* the challenge of new technology will be in great demand. At this writing, the Internet links 60 million people in 140 countries, with a growth rate of approximately 10 percent per month.[24] Growing pains notwithstanding, the Net is an unequaled means of global communication that holds extraordinary promise. The sharpest increases in stocks reported in the last two years have been for Internet-related companies.[25]

New pay structures in the workplace, like profit sharing, stock options, and employee ownership, favor change-seeking Edisonians who want to ride the waves of growth they help generate for their companies. Currently, the principle of financial partnership is taking the place of guaranteed salary. "Shared risks, shared income" is in the process of replacing "a fair day's work for a fair day's pay."[26]

The Dynamo who is hard-driving and works at top speed profits handsomely when his income is tied directly to the results of his own efforts. It is to his benefit to trade predictability for the potential to make more money.

The Dynamo who takes chances with ease has a marked advantage. Tom Peters concludes:

> Success will come to those who love chaos—constant change— not those who attempt to eliminate it. The fleet-of-foot, value-adding, niche-market creator thrives on the very uncertainty that drives others to distraction.[27]

Communicating a Vision

The Edison-trait child has a gift for metaphoric thought and visual imagery. He sees a world of stories and pictures. The Edisonian who develops his communication skills fully is a persuasive and powerful force in the twenty-first-century workplace.

A new model of production is emerging in today's marketplace. It is "simultaneous and synchronized," not sequential. As Toffler describes it, "Information gained from sales and marketing people feeds the engineers, whose innovations need to be understood by the financial people, whose ability to raise capital depends on how well satisfied customers are, which depends on how well scheduled the company's trucks are. . . ."[28] The people who make the product need to connect with the ones who sell it, who need to connect with the ones who deliver it . . . all at the same time.

Boyett and Conn agree that to succeed, workers must be able to clearly communicate their individual visions, so they can create their shared vision.[29]

A person with a talent to communicate in verbal pictures is an asset in the workplace. A person with a talent to communicate a shared vision is a *leader* who can attract and motivate others.

A leader uses stories, anecdotes, and parables to excite and unify workers in a singular purpose, a common goal. Leadership expert John Gardner says that effective leaders deal with "that partly conscious, partly buried world of needs and hopes, ideals and symbols. . . . [T]hey retell stories that carry shared meanings."[30] Management experts Warren Bennis and Burt Nanus explain how leaders "invent images, metaphors, and models." Leaders are "intense personalities" who "are so intent on what they are doing that, like a child completely absorbed with creating a sand castle, they draw others in."[31] In this sense, an Edisonian is a natural-born leader.

THE VISUALIZATION OF PERSONAL SUCCESS

Ultimately, it is divergent thinking that fortifies us to be adaptive, creative writers of our own stories. The ability to visualize holds the promise of personal empowerment for living life. When your mind's eye can see a personal goal as already accomplished, you are well on your way to the achievement of your goal.

Elite athletes visualize their goals as achieved. Sports psychologists have documented the effectiveness of this method. Neuroscientists are now discovering why this is so. Neural events, changes that occur inside the brain, are essentially the same for real or imagined experience.[32]

Edisonians have a powerful gift in their aptitude for visualization. With hard work and follow-through, they can create new realities inside and outside their own brains. They have the ability to see many possible futures, and to adapt themselves to the best ones for them.

Cherish your Edison-trait child and nurture his individuality. He shares characteristics with Edisonian celebrities, yet he is not Bill Gates. He is who he is. He has his own visions and struggles and purpose in life.

Edisonians have the determination and stamina to make their personal desires come true. They keep a strong vision of the future as they want to see it. This empowers them to work and create the future they see.

As Thomas Edison himself once said: "If we did all the things we are capable of doing, we would literally astonish ourselves."

Notes

Introduction

1. P. Mint, *Thomas Edison: Inventing the Future* (New York: Fawcett Columbine, 1989); T. Rowland-Entwistle, *Children of History: Thomas Edison* (New York: Marshall Cavendish, 1988).
2. *The Diagnostic and Statistical Manual of Mental Disorders,* 4th ed. (Washington, D.C.: American Psychiatric Association, 1994), hereafter referred to as the *DSM-IV,* is the authoritative reference in the United States for the definitions and descriptions of all mental disorders, including Attention Deficit Disorder. In the *DSM-IV,* Criterion D for ADD states: "There must be clear evidence of clinically significant impairment in social, academic, or occupational functioning" (p. 84).
3. See Chapter 13, Notes 7 and 11.
4. The *DSM-IV* estimates the prevalence rate for ADD at 3–5 percent for school-age children (p. 82). For children who demonstrate symptoms but may not necessarily meet the full diagnostic criteria as defined by the *DSM-IV,* prevalence rates are much higher. For example, Larry Silver, M.D., former director of the National Institute of Mental Health, estimates a prevalence rate of 10–20 percent, or as high as 30 percent. See *Dr. Larry Silver's Advice to Parents on Attention-Deficit Hyperactivity Disorder* (Washington, D.C.: American Psychiatric Association Press, 1993), p. 10.
5. Robert Brooks, Ph.D., "Fostering the Self-Esteem of Children with ADD: The Search for Islands of Competence," a general session at the Fifth An-

nual Conference of CH.A.D.D. (Children and Adults with Attention Deficit Disorder), in San Diego, October 16, 1993.

6. Claudia Wallace, "Living in Overdrive," *Time,* July 18, 1994, p. 44.

7. Jane Leavy, "Ritalin: Are We Overmedicating Our Kids?" and "With Ritalin, the Son Also Rises," *Newsweek,* March 18, 1996, p. 51.

8. G. Weiss et al., "Psychiatric Status of Hyperactives as Adults: A Controlled Prospective 15-Year Follow-up of 63 Hyperactive Children," *Journal of the American Academy of Child and Adolescent Psychiatry* 24 (1985): 211–20. Also, G. Weiss and L. Hechtman, *Hyperactive Children Grown Up* (New York: Guilford Publications, 1993).

9. See Chapter 13, Notes 20–23.

PART I—YOUR CHILD'S INVENTIVE MIND

Chapter 1—Does Your Child Have the Edison Trait?

1. C. Lampton, *Thomas Alva Edison* (New York: Franklin Watts, 1988); P. Mint, *Thomas Edison: Inventing the Future* (New York: Fawcett Columbine, 1990).

2. The following are sources for the biographical sketch of Anne Morrow Lindbergh: Roxane Chadwick, *Anne Morrow Lindbergh: Pilot and Poet* (Minneapolis: Lerner Publications, 1987); Dorothy Herrmann, *Anne Morrow Lindbergh: A Gift for Life* (New York: Ticknor & Fields, 1992); Anne Morrow Lindbergh, *Bring Me a Unicorn: Diaries and Letters of Anne Morrow Lindbergh, 1922–1928* (New York: Harcourt Brace Jovanovich, 1972), *Gift from the Sea* (New York: Vintage Books, 1972), and *The Unicorn and Other Poems, 1935–1955* (New York: Vintage Books, 1972); Joyce Milton, *Loss of Eden: A Biography of Charles and Anne Morrow Lindbergh* (New York: HarperCollins, 1993).

3. The following are sources for the biographical sketch of Henry Ford: James Brough, *The Ford Dynasty: An American Story* (New York: Doubleday, 1977); Roger Burlingame, *Henry Ford: A Great Life in Brief* (New York: Alfred A. Knopf, 1954); Richard Crabb, *Birth of a Giant: The Men and Incidents That Gave America the Motorcar* (New York: Chilton Book Co., 1969); Jacqueline L. Harris, *Henry Ford* (New York: Franklin Watts, 1984); Barbara Mitchell, *We'll Race You Henry: A Story About Henry Ford* (Minneapolis: Carolrhoda Books, 1986); Kenneth Richards, *Henry Ford* (Chicago: Children's Press, 1967); William C. Richards, *The Last Billionaire: Henry Ford* (New York: Charles Scribner's Sons, 1948).

4. The following are sources for the biographical sketch of Jesse Owens: William J. Baker, *Jesse Owens: An American Life* (New York: Free Press, 1986); Richard D. Mandell, *The Nazi Olympics* (New York: Macmillan, 1971); *North American Biographies: Athletes* (Danbury, Conn.: Grolier Educational Services, 1994); Jesse Owens and Paul Neimark, *The Jesse Owens Story* (New York: Putnam, 1970), and *I Have Changed* (New York: William Morrow, 1972); David Wallechinsky, *The Complete Book of the Olympics* (Boston: Little, Brown, 1992).

5. Russell Barkley, Ph.D., quoted in M. Fowler, *CH.A.D.D. Educators' Manual* (Plantation, Fla.: CH.A.D.D. National Education Committee, 1992; distributed by CASET Associates, Ltd.), pp. 13–14.

Chapter 2—Children Who Are Divergent-Thinking-Dominant

1. The scientist-practitioner model, also known as the Boulder model, emerged from the Boulder Conference in 1949, when psychologists endorsed a training model that would combine the scientific foundation of psychology with its practice applications, so that clinical psychologists would be trained to be both scientists and practitioners. See V. Raimy, ed., *Training in Clinical Psychology* (New York: Prentice Hall, 1950). Arizona State University, like most other traditional university settings, subscribed to the Boulder model, which has evolved through the years to a "clinical scientist" model, which encourages the application of scientific knowledge and the scientific attitude in day-to-day clinical practice. See G. Stricker and S. Trierweiler, "The Local Clinical Scientist," *American Psychologist* 50 (Dec. 1995): 995–1002.

2. The account of brainstorming presented in the text is derived from my original notes of the conference conducted by Julien Edny, Ph.D., at the Department of Psychology, Arizona State University, in 1975. The Osborn method has four ground rules: (1) All criticism is ruled out; (2) "Freewheeling" is encouraged; (3) Strive for quantity of ideas; (4) Cross-fertilization and idea development are the goals. See Alex Osborn, *Applied Imagination* (New York: Charles Scribner's Sons, 1963).

3. D. H. Lawrence quoted in Carl Sagan, *The Dragons of Eden* (New York: Random House, 1977), pp. 182–83.

4. See Chapter 13, Note 30.

5. Sagan, *The Dragons of Eden,* p. 183.

6. Morris Berman, *The Reenchantment of the World* (Ithaca, N.Y.: Cornell University Press, 1981), p. 16.

7. The assignment was given by Mr. Frank Verga, an award-winning elementary school teacher with the Encinitas Union School District.

8. For a clear but somewhat technical description of the utility of metaphoric language in hypnosis, see D. Corydon Hammond, Ph.D., ed., *The Handbook of Hypnotic Suggestions and Metaphors* (New York: W. W. Norton, 1990), Chapter 2. The concept of metaphoric language has been considered and treated by scholars of many disciplines. "Fictional thinking" is a translation of a term believed to have been coined by the German philosopher Hans Vaihinger. Writer and attorney Gerry Spence notes that Vaihinger's *The Philosophy of "As If"* is an "important but, in America, little-known book." Spence also notes that Joseph Campbell, Gabriel García Márquez, and the Nobel Prize winner Jorge Luis Borges "have all made the same argument, that 'fictional thinking' is the original form of human thought, that it harkens to our genes." See Spence's *How to Argue and Win Every Time* (New York: St. Martin's Press, 1995), pp. 114–15.

9. In Carl Sagan's words: "We might say that human culture is the function of the corpus callosum." See his *The Dragons of Eden,* p. 185.

10. The "humorous film" study was conducted by Alice Isen, Ph.D., and her colleagues in the psychology department at the University of Maryland. It is cited in the March 1989 issue of *Psychology Today.*

11. The "problems-as-games" study was conducted by Mary Ann Glyn, Ph.D., a professor of organizational behavior at Yale University. It is cited in the March 1989 issue of *Psychology Today.*

12. Personal communication from former Air Force Commander Alan K. Reeter; reprinted with permission.

Chapter 3—*The Nature of Attention*

1. *The Perfect Tribute,* video recording by Procter & Gamble Productions, 1991. See also B. J. Armento et al., *A More Perfect Union* (Boston: Houghton Mifflin, 1991), p. 355.

2. Robert Ornstein, *The Evolution of Consciousness* (New York: Prentice Hall, 1991), p. 264.

3. Alvin Toffler, *The Third Wave* (New York: William Morrow, 1980), p. 182.

4. Hallowell and Ratey are quoted in Claudia Wallace, "Living in Overdrive," *Time,* July 18, 1994, p. 48.

5. Teresa M. Amabile, *Growing Up Creative* (New York: Crown, 1989).

6. Lecture by Dorothy Johnson, M.D., F.A.A.P., sponsored by the Encinitas Union School District, at Ocean Knolls Elementary School auditorium, Encinitas, Calif., March 16, 1994.

7. Thom Hartmann, *Attention Deficit Disorder: A Different Perception* (Novato, Calif.: Underwood-Miller, 1993).

8. See ibid. for references on the evidence that the Edison-trait profile, including Hunter qualities, is hereditary. See also Chapter 13, Notes 20–23.

9. See Hartmann, *Attention Deficit Disorder,* pp. 22–23.

10. Quoted in Wallace, "Living in Overdrive," *Time,* July 18, 1994, p. 48.

11. Holly Brubach, "The Restless Ones," *The New York Times Magazine,* September 25, 1994, p. 57.

12. Thom Hartmann, *ADD Success Stories* (Grass Valley, Calif.: Underwood, 1995).

13. See Note 8.

14. G. Bruce Knecht, "Budget Ax Threatens Edison Museum," *The Wall Street Journal,* October 25, 1995, p. A16.

15. Michael Lewis, *Liar's Poker: Rising Through the Wreckage on Wall Street* (New York: Bantam Audio, 1987).

PART II—EIGHT STEPS TO HELP YOUR EDISON-TRAIT CHILD

Chapter 4—*Step One: Believe In Your Child*

1. Charlotte Tomkins, "Laugh Lines," *Los Angeles Times,* March 29, 1995, p. E2.

2. Martin Seligman, Ph.D., *Learned Optimism* (New York: Alfred A. Knopf, 1991), and *The Optimistic Child* (Boston: Houghton Mifflin, 1995). Seligman, a University of Pennsylvania psychologist, is an accomplished research scientist and author. He first identified a relationship between depression and learned helplessness, and then went on to investigate the positive effects of learned optimism. Results of his work have been applied in business and industry, education, and sports psychology. In *The Optimistic Child,* Seligman describes a program that helps children rethink failure. Children are taught (1) to catch themselves if they attribute failure to themselves, and instead look at situation-specific causes they can change, and (2) to argue with their negative thoughts as if a third person were doing the arguing.

Chapter 5—Step Two: Watch What You Say

1. R. P. Hastings et al., "An Analysis of Labels for People with Learning Disabilities," *British Journal of Clinical Psychology* 32 (Nov. 1993): 463–65.

Chapter 6—Step Three: Build a Parent-and-Child Team

1. Adele Faber and Elaine Mazlish, *How to Talk So Kids Will Listen & Listen So Kids Will Talk* (New York: Avon Books, 1980).
2. The story of the boy, the old man, and the bird has been retold by many. Recently it was related by Gerry Spence in *How to Argue and Win Every Time* (New York: St. Martin's Press, 1995), pp. 141–42.
3. Penelope Leach, *Children First* (New York: Alfred A. Knopf, 1994).
4. Andree A. Brooks, *Children of Fast-Track Parents* (New York: Viking, 1989).
5. In one study of sixth- and seventh-graders, adolescents who believed their parents asserted and did not relax their power and restrictiveness rated higher in an extreme form of peer orientation. In other words, teens need a confidant. If they feel that they cannot go to their parents, they seek the company and advice of their peers to a much greater degree. A. J. Fuligni and S. Jacquelynne, "Perceived Parent-Child Relationships and Early Adolescents' Orientation Toward Peers," *Developmental Psychology* 29 (July 1993): 622–32.

Chapter 7—Step Four: Encourage Your Child's Interests

1. John Holt, *How Children Learn* (New York: Delta, 1989), p. 76.
2. Ibid., p. 134.
3. Kahlil Gibran, *The Prophet* (New York: Alfred A. Knopf, 1981).
4. George Leonard, *The Ultimate Athlete* (New York: Viking, 1975).
5. P. Goldberg, *The Intuitive Edge* (Los Angeles: Jeremy Tarcher, 1983), p. 118.

Chapter 8—Step Five: Teach Your Child Self-control

1. F. Iaboni et al., "Effects of Reward and Response Costs on Inhibition in ADHD Children," *Journal of Abnormal Psychology* 104 (Feb. 1995): 232–40.

2. A more complex version of the "Y-man" technique may be found in Dorothy Johnson, *I Can't Sit Still* (Santa Cruz, Calif.: ETR Associates, 1992), pp. 75–81. The simpler version presented here is from a talk Dr. Johnson gave in Encinitas, Calif. (see Chapter 3, Note 6).
3. *New Grolier Multimedia Encyclopedia* (New York: Grolier Inc., 1993).
4. E. J. Langer, "The Illusion of Control," *Journal of Personality and Social Psychology* 32 (1975): 311–28.
5. Robert Ornstein, *The Evolution of Consciousness* (New York: Prentice Hall, 1991), p. 211.
6. See Chapter 3, Note 6.

Chapter 9—Step Six: Coach Your Child to Learn How to Achieve

1. Right to Privacy Act. According to both federal and state educational codes, your local school district must provide annual notification of certain parental rights, including privacy rights of parents and students (ECS 49063).
2. Thomas Edison is quoted by Robert Ornstein in *The Evolution of Consciousness* (New York: Prentice Hall, 1991), p. 246.
3. Zentall's philosophy and practice are discussed in E. Hallowell and J. Ratey, *Driven to Distraction* (New York: Touchstone, 1994), p. 282.
4. A. L. Kahle and M. L. Kelley, "Children's Homework Problems: A Comparison of Goalsetting and Parent Training," *Behavior Therapy* 25 (1994): 275–90.
5. R. M. Gagne, *The Conditions of Learning,* 2nd ed. (New York: Holt, Rinehart & Winston, 1973).
6. R. M. Gagne and H. Foster, "Transfer of Training from Practice on Components in a Motor Skill," *Journal of Experimental Psychology* 39 (1949): 47–68.
7. "A Remarkable Reading Program," editorial in the *San Diego Union Tribune,* June 16, 1994.

Chapter 10—Step Seven: Take Care of Yourself

1. Hans Selye, *Stress Without Distress* (New York: Lippincott & Crowell, 1974).
2. Hans Selye, *The Stress of Life* (New York: Lippincott & Crowell, 1968), p. 162.

Chapter 11—Step Eight: Take Care of Your Family

1. D. W. Smith and D. M. Brodzinsky, "Stress and Coping in Adopted Children: A Developmental Study," *Journal of Clinical Child Psychology* 23 (March 1994): 91–99.

PART III—A PARENT'S GUIDE TO RESOURCES
Chapter 12—*Your Edison-Trait Child at School*

1. Carol Dweck, Ph.D., a Columbia University psychologist, has conducted most of her research with students in the New York City school system. Her studies are discussed in Bridget Murray, "Children Can Excel When They Learn from Mistakes," *APA Monitor* 26 (Nov. 1995): p. 42. The *APA Monitor* is the monthly newspaper of the American Psychological Association.

2. Gloria Steinem, *Revolution from Within* (Boston: Little, Brown, 1992), p. 121.

3. William Glasser, *Schools Without Failure* (New York: Harper & Row, 1969), pp. 97, 31.

4. The cover story of the October 7, 1996, issue of *U.S. News & World Report* was "Fixing Schools: The Debate That Really Matters," by T. Toch and M. Daniel. It reviewed the debate between convergent-thinking methods that stress content, recitation work, and cultural literacy (as represented by educator E. D. Hirsch, Jr.) versus divergent-thinking methods that stress learning how to learn, hands-on work, and student-relevant topics (as represented by educator Theodore Sizer). It concluded that "school reform doesn't have to be an either/or proposition. In fact, it shouldn't be. Both Hirsch, with his traditionalist allies, and Sizer, with his progressive followers, have valuable contributions to make" (p. 60).

5. Sydney Zentall, Ph.D., teaches psychology at Purdue University. Her response appeared in "Ask CH.A.D.D.," a regular column of *CH.A.D.D.er* (the newsletter of CH.A.D.D., Children and Adults with Attention Deficit Disorder), October–November 1994.

6. John Holt, *How Children Learn* (New York: Delta, 1989).

7. Holt cites the example of Janet Sarkett, a mother from Arizona, who wrote to *Growing Without Schooling* about how her four-and-a-half-year-old son learned to read. In ibid., pp. 251–52.

8. Tony Buzan, *The Mind Map Book* (New York: Dutton, 1993); and *Use Both Sides of Your Brain* (New York: Dutton, 1974). Supplementary resource materials now include books, a video, computer software, and a children's coloring book.

9. Holt, *How Children Learn,* p. 278.

10. The example Holt cites is from the prospectus of the Green Valley School, written by George von Hilsheimer. Ibid., p. 277.

11. Seymour Papert, *The Connected Family* (Marietta, Ga.: Longstreet Press, Inc., 1996).

12. Glasser, *Schools Without Failure.*

13. Most school districts that use portfolios also use grades. Some experimental schools now use portfolios only, for example, the ACT (Academic Competitiveness Through Technology) Academy of the McKinney Independent School District, in McKinney, Texas, which is a federally funded demonstration program. The program runs K through twelfth grade, and

colleges are expected to accept portfolios instead of grade-point averages. See Kevin Helliker, "Texas Tech," *The Wall Street Journal,* Special Supplement: "Technology in the Classroom," November 13, 1995, pp. R18, R20.

14. While policies differ from district to district, most schools follow these guidelines: Group testing occurs in March for placement in GATE for the following academic year. A student may take the test for the first time in the third grade (for fourth-grade placement). Once a student qualifies, he does not have to be retested. A student who doesn't achieve qualifying scores but who wants to enter the program may be retested at the next group administration (next year), or he may obtain a private evaluation at his own expense.

15. On the Wechsler Intelligence Scale for Children, Third Revision, this is the approximate equivalent of 2 standard deviations above the mean.

16. See Chapter 14, Note 14, for a discussion of and references for current theories of multiple intelligence.

17. This issue is treated by Howard Gardner in *Multiple Intelligences: The Theory in Practice* (New York: Basic Books, 1993), pp. 176–77. Also, an interesting point is raised in James T. Webb and Diane Latimer, "ADHD and Children Who Are Gifted," *Exceptional Children* 60 (Oct.–Nov. 1993): 183–84. In discussing the qualities that determine giftedness, the authors describe the characteristics of an Edison-trait profile, including "much energy focussed on whatever truly interests them, . . . specific interests [that] may not coincide with the desires and expectations of teachers and parents—an active questioning of rules, customs, and traditions, and power struggles and behaviors that can cause discomfort for parents, teachers, and peers" (p. 184).

18. There are two laws that apply here. The Individuals With Disabilities Education Act (IDEA) and Section 504 of the Rehabilitation Act of 1973. To be eligible for services under the IDEA, a child must be found to have one or more of the thirteen disability categories specified in the Act and be found to need special education. To be eligible for services under Section 504 of the Rehabilitation Act of 1973, a child must have a disability that "substantially limits a major life activity" and must be found to need special education. All children covered by IDEA are covered by Section 504. Some children are covered by Section 504, but not IDEA.

19. If your child attends private school, you are responsible for transporting him to and from the public school at the specified time that special services can be made available to him, but the services themselves are paid for by the district.

20. On April 29, 1993, the Office of Civil Rights (OCR) issued the statement: "There is no absolute right to an evaluation on demand—not for ADD or any other suspected disability. However, a school district is obligated to evaluate any child it suspects of having a disability that substantially limits a major life activity such as learning. If a parent requests that his child be evaluated and the school district refuses to evaluate the child because it does not believe the child is in need of regular education with supplementary service or special education and related services, the

school district must inform the parent of his or her right to due process to challenge its decision not to evaluate."

This statement clarified some confusion that had arisen following a previous memorandum on September 16, 1991, issued jointly by the OCR and the U.S. Department of Education's Office of Special Education Programs (OSEP).

See "OCR Issues New ADD Memorandum—Tones Down Schools' Responsibilities," *The Schools' Advocate: The Special Education Law Reporter Emphasizing Legal Advice for Schools* 8 (Aug. 1993): 689–90; and *The Special Educator,* August 11, 1993, pp. 11–12 (LRP Publications, Horsham, Pa.).

On March 14, 1994, a response letter was issued jointly by the OCR and the OSEP reaffirming selected aspects of the September 16, 1991, memorandum. For a review of this statement, see Matthew D. Cohen, "The Advocate," *CH.A.D.D.er,* October–November 1994, pp. 6–7.

21. For a list of standardized intelligence tests, see Chapter 14, Note 12. For a list of standardized achievement tests, see Chapter 14, Note 17. These achievement tests are all "norm-based," i.e., your child's score is compared to the scores of other children of the same gender and age. An IEP evaluation is likely to include some "curriculum-based" achievement tests, too. "Curriculum-based measurement" is a way of assessing the knowledge your child should have in particular subjects at particular grade levels. An example of a curriculum-based test is the Brigance Comprehensive Inventory of Basic Skills. Curriculum-based measurement is a growing field in special education because the emphasis is on individual learning, not peer comparison.

22. To get a picture of the usual range of recommendations that an IEP team makes, here is some current data for children who were evaluated recently. This data was collected to assess the needs of students who had previously been diagnosed with ADD: In about 50 percent of cases, the team gives the teacher a list of suggestions to modify the child's regular classroom instruction. In about 43 percent of cases, the team gives the teacher a suggestion list, but also schedules some time for the child with a resource specialist. For example, the child might leave class twice a week to attend small-group language therapy or she might get tutorial help from a special education teacher who visits the classroom for several hours each week. In about 7 percent of cases, the child will need to receive some or most of her instruction in a specialized classroom. This information was released by the Council on Exceptional Children (CEC), as reported by the Professional Group for ADD and Related Disorders (PGARD), in "The ADD Controversy—What Did CEC Say?" *Exceptional Children* 60 (Oct.–Nov. 1993): 181–82.

23. A list of "reasonable accommodations" associated with Section 504 regulations is specified in Kathy Hubbard, MSW, "Bringing Section 504 into the Classroom," *CH.A.D.D.er,* October–November 1994, pp. 8–9. A useful checklist for assessing a child's eligibility under IDEA and Section 504 is provided by Perry A. Zirkel in *The Special Educator,* May 17, 1994, p. 285 (LRP Publications, Horsham, Pa.).

Chapter 13—What Is ADD?

1. The *DSM-IV* (see Introduction, Note 2) estimates the prevalence rate for ADD at 3–5 percent for school-age children (p. 82). According to the 1990 census, the total population of five- to twelve-year-old children is 45,249,989 persons. Four percent of 45,249,989 is 1.8 million children.
2. The terms "ADD" and "ADHD" are sometimes used interchangeably, and there is a popular misconception—a logical one—that ADD means Attention Deficit Disorder without hyperactivity and ADHD means Attention Deficit Disorder with hyperactivity. Technically speaking, ADD is a vestigial term. The *DSM-IV* does not use the term at all. Instead, the *DSM-IV* uses the term "Attention-deficit Hyperactivity Disorder," or ADHD, as an umbrella term to describe *all* forms of the disorder today. This means that a child can have ADHD even if there is not a single sign of hyperactivity, and this is a source of confusion. The reason why the *DSM-IV* uses the term ADHD exclusively is found in the history of how ADHD evolved as a diagnosis in the last three editions of *The Diagnostic and Statistical Manual of Mental Disorders*.

   Attention Deficit Disorder (ADD) was first introduced as a diagnosis in 1980, in the third edition of the manual, the *DSM-III*. Two kinds were defined: "Attention Deficit Disorder (ADD) With Hyperactivity" and "Attention Deficit Disorder (ADD) Without Hyperactivity."

   In 1987, when the third edition was revised, the *DSM-III-R*, as it was called, listed criteria for only one type of the disorder: "Attention-deficit Hyperactivity Disorder" or "ADHD." Another kind was mentioned, "Undifferentiated Attention-deficit Disorder," but with no list of criteria, because, as *DSM-III-R* nosologists noted, "Research is necessary to determine if this is a valid diagnostic category and, if so, how it should be defined."

   Over the course of the next seven years, interest in the field expanded rapidly, producing voluminous research studies, journal articles, and educational materials. Consistent with the major category name given in the *DSM-III-R*, these reports were referenced under the heading "Attention-deficit Hyperactivity Disorder," or "ADHD." Meanwhile, cases of "Undifferentiated Attention-deficit Disorder" were being diagnosed with increasing frequency, demonstrating the validity of that construct, but it was not used as a heading in journals and other reference sources.

   In June of 1994, when the fourth edition of the manual came out, the *DSM-IV* gave full criteria for three distinct types of the disorder: two with hyperactivity and one without. However, by this time the heading "ADHD" had become entrenched in relevant databases, medical record keeping, and psychiatric terminology. Hence, the *DSM-IV* incorporated "ADHD" into the title of all three types, the technical names of which are: (1) ADHD Inattentive Type (having no hyperactivity), (2) ADHD Hyperactive-Impulsive Type, and (3) ADHD Combined Type.
3. See Note 1.
4. *DSM-IV,* p. 83.

5. E. Copeland and V. Love, *Attention Without Tension* (Atlanta: 3 C's of Childhood, 1992), p. 4.

6. According to the *DSM-IV,* comorbidity exists "in a substantial proportion of children referred to clinics with ADHD." It is commonly accepted that over 50 percent of those diagnosed with ADD also meet diagnostic criteria for one or more additional psychiatric disorders. See also J. M. Halperin et al., "Ritalin: Diagnostic Comorbidity and Attentional Measures," in L. I. Greenhill and B. B. Osman, eds., *Ritalin: Theory and Patient Management* (New York: Mary Ann Liebert, 1991), pp. 15–24.

   Comorbidity includes the co-occurrence of ADD with disruptive behavior disorders such as oppositional defiant disorder and conduct disorder; anxiety disorders, especially obsessive-compulsiveness; mood disorders, especially depression and manic depression; learning and communication disorders, particularly auditory processing problems; sleep and awakening disorders; Tourette's disorder; Asperger's syndrome; pervasive developmental disorder; substance abuse; and borderline personality disorder.

   For a comprehensive professional review of comorbidity, see Thomas E. Brown, Ph.D., ed., *Attention Deficit Disorders and Comorbidities in Children, Adolescents, and Adults* (Washington, D.C.: American Psychiatric Press, 1996). Dr. Brown wrote a review article in laypersons' terms called "The Many Faces of ADD: Comorbidity," which appeared in *Attention!,* Fall 1994, pp. 29–36. *Attention!* is the quarterly journal of CH.A.D.D., Children and Adults with Attention Deficit Disorder.

7. R. Edwards, "Is Hyperactivity Label Applied Too Frequently?" *APA Monitor* 26 (Jan. 1995). See also M. Gordan, "Certainly Not a Fad, but It Can Be Overdiagnosed," *Attention!,* Fall 1995, pp. 20–22.

8. According to Paul Genova, M.D., a psychiatrist and a columnist for the *Psychiatric Times:* "I also predict that Attention-Deficit/Hyperactivity Disorder will become the fad diagnosis of the late '90's. ADHD is a very well-defined condition, which lends itself to a short-term, biological treatment that managed care prefers in an era of scarce resources." "ADD in the Late 90's," *Family Therapy Networker,* May–June 1995.

   See also "Managed Care's Focus on Psychiatric Drugs Alarms Many Doctors," *The Wall Street Journal,* December 1, 1995.

9. Claudia Wallace, "Living in Overdrive," *Time,* July 18, 1994, p. 44.

10. R. Vatz, "Attention Deficit Delirium," *The Wall Street Journal,* July 27, 1994.

11. L. Hancock, "Mother's Little Helper," *Newsweek,* March 18, 1996, p. 52.

12. See Note 9.

13. Ann Landers column, "Readers Make Some Suggestions on Dealing with Child's Tantrums," December 26, 1994.

14. ADD is referred to as the "disease of the hour" in N. Angier, "The Debilitating Malady Called Boyhood," *The New York Times,* July 24, 1994. ADD as the yuppie flu of the nineties was the "thread" of an on-line conversation at alt.support.attn-deficit on the Internet in 1995.

15. In the national media, for example, H. Brubach, "The Restless Ones," *The New York Times Magazine,* September 25, 1994, p. 57: "ADD is by my reck-

oning epidemic among those of us who work in the fashion business, and the traits that make it so hard for people with ADD to get on in the world are the very traits that make people get ahead in the world of fashion." These designers who are "ahead in the world of fashion" are not suffering an occupational dysfunction. In fact, the opposite seems to be true. They are encountering *more* success than the norm in their daily functioning.

16. At parent-teacher conferences, for example, in my role as a consultant, I have heard bright underachieving students described as having "a little bit of ADD." These students give indications that they could be getting "A"'s but instead they get "B"'s or "C"'s, usually because they do not do well on timed tests, or because they don't follow instructions correctly, or because they forget to hand in assignments. While these problems need to be addressed, they do not constitute a significant impairment, which is the litmus test for a mental disorder. In Hancock, "Mother's Little Helper," Dr. Bruce Epstein, a St. Petersburg pediatrician, reported that parents "of normal children" had asked him for Ritalin to improve their children's grades. "When I won't give it to them, they switch doctors. They find someone who will."

17. "Neither deviant behavior . . . nor conflicts that are primarily between the individual and society are mental disorders unless the deviance or the conflict is a symptom of a dysfunction in the individual" *DSM-IV* (see Introduction, Note 2), p. xxii.

18. In the Winter 1995 issue of *Attention!,* CH.A.D.D. president JoAnne Evans stated the organization's official stance, based on the conclusions of its professional advisory board: "A multi-modal approach is absolutely essential to achieve optimal results. Our strong position is based on current scientific literature that supports the multi-modal concept" (p. 3). Currently the NIMH Multimodal Treatment Study is under way to study the long-term intervention (up to two years) of multimodal treatment at six sites around the country, including the University of California at Berkeley, where it is conducted by Stephen Hinshaw, Ph.D.

19. See Introduction, Note 8.

20. Family studies include J. Biederman, et al., "Family-genetic and Psychosocial Risk Factors in *DSM-III* Attention Deficit Disorder," *Journal of the American Academy of Child and Adolescent Psychiatry* 29 (1990): 526–33, and "A Family Study of Patients with Attention Deficit Disorder and Normal Controls," *Journal of Psychiatric Research* 20 (1986): 263–74. As reported in *Time,* July 18, 1994: "Interest in the genetics of ADHD is enormous. In Australia a vast trial involving 3,400 pairs of twins between the ages of 4 and 12 is examining the incidence of ADHD and other behavioral difficulties. At NIMH, [Alan] Zametkin's group is recruiting 200 families who have at least two members with ADHD" (p. 46). See also Alan Zametkin, "Attention Deficit Disorder: Born to be Hyperactive," *Journal of the American Medical Association* 273 (1995): 1871–74.

21. E. H. Cook et al., "Association of Attention-Deficit Disorder and the Dopamine Transporter Gene," *American Journal of Human Genetics* 56 (1995): 993–99. Also, D. E. Comings et al., "The Dopamine D2 Recep-

tor Locus as a Modifying Gene in Neuropsychiatric Disorders," *Journal of the American Medical Association* 266 (1991): 1793–99.

22. See Notes 20 and 21. Also, a small percentage of ADD cases (according to *Time,* July 18, 1994, less than 10 percent) have other causes, such as trauma, infection, neurotoxin exposure, drug exposure in utero, and fetal distress. These cases are difficult to treat, and although technically the diagnosis of record is ADD, they are generally regarded as a disparate variation of the syndrome. In professional literature, these cases are usually referred to as being caused by "organic factors due to physiological insult or injury." See, for example, Copeland and Love, *Attention Without Tension,* p. 17.

23. E. Carlson et al., "A Developmental Investigation of Inattentiveness and Hyperactivity," *Child Development* 66 (Feb. 1995): 37–54. See also Eric Taylor, "The Risks for ADD," keynote address at the Eighth Annual Conference of CH.A.D.D. (Chicago, Ill., Nov. 15, 1996), for evidence drawn from a long-term follow-up study in a nontreated population indicating how biological risks and psychosocial risks must interact for the disorder to occur.

24. "The Disability Named ADD," CH.A.D.D. Fact Sheet No. 1, 1993.

25. Claudia Wallace, "Living in Overdrive," *Time,* July 18, 1994, poses the question: "Is ADD truly a disorder? Just because something responds to a drug doesn't mean it is a sickness" (pp. 47–48).

26. "An Interview with Judith Rapoport, M.D.," *Attention!* (Winter 1996), p. 8.

27. See Joel L. Swerdlow, "Quiet Miracles of the Brain," *National Geographic,* June 1995, pp. 2–41.

28. C. A. Mann et al., "Quantitative Analysis of EEG in Boys with Attention Deficit Hyperactivity Disorder: Controlled Study with Clinical Implications," *Pediatric Neurology* 8 (1992): 30–36.

29. Detection of the absence of "right greater than left asymmetry" is reported by F. Castellanos, et al., "Quantitative Morphology of the Caudate Nucleus in Attention Deficit Hyperactivity Disorder," *American Journal of Psychiatry* 151 (Dec. 1994): 1791–96. It is also reported in a series of studies by G. Hynd et al., summarized in C. Riccio et al., "Neurological Basis of Attention Deficit Hyperactivity Disorder," *Exceptional Children* 60 (Oct.–Nov. 1993): 118–24.

30. Thomas R. Blakeslee, *The Right Brain* (New York: Doubleday, 1980). The entire text of the book explains the differential and cooperative functioning of the two brain hemispheres. See p. 33 for a succinct description of convergent vs. divergent thinking.

31. Evidence of the role of the corpus callosum is reported by J. N. Giedd et al., "Quantitative Morphology of the Corpus Callosum in Attention Deficit Hyperactivity Disorder," *American Journal of Psychiatry* 15 (May 1994): 665–69; see also Note 29. To understand the role of the corpus callosum in the dynamic distribution of attention, particularly with reference to individual differences and the developmental changes associated with interhemispheric interaction, see M. Hoptman and R. Davidson,

"How and Why Do the Two Cerebral Hemispheres Interact?," *Psychological Bulletin* 116 (Sept. 1994): 195–219.

32. Blood-flow studies are reported by H. C. Lou et al., "Focal Cerebral Hypoperfusion in Children with Dysphasia and/or Attention Deficit Disorder," *Archives of Neurology* 41 (1984): 825–29; and H. C. Lou et al., "Striatal Dysfunction in Attention Deficit and Hyperkinetic Disorder," *Archives of Neurology* 46 (1989): 48–52. These studies document the findings that subjects who have ADD, as compared with subjects who do not, have comparatively less blood flow in the right hemisphere (or comparatively more in the left one). For an explanation of the relationship between these findings and brain asymmetry, see Note 29.

33. A. R. Zametkin et al., "Cerebral Glucose Metabolism in Adults with Hyperactivity of Childhood Onset," *New England Journal of Medicine* 323 (Nov. 1990): 1364–66.

34. A. R. Zametkin et al., "Brain Metabolism in Teenagers with Attention-Deficit Hyperactivity Disorder," *Archives of General Psychiatry* 50 (May 1993): 338; and E. M. Liebenaur et al., "Reduced Brain Metabolism in Hyperactive Girls," *Journal of the American Academy of Child and Adolescent Psychiatry* 33 (1994): 858–68. The failure to replicate previous PET-scan findings is discussed by Dr. Emily Szumowski in the "ADD Journal Club" column of *Attention!,* Spring 1995, pp. 44–45.

35. H. T. Chugani et al., "Positron Emission Tomography Study of Human Brain Functional Development," *Annals of Neurology* 22 (1987): 487–97.

36. J. A. Matochik et al., "Effects of Acute Stimulant Medication on Cerebral Metabolism in Adults with Hyperactivity," *Neuropsychopharmacology* 8 (1993): 377–86.

37. J. A. Matochik et al., "Cerebral Glucose Metabolism in Adults with Attention Deficit Hyperactivity Disorder After Chronic Stimulant Treatment," *American Journal of Psychiatry* 5 (1994): 658–64.

38. For example, *Journal of Attention Disorders,* published quarterly by Mental Health Systems, C. Keith Connors, Ph.D., editor; the *ADHD Report,* published bimonthly by Guilford Publications, Russell A. Barkley, Ph.D., editor; and the official publications of CH.A.D.D., which include *Attention!* (a quarterly magazine), *CH.A.D.D.er* (a quarterly newsletter), and the proceedings of its annual national and international conferences. Also, the American Psychological Association (APA) has published a special volume in its series *PsychInfo: Bibliographies in Psychology,* R. Resnick and K. McEvoy, eds., *Attention Deficit/Hyperactivity Disorder: Abstracts of the Psychological and Behavioral Literature, 1971–1994* (Washington, D.C.: APA, 1994).

39. The following are some of the theories used to explain ADD:

Robert D. Hunt, M.D., and his associates have developed a clinical model of three discrete neurobiological subtypes, each of which involves a major brain system mediated by a corresponding neurotransmitter: (1) cognitive (corresponding neurotransmitter: dopamine), (2) arousal (norepinephrine), and (3) behavioral inhibition (serotonin). Each brain system corresponds to a distinctive constellation of symptoms: (1) inattentiveness, (2) impulsivity, and (3) hyperactivity. This would explain why various medicines and their combinations are more or less effective for treating different kinds of behaviors associated with ADD. R. Hunt et al., "Neurological Subtypes of ADHD," *CH.A.D.D.er,* Fall–Winter 1993, pp. 7–10.

Larry Silver, M.D., postulates a "faulty filter" in what is known as the "reticular activating system" of the brain. This system is mediated by neurotransmitters, whose activity would be boosted by the use of stimulant medication. Thus the model fits with the fact that stimulants modify behaviors associated with ADD. L. Silver, *Dr. Larry Silver's Advice to Parents on Attention-Deficit Hyperactivity Disorder* (Washington, D.C.: American Psychiatric Press, 1992).

There are several variations of a model called the *optimal arousal model,* in which the brain of a person with ADD is thought of as being "understimulated." This would explain both why stimulant medicines are effective and why novelty and multisensorial experience can enhance learning. Sydney Zentall, Ph.D., suggests an "underaroused" brain, in which frontal regions do not receive enough input from lower regions. Paul Wender, M.D., an early pioneer in the field, conceptualized an "underactivated" reward center in the brain. These theories are summarized by Edward Hallowell, M.D., and John Ratey, M.D., in their overview of biological evidence of ADD in *Driven to Distraction* (New York: Touchstone, 1994), pp. 274–85.

40. There are several variations of the disinhibition model. The one proposed by Russell Barkley, Ph.D., regards ADD-with-hyperactivity and ADD-without-hyperactivity as distinct disorders. Barkley views ADD with hyperactivity as a frontal lobe "deficit" in a person's ability to inhibit responses. R. Barkley, "More on the New Theory of ADHD," *The ADHD Report* 2 (April 1994): 1–4.

In the wider area of experimental neurophysiology, disinhibition is being hypothesized to explain a full range of neurochemical occurrences. Researchers are attempting to define a comprehensive system of ascending pathways of brain arousal and descending pathways of brain inhibition. The ascending pathways are believed to activate brain regions, while the descending pathways deactivate the same regions, including subcortical structures. In this context, ADD as well as other neurological interruptions would be interpreted as the manifestations of interference in the system. C. Riccio et al., "Neurological Basis of Attention Deficit Hyperactivity Disorder," *Exceptional Children* 60 (Oct.–Nov. 1993): 118–24.

41. Hallowell and Ratey, *Driven to Distraction,* p. 282.

42. Address by Carla Shatz, Ph.D., president, Society for Neuroscience, at "A Lifetime of Brain Fitness," sponsored by the Dana Alliance for Brain Initiatives, at the Salk Institute Auditorium, La Jolla, Calif., November 12, 1995.

43. Ibid. For further evidence of brain plasticity throughout the life span, see the findings by Jeffrey Schwartz, M.D., and his associates at UCLA on PET-scan findings of brain differences before and after therapy, summarized in the "Brainwatch" report by J. Clausiusz, *Discover,* June 1996, p. 36.

44. Ron Reeve, Ph.D., associate professor, University of Virginia, in *CH.A.D.D. Educators Manual* (Plantation, Fla.: CH.A.D.D. National Education Committee, 1992; distributed by CASET Associates, Ltd.), p. 11.

45. C. Green, *Thomas Alva Edison: Bringer of Light* (Chicago: Children's Press, 1985); C. Lampton, *Thomas Alva Edison* (New York: Franklin Watts, 1988); T. Rowland-Entwistle, *Children of History: Thomas Edison* (New York: Marshall Cavendish, 1988).

Chapter 14—Professional Diagnosis, Testing, and Counseling

1. See Introduction, Note 2.
2. The following are some of the standardized rating scales currently used and the behaviors they measure:

ACTeRS (ADD-H: Comprehensive Teachers [and Parents] Rating Scale), parent and teacher forms: *Attention, Hyperactivity, Social Skills, Oppositional Behavior.* Developed by R. Ullmann, M.Ed., E. Sleator, M.D., R. Sprague, Ph.D.; first published in 1986; normed for children grades K–8; distributed by MetriTech, Inc., Champaign, Ill.

ADDES (Attention Deficit Disorder Evaluation Scale), home and school versions: *Inattentiveness, Impulsivity, Hyperactivity.* Developed by S. McCarney, Ph.D.; revised in 1995; normed for children ages 4.0–20 (home version) and 4.5–20 (school version); distributed by Hawthorne, Columbia, Missouri.

Hawthorne Educational Services, Inc. has also published the following ADHD rating scales:

ECADDES (The Early Childhood Attention Deficit Disorders Evaluation Scale), nationally standardized on 4,883 children ages 24 through 84 months; school and home version rating forms; intervention manuals providing goals, objectives, and interventions.

ADDES-S (The Attention Deficit Disorders Evaluation Scale Secondary-Age Student), nationally standardized on 1,280 students ages 11.5 through 18 years; school and home version rating forms; intervention manuals providing goals, objectives, and interventions.

A-ADDES (The Adult Attention Deficit Disorders Evaluation Scale), nationally standardized on 6,074 adults ages 18 through 65+ years; self-report, home, and work version rating forms; intervention manual.

ADHDT (Attention-Deficit/Hyperactivity Disorder Test), a single-form test: *Hyperactivity, Impulsivity, Inattention.* Developed by J. Gilliam, Ph.D.; published in 1995; normed for children ages 3–23; distributed by Pro-Ed, Austin, Tex.

ANSER (Aggregate Neurobehavioral Student Health and Educational Review); parent and school versions of Form 1 (ages 3–5), Form 2 (ages 6–11), Form 3 (ages 12 and older), and Form 5 (follow-up questionnaire, all ages); self-administered version of Form 4 (age 9½ and older) and Form 6 (same): a series of questionnaires to obtain information about the development and health as well as the behaviors of children ages 3–adolescence. Developed by Melvin D. Levine, M.D.; originally published in 1980, revised in 1986 and 1992; normed for a selected section of Form 2; distributed by Educators Publishing Service, Inc., Cambridge, Mass.

CRS (Connors Rating Scale), parent (CPRS) and teacher (CTRS) forms, long and short versions: CPRS-93 (parent long version, 1970)— seven scales, including Restless-Disorganized and Hyperactive-Immature; CPRS-48 (parent short version, 1978)—five scales, including Impulsive-Hyperactive; CTRS-39 (teacher long version, 1969)—six scales, including Hyperactivity and Daydream-Attention Problem; CTRS-28 (teacher short version, 1978)—three scales, including Hyperactivity and Inattentive-Passivity. Developed by C. Keith Connors, Ph.D.; dates of publication listed above for each scale; normed for children ages 3 to 17 on the short versions, ages 6 to 14 on the CPRS-93 (parent long version, 93 items), ages 3 to 14 on the CTRS-39 (teacher long version, 39 items); distributed by a number of publishers, including Pro-Ed, Austin, Tex.; Psychological Assessment Resources, Inc., Odessa, Fla.; Psychological and Educational Publications, Inc., Burlingame, Calif.; NCS Assessments, Minneapolis, Minn.; the Psychological Corporation, San Antonio, Tex.

3. See Introduction, Note 4. A prevalence rate of 3–5 percent means that if diagnosed correctly, in a class of 30 students there is likely to be only 1 student whose symptoms are so extreme that she qualifies for the diagnosis.

4. Some of the **CPTs** (continuous performance tests) currently used include:

   Connors: IBM-compatible; test time, 14 minutes; normed for ages 4–19 and older. Developed by C. Keith Connors, Ph.D.; distributed by MHS, North Tonawanda, N.Y.

   GDS (Gordon Diagnostic System): Self-contained portable microprocessor; CPT test time, 9 minutes, "delay" task test time, 8 minutes; normed for ages 4–16 and adults. Developed by Michael Gordon, Ph.D.; distributed by Gordon Systems, Inc., DeWitt, N.Y.

   IVA (Intermediate Visual and Auditory): IBM-compatible with Soundblaster card; test time, 13 minutes; normed for ages 5–90. Developed by Joseph A. Sandford, Ph.D., and Ann Turner, M.D.; distributed by Braintree, Richmond, Va.

   TOVA (Tests of Variables of Attention): Macintosh- or IBM-compatible; test time, 23 minutes; normed for ages 4–16 and adults. Distributed by Universal Attention Disorders, Inc., Alamitos, Calif.

5. R. Gomez and A. Sanson, "Effects of Experimenter and Mother Presence on Attentional Performance and Activity of Hyperactive Boys," *Journal of Abnormal Psychology* 22 (Oct. 1994): 517–29. See also J. van der Meere et al., "Sustained Attention, Activation and MPH in ADHD: A Research Note," *Journal of Child Psychology and Psychiatry and Allied Disciplines* 36 (May 1995): 697–703.

6. H. Koelega, "Is the Continuous Performance Task Useful in Research with ADHD Children? Comments on a Review," *Journal of Child Psychology and Psychiatry and Allied Disciplines* 36 (Nov. 1995): 1477–85.

7. M. Fischer, R. Newby, and M. Gordon, "Who Are the False Negatives on Continuous Performance Tests?," *Journal of Clinical Child Psychology* 24 (December 1995): 427–33. This study examined children who were already diagnosed with ADD. The predominant symptom for those with

"abnormal" CPT scores was inattention and the predominant symptoms for those with "normal" CPT scores were conduct and psychosomatic problems. Children with ADD who were inattentive tended to respond better to psychostimulants, especially at high doses, than the children with ADD who had conduct and psychosomatic problems.

K. Hooks, R. Milich, and E. P. Lorch, "Sustained and Selective Attention in Boys with Attention Deficit Hyperactivity Disorder," *Journal of Clinical Child Psychology* 23 (March 1994): 69–77. This study compared a group of children who were already diagnosed with ADD with a control group of children who had no diagnosis. The two groups did not differ on measures of selective attention. The group who was diagnosed with ADD did not sustain scores of two of the measures for the same length of time as the control group did.

8. Van der Meere et al., "Sustained Attention, Activation and MPH in ADHD: A Research Note."

9. C. K. Connors et al., "Information Processing Deficits in ADHD: Effect of Stimulus Rate and Methylphenidate," paper presented at the 32nd Annual Meeting of the American College of Neuropsychopharmacology, December 13–17, 1993, Honolulu, Hawaii.

10. For a basic evaluation, the two most popular projective drawings for children are the Draw A Person and the Kinetic Family Drawings.

    Draw A Person: Screening Procedure for Emotional Disturbance (1991) is a standardized scoring system for ages 6–17, normed on a sample of 2,260. Developed by Jack A. Naglieri, Timothy J. McNeish, and Achilles N. Bardos.

    A method of analysis for **Kinetic Family Drawings** is contained in Robert C. Burns and S. Harvard Kaufman, *Actions, Styles and Symbols in Kinetic Family Drawings (K-F-D): An Interpretative Manual* (New York: Brunner/Mazel, 1972).

    A range of tests, including many other projective techniques, is available to psychologists if the findings of a basic evaluation suggest that there should be further assessment of a clinically significant emotional disturbance.

11. Wechsler Intelligence Scale for Children, 3rd ed. (San Antonio: The Psychological Corporation, 1991).

12. The following are some of the standardized individual intelligence scales for children currently used:

    KABC (Kaufman Assessment Battery for Children), 1983; normed for children ages 2.5–12.5. Developed by Alan S. Kaufman, Ph.D., and Nadeen L. Kaufman, Ph.D.; distributed by American Guidance Service, Circle Pines, Minn.

    Stanford–Binet (Stanford–Binet Intelligence Scale), 4th ed., 1986; normed for children ages 2–23. Developed by R. L. Thorndike, Ph.D.; E. P. Hagen, Ph.D.; and J. M. Sattler, Ph.D.; distributed by the Riverside Publishing Company, Chicago, Ill.

    WISC-III (Wechsler Intelligence Scale for Children), 3rd ed., 1991; normed for children ages 6–16. Originally developed by David

Wechsler, Ph.D.; distributed by the Psychological Corporation, San Antonio, Tex.

WPPSI (Wechsler Preschool and Primary Scale of Intelligence), rev. 1989; normed for children ages 3–7.3 years. Originally developed by David Wechsler, Ph.D.; distributed by the Psychological Corporation, San Antonio, Tex.

13. "Wechsler Intelligence Scale for Children: Third Edition (WISC-III)," B. A. Bracken and R. S. McCallum, eds., *Journal of Psychoeducational Assessment: A Monograph in the Advances of Psychoeducational Assessment Series* (Brandon, Vt.: Clinical Psychology Publishing Co., 1993).

14. The theory of multiple intelligences (MI) was originally proposed by Howard Gardner in his classic work, *Frames of Mind: The Theory of Multiple Intelligences* (New York: Basic Books, 1983). Gardner proposed 7 basic intelligences: linguistic, musical, logical-mathematical, spatial, bodily-kinesthetic, intrapersonal, and interpersonal. Since the publication of this book, research in the area has proliferated. For a list of books, monographs, magazines, newsletters, and contact persons specializing in MI theory or conducting MI projects, see Howard Gardner, *Multiple Intelligences: The Theory in Practice* (New York: Basic Books, 1993). Harvard Project Zero maintains an up-to-date list of schools and teachers that are involved in experiments with multiple intelligences: Harvard Project Zero Development Group, Longfellow Hall, Appian Way, Cambridge, MA 02138.

Gardner and his colleagues advocate the assessment of learning "in context." They maintain that the proper way to obtain accurate information about the skills and potentials of individuals is in the ordinary performance of relevant tasks. This method holds a number of advantages over the results of "decontextualized" formal tests, which are heavily biased in favor of only a few kinds of intelligence.

Another theory of multiple intelligences has been proposed by Robert Sternberg, in *Beyond IQ: A Triarchic Theory of Human Intelligence* (New York: Cambridge University Press, 1985). Sternberg proposes three intelligences: analytic, creative, and practical. One form of practical intelligence, called "tacit knowledge," is "action-oriented knowledge, acquired without direct help from others, that allows individuals to achieve goals they personally value." Tests of tacit knowledge appear to correlate significantly with job performance, particularly in business management. Tacit knowledge has been shown to be a better predictor of success after school than school performance as measured by academic grades.

Among best-selling books, theories of multiple intelligence have their critics—R. J. Hernstein and C. Murray, *The Bell Curve: Intelligence and Class Structure in American Life* (New York: Free Press, 1994)—and their supporters—D. Goleman, *Emotional Intelligence* (New York: Bantam Books, 1995). After reviewing the intelligence debate at its November 1994 meeting, the Board of Scientific Affairs (BSA) of the American Psychological Association (APA) established a task force to draft an authoritative and up-to-date report. The following year, this report was published in the monthly journal of the APA: U. Neisser et al., "Intelligence: Knowns and Unknowns," *American Psychologist* 51 (Feb. 1996): 77–101.

15. A. D. Anastopoulos, M. Spisto, and M. C. Maher, "The WISC-III Third Factor: A Preliminary Look at Its Diagnostic Utility," *The ADHD Report* 2 (Feb. 1994): 4–5.

16. Russell A. Barkley, "Can Neuropsychological Tests Help Diagnose ADD/ADHD?" *The ADHD Report* 2 (Feb. 1994): 1–3.

17. Achievement tests are administered routinely as part of the school evaluation that you and your child's teacher may request to assess the need for an individualized educational program (IEP) for your child. Some commonly used achievement tests are Diagnostic Achievement Battery, 2nd ed. (DAB-2); Peabody Individual Achievement Test–revised (PIAT-R); Kaufman Test of Educational Achievement (K-TEA); Test of Academic Performance (TAP); Test of Written Language (TOWL); Wechsler Individual Achievement Test (WIAT); Wide Range Achievement Test, 3rd ed. (WRAT3); Woodcock-Johnson Achievement Battery; Woodcock Reading Mastery Tests.

18. The criteria for a "learning disability" in the state of California are found in the California Administrative Code, Title V, Section 3030. This section defines the terms "basic psychological processes" and "severe discrepancy between ability and achievement." It states that the decision as to whether or not a "severe discrepancy exists shall be made by the individualized education program team."

19. M. Poplin, "Looking Through Other Lenses and Listening to Other Voices: Stretching the Boundaries of Learning Disabilities," *Journal of Learning Disabilities* 28 (Aug.–Sept. 1995): 392–98.

20. C. Dudley-Marling and D. Dippo, "What Learning Disability Does: Sustaining the Ideology of Schooling," *Journal of Learning Disabilities* 28 (Aug.–Sept. 1995): 408–14.

21. *Journal of Learning Disabilities* 28 (Aug.–Sept. 1995).

22. L. G. Denti, and M. S. Katz, "Escaping the Cave to Dream New Dreams: A Normative Vision for Learning Disabilities," *Journal of Learning Disabilities* 28 (Aug.–Sept. 1995): 415–24. Also, D. Hearne and S. Stone, "Multiple Intelligences and Underachievement: Lessons from Individuals with Learning Disabilities," *Journal of Learning Disabilities* 28 (Aug.–Sept. 1995): 425–38.

23. W. L. Moss and W. A. Sheiffele, "Can We Differentially Diagnose an Attention Deficit Disorder Without Hyperactivity from a Central Auditory Processing Problem?" *Child Psychiatry and Human Development* 25 (Winter 1994): 85–96. See also D. Geffner, J. Lucker, and W. Koch, "Evaluation of Auditory Discrimination in Children With ADD and Without ADD," *Child Psychiatry and Human Development* 26 (Spring 1996): 169–80. In noise conditions (under distraction), subjects performed worse in speech discrimination (auditory) but not in picture pointing (visual).

24. Roger Shepherd, Ph.D., a researcher of spatial intelligence, has shown that the amount of time it takes to judge whether two forms are in fact identical is tied directly to the number of degrees through which one form must be displaced to coincide with the other. Reaction time is gen-

erally considered a measure of spatial ability. An individual who is high in spatial intelligence will tend to rotate a form or figure quickly and with great facility. To such an individual, the form or figure is central. The rotation is a modification.

For example, Eskimos are unusually high in spatial intelligence. At least 60 percent of Eskimo children reach as high a score in spatial ability as the top 10 percent of Caucasian children. Adult Eskimos are known to be able to read upside down. They view form as central, and rotation as a fluid, nonessential modification. See Gardner, *Frames of Mind*.

The value of this ability is evident in the specialized training of spatial intelligence for present-day tasks. For example, "bioflight" is a system of three-dimensional spatial orientation developed by Ray Bright, Ph.D., of California State University, Chico, for use with competitive gymnasts, some of whom have won Olympic and other world-class titles. In bioflight, students "unlearn" the concepts of "up," "down," "clockwise" and "counterclockwise." Instead they train themselves to think in terms like "axis," "rotate," "translation of movement." Principles of bioflight are also used by acrobatic pilots, skydivers, and astronauts.

25. V. I. Douglas and P. A. Parry, "Effects of Reward and Nonreward on Frustration and Attention in Attention Deficit Disorder," *Journal of Abnormal Child Psychiatry* 3 (June 1994): 281–302.
26. See Introduction, Note 5.
27. The ADD Forum can be accessed through CompuServe (GO ADD). CompuServe, on the Internet: http://www.compuserve.com

Chapter 15—Medicating a Child Who Has ADD: A Personal Decision

1. "An Interview with Howard Abikoff, Ph.D.," in *Attention!* (Winter 1995), p. 7, reviews studies in which the effects of medication are compared with the effects of behavior therapy, for periods of six weeks, eight weeks, or four months. See also Lisa J. Bain, *A Parent's Guide to Attention Deficit Disorders* (New York: Delta, 1991), Chapter 6, "Medical Management."
2. According to CIBA's 1992 revision of the package insert for Ritalin: "Sufficient data on safety and efficacy of long-term use of Ritalin in children are not yet available."
3. According to CIBA's 1992 revision of the package insert for Ritalin: "The mode of action is not completely understood, but Ritalin presumably activates the brain stem arousal system and cortex to produce its stimulant effect. There is neither specific evidence which clearly establishes the mechanism whereby Ritalin produces its mental and behavioral effects in children, nor conclusive evidence regarding how these effects relate to the condition of the central nervous system."

In one study, PET scans revealed that the regional distribution of methylphenidate (Ritalin) was "almost identical" to that of cocaine. The two drugs competed for the same binding sites, and there were similarities in their affinity to the dopamine transporter, their absolute rate of brain uptake, and the rapidity with which they entered the brain. They differed only in their rate of clearance from the brain. N. D. Volkow et al., "Is Methylphenidate Like Cocaine? Studies on Their Pharmacokinetics and Distribution in the Human Brain," *Archives of General Psychiatry* 52 (June 1995): 456–63.

4. Estimates of known benefits vary. Here is a sampling:

William A. Kehoc, "Attention-Deficit/Hyperactivity Disorder and Stimulants: Information for the Pharmacist," *Pharmacist's Letter* No. 120113 (Jan. 1996): "Approximately ⅔ to ¾ of children show at least some benefit from stimulant treatment."

Harvey C. Parker and George Storm, *Medical Management of Children with Attention Deficit Disorders—Commonly Asked Questions,* published and distributed by Children and Adults with Attention Deficit Disorders (CH.A.D.D.) and the American Academy of Child and Adolescent Psychiatry (AACAP), 1991: "Seventy to eighty percent of ADD children respond in a positive manner to psychostimulant medication."

James Swanson, Ph.D., professor of pediatrics, psychiatry, and special sciences, University of California at Irvine, and past president of the Professional Group for Attention and Related Disorders (PGARD), on *60 Minutes,* December 8, 1995: "I think stimulant medication is very effective with a percentage of children with ADHD. Now I think that percentage is lower than most people. I think that most people think that 90 percent of ADHD children get better with medication. I think it's more like 60 percent."

Some studies have demonstrated placebo effects. For example, all parent ratings, as measured by the Connors, decrease in severity from baseline to placebo conditions. M. Fischer and R. F. Newby, "Assessment of Stimulus Response in ADHD Children Using a Refined Multimethod Clinical Protocol," *Journal of Clinical Child Psychology* 20 (1991): 232–44.

In two other studies, observers could not tell the difference in social interactions of hyperactive boys when blind to their medication status. D. Granger, C. K. Whalen, and B. Henker, "Malleability of Social Impressions of Hyperactive Children," *Journal of Abnormal Child Psychology* 6 (Dec. 1993): 631–47; "Perceptions of Methylphenidate Effects on Hyperactive Children's Peer Interactions," *Journal of Abnormal Child Psychology* 21 (Oct. 1993): 535–49.

5. In addition to loss of appetite and trouble sleeping, other common side effects of Ritalin include increased restlessness, headaches, stomachaches, or weight loss.

Suppression of growth may be a problem. The following warning appears on the package insert for Ritalin: "Although a causal relationship has not been established, suppression of growth (i.e., weight gain, and/or height) has been reported with the long-term use of stimulants in children."

Tics and seizures are concerns. Research on the development and worsening of tics and Tourette's disorder is cited in Notes 13–15.

According to *FDA Talk Paper,* January 12, 1996, on the basis of the results of animal studies, the FDA alerted health professionals that methylphenidate (Ritalin) might be carcinogenic. The FDA still considers it a safe drug but is requiring additional information in the package insert, having manufacturers send out a letter to doctors who prescribe the drug, and calling for further studies.

See the 1992 CIBA package insert for Ritalin for a detailed list of contraindications, warnings, precautions, and adverse reactions.

6. This may be done informally or conversationally, or it may be done formally by completing standardized parent and teacher rating scales periodically. See Chapter 14, Note 2.

7. McGough and Cantwell, "Current Trends in the Medication Management of ADD," p. 17.

8. T. Mandelkorn and G. Storm, "What Parents and Educators Need to Know About Medication," paper presented at the Fifth Annual CH.A.D.D. Conference, San Diego, Calif., October 16, 1993.

9. Package insert (1992) for Ritalin.

10. A third, infrequently prescribed stimulant is Adderall, a combination of dextroamphetamine and amphetamine. Adderall comes in 10- and 20-milligram tablets and its effect can last about six hours. The use of Adderall to reduce ADD symptoms is new, but the drug itself is not. It is the same formula as Obetrol, a drug promoted years ago to reduce obesity. See *Pharmacist's Letter* No. 10109, 1994. For a detailed list of contraindications, warnings, precautions, and adverse reactions, see the package insert for Adderall, which is manufactured by Richmond Pharmaceutical Co., Inc., Florence, Ky.

11. Dexedrine (dextroamphetamine) comes in "spansules," which are long acting (six to eight hours) but have a slow onset of action (one to two hours). Dexedrine also comes in tablet form, which is shorter acting, with a quicker onset of action. Some clinicians prefer Dexedrine spansules to Ritalin in its sustained or time-released form, when the aim is to avoid the need for a lunchtime dose at school. Mandelkorn and Storm, "What Parents and Educators Need to Know About Medication." For a detailed list of contraindications, warnings, precautions, and adverse reactions, see the 1992 revision of the package insert for Dexedrine, manufactured by SmithKline Beecham Pharmaceuticals, Philadelphia, Pa.

12. Cylert (pemoline) is generally tried only if the other stimulants are ineffective. This is because it has been known to cause mild liver damage. A child should take a liver-function blood test prior to taking Cylert and at least every six months while on the drug. Mandelkorn and Storm, "What Parents and Educators Need to Know About Medication." For a detailed list of contraindications, warnings, precautions, and adverse reactions, see the 1991 revision of the package insert for Cylert, manufactured by Abbott Laboratories, Chicago, Ill.

13. P. Lipkin, I. J. Goldstein, and A. R. Adesman, "Tics and Dyskinesias Associated with Stimulant Treatment in Attention Deficit Hyperactivity Disorder," *Archives of Pediatrics and Adolescent Medicine* 148 (1994): 859–61.

14. K. Gadow et al., "School Observation of Children With Attention-deficit Hyperactivity Disorder and Comorbid Tic Disorder: Effects of

Methylphenidate Treatment," *Journal of Developmental and Behavioral Pediatrics* 16 (June 1995): 167–76.

15. There is clinical evidence that Ritalin may lower the convulsive threshold, particularly in persons who have had seizures, or who have had EEG abnormalities but no seizures. James J. McGough and Dennis P. Cantwell, "Current Trends in the Medication Management of ADD," *Attention!* (Winter 1995): 18; Harvey C. Parker and George Storm, *Medical Management of Children with Attention Deficit Disorders.*

16. For a detailed list of contraindications, warnings, precautions, and adverse reactions, see the 1994 revision of the package insert for Prozac, manufactured by Dista Products Co., Division of Eli Lilly, Indianapolis, Ind.; the 1993 revision for Paxil, SmithKline Beecham, Philadelphia, Pa.; 1994 revision for Wellbutrin, Burroughs Wellcome Co., Research Triangle Park, N.C.

17. Clinical trials of efficacy for Prozac (fluoxetine) were conducted on adults 18 years and older. Under "Usage in Children" the package insert states: "Safety and effectiveness in children have not been established." For a detailed list of contraindications, warnings, precautions, and adverse reactions, see the 1994 revision of the package insert for Prozac.

18. Package insert for Prozac.

19. For a detailed list of contraindications, warnings, precautions, and adverse reactions, see 1991 revision of the package insert for Tofranil, Abbott Laboratories, Chicago, Ill.; Elavil, 1993 version, Stuart Pharmaceuticals of Merck & Co., Inc., Wilmington, Del.; Pamelor, 1994 revision, Sandoz Pharmaceuticals Corp., East Hanover, N.J.; and Norpramin, 1994 revision, Merrill Dow Pharmaceuticals, Kansas City, Mo.

20. *Pharmacist's Letter* No. 101010, 1994. See also Mandelkorn and Storm, "What Parents and Educators Need to Know About Medication." See also Note 17.

21. Package insert (1991) for Tofranil.

22. At one time Catapres (clonidine) was prescribed primarily as an antihypertensive drug; in other words, it was used to treat high blood pressure. Because of clinical reports of its positive effects on oppositional defiant behavior and anger management, it is increasingly being used to treat excess aggression in children who have ADD. There are also clinical reports of its decreasing facial and vocal tics in Tourette's disorder. Common side effects include tiredness, dizziness, and dry mouth. Tablets are short acting, about 4 hours. Administration through use of a patch applied to the back of the shoulder lasts about 5 days. Many children cannot tolerate patches and they are expensive. Mandelkorn and Storm, "What Parents and Educators Need to Know About Medication." For a detailed list of contraindications, warnings, precautions, and adverse reactions, see the 1993 revision of the package insert for Catapres, Boehringer Ingelheim Pharmaceuticals, Ridgefield, Conn.

23. Tenex (guanfacine), like clonidine, is actually an antihypertensive agent that acts on the central nervous system. For a detailed list of contraindications, warnings, precautions, and adverse reactions, see the package insert for Tenex (Philadelphia, Pa.: Wyeth-Ayerst Laboratories).

24. The use of Corgard (nadolol) to control the side effects of Ritalin is suggested by the psychiatrists E. M. Hallowell and J. J. Ratey, *Driven to Distraction* (New York: Touchstone, 1994). For a detailed list of contraindications, warnings, precautions, and adverse reactions, see the 1992 revision of the package insert for Corgard, Bristol Laboratories, Princeton, N.J.

25. Mortimer D. Gross, "Origin of Stimulant Use for Treatment of Attention Deficit Disorder," *American Journal of Psychiatry* 152 (Feb. 1995): 298–99.

26. Daniel J. Safer, Julie M. Zito, and Eric M. Fine, "Increased Methylphenidate Usage for Attention Deficit Disorder in the 1990s," *Pediatrics* 98 (1996): 1084–88. According to the authors, the DEA production quota in the United States increased from 1,768 kg in 1990 to 10,410 kg in mid-1995, a sixfold rise. Use as reported by a selected sample of computerized databases, however, shows an approximate increase of 2.5-fold. These databases are: Baltimore County Public Schools in 1991, 1993, and 1995; Maryland Medicaid enrollment from 1990 to 1994; the Automated Reports Consolidated Orders System (ARCOS) for 1990 to 1993; estimates from the National Prescription Audit projected from samples through 1994; the Scott-Levin National Physician's Drug and Diagnosis Audit for the number of office visits for ADD youth receiving prescriptions through 1994; a triplicate prescription survey in Michigan for February and March 1992, and in New York in 1991; and the Northwest region Kaiser-Permanente dataset for HMO enrollees in 1991. See also Daniel J. Safer, "Medication Usage Trends for ADD," *Attention!*, Fall 1995, pp. 11–15.

27. Ben F. Feingold, *Why Your Child Is Hyperactive* (New York: Random House, 1974), p. 65.

28. Dr. Paul McHugh is quoted in L. Hancock, "Mother's Little Helper," *Newsweek*, March 18, 1996, p. 52.

29. Hancock, "Mother's Little Helper."

30. Ibid. Also, in the April/May 1996 issue of *CH.A.D.D.*, the executive director of that organization reported that on March 11, 1996, CH.A.D.D. and the American Academy of Neurology (AAN) withdrew their petition to the Drug Enforcement Agency (DEA) to ease restrictions on the regulation of psychostimulants. This petition, filed on October 11, 1994, had asked the DEA to reschedule methylphenidate from Schedule II to Schedule III. Methylphenidate remains a Schedule II narcotic at this writing.

31. According to Dr. Judith Rapoport, chief of the child psychiatry branch at the National Institute of Mental Health, research there has demonstrated that all children "have the same kind of response to stimulants," and because of this, a child's response to stimulants may *not* be used as a diagnostic test for ADD. "An Interview with Judith Rapoport, M.D.," in *Attention!* (Winter 1996): 7. In controlled research studies, parents and teachers rate both ADD and non-ADD groups as improved under medication, with ADD groups showing more improvement. See R. Klorman et al., "Clinical and Cognitive Effects of Methylphenidate on Children with Attention Deficit Disorder as a Function of Aggression/Oppositionality and Age," *Journal of Abnormal Psychology* 103 (May 1994): 206–21. See also Lisa J. Bain, *A Parent's Guide to Attention Deficit Disorders,* Chapter 6, "Medical Manage-

ment," for further discussion of the fact that "non-ADHD children tend to become more attentive when given stimulants" (p. 93).

32. One recent review article for pharmacists sums it up this way: "We used to consider the response of an ADHD child to stimulants 'paradoxical' in that they appeared to slow down rather than speed up as a 'normal' child might. However, more recent research has found that 'normals' respond to usual doses of stimulants in similar ways as ADHD children. This is probably because attention and hyperactivity/impulsivity are processes that involve neurotransmission by both dopamine (DA) and norepinephrine (NE) and stimulants affect both of these systems. Increases of DA and NE appear to improve and aid in the control of activity." William A. Kehoc, "Attention-Deficit/Hyperactivity Disorder and Stimulants: Information for the Pharmacist," *Pharmacist's Letter* No. 120113 (Jan. 1996).

33. G. Weiss, *Attention-Deficit Hyperactivity Disorder* (Philadelphia: W. B. Saunders, 1992).

34. L. DeMilio, "Psychiatric Syndromes in Adolescent Substance Abusers," *American Journal of Psychiatry* 146 (1989): 1212–14.

35. T. E. Wilens and C. E. Lineham, "ADD and Substance Abuse," *Attention!,* Winter 1995, recommends "at least one month of abstinence" in assessing ADD symptoms (p. 27).

36. D. Cantwell, "Psychiatric Illness in the Families of Hyperactive Children," *Archives of General Psychiatry* 27 (1972): 414–17. Also, D. E. Comings et al., "The Dopamine D_2 Receptor Locus as a Modifying Gene in Neuropsychiatric Disorders," *Journal of the American Medical Association* 266 (1991): 1793–99.

37. In California, a physician writes orders for Ritalin on a triplicate form. Each physician is allocated a quota of these triplicate forms for prescribing controlled substances. One copy goes to the California Bureau of Narcotic Enforcement, one is filed at the pharmacy, and one is kept by the physician.

38. F. Sallee and C. L. Divan, "Current Pharmacy Topics: A Continuing Education Program for Pharmacists," in *Attention-Deficit/Hyperactivity Disorder: The Pharmacist's Role* (Champaign, Ill.: Grotelueschen Associates, 1995), p. 17.

39. J. Rosenberg, "From the Newsroom to Your Living Room," *Attention!,* Winter 1996, pp. 33–34, included mention of 1995 coverage by *20/20* and *Newsweek*. Also, in March 1995, *USA Today* ran a story about a teen in Michigan who was arrested for selling his Ritalin to another student. As reported by ABC News and *Newsweek* magazine, in April of 1995, a 17-year-old boy died of a Ritalin overdose. On December 19, 1995, Knight-Ridder Newspapers, a nationally syndicated news service, released a story that included the information that at St. Ann Catholic School in West Palm Beach, Florida, four children were expelled for sharing Ritalin. On March 18, 1996, *Newsweek* ran an article reporting that high doses of Ritalin, snorted or injected, can become addictive, but that the number of abusers at this time appeared to be negligible. As reported by ABC News in 1996, CIBA Pharmaceuticals distributed over 200,000 copies of *The Three R's of Ritalin* to physicians and pharmacists, warning them about the dangers of diversion of prescribed Ritalin.

40. Hancock, "Mother's Little Helper," p. 52.

41. Wilens and Lineham, "ADD and Substance Abuse," pp. 24–31.

42. Claudia Wallace, "Living in Overdrive," *Time,* July 18, 1994, p. 47.

43. The statement "In fact, emotional difficulties, including substance abuse, are more likely to occur when a child with ADD is *not* treated" appears on CH.A.D.D. Fact Sheet No. 3.

    The Merrow Report, broadcast on PBS on October 20, 1995, reported that this statement was not supported by research and was included owing to the influence of CIBA Pharmaceutical Co. on CH.A.D.D.

    A letter sent to CH.A.D.D. membership cosigned by its president and executive director, on October 9, 1995, refuted a number of points made by *The Merrow Report,* which was to be broadcast the following week. CH.A.D.D. stated that since its founding in 1987, its total revenue had been $7.7 million, of which a total of $820,000 had come from CIBA, along with other grants from Abbott, SmithKline Beecham, Pfizer, and GlaxoWellcome. They stated that 1993 corporate contributions accounted for 15 percent of total revenue and estimated that in 1994 it was "approximately 20%."

    A news story by Gail S. Hand, released by Knight-Ridder Newspapers, December 19, 1995, noted that while CH.A.D.D. says this practice is no different from other drug makers' educational grants to consumer groups, "the DEA has expressed concern about the relationship."

44. Wallace, "Living in Overdrive," p. 44.

45. M. N. Verbaten et al., "Methylphenidate Influences on Both Early and Late ERP Waves of ADHD Children in a Continuous Performance Test," *Journal of Abnormal Child Psychology* 22 (1994): 561–78. Experimental findings such as these show a significant increase in percentage of hits on a CPT. Nonetheless CPT scores must be interpreted with caution. (See the section on CPTs in Chapter 14, p. 218.)

46. R. J. Sternberg and T. I. Lubart, "Investing in Creativity," *American Psychologist* 51 (July 1996): 677–88.

47. Bain, *A Parent's Guide to Attention Deficit Disorders,* p. 96.

48. Thom Hartmann, *Attention Deficit Disorder: A Different Perception* (Novato, Calif.: Underwood-Miller, 1993), pp. 60–61. Hartmann relates the responses of a novelist, a public speaker, and a magazine reporter, all of whom describe the loss of spontaneity that accompanies the gain in concentration they experience when they take Ritalin.

49. "Pay Attention," *60 Minutes,* December 8, 1996.

50. Wallace, "Living in Overdrive," p. 50.

51. Mary Fowler, *CH.A.D.D. Educators Manual* (Plantation, Fla.: CH.A.D.D. National Education Committee, 1992; distributed by CASET Associates, Ltd.), p. 34.

52. Ibid., p. 19.

Chapter 16—Controversial Theories and Methods

1. D. M. Eisenberg et al., "Unconventional Medicine in the United States," *New England Journal of Medicine* 328 (Jan. 8, 1993): 246–52.

2. Ben F. Feingold, *Why Your Child Is Hyperactive* (New York: Random House, 1974).

3. See Chapter 13, Note 2.

4. Feingold, *Why Your Child Is Hyperactive*.

5. On May 13, 1974, in Redwood Valley, Calif., 11 children ages 3–17 went on the K-P diet. They remained under 24-hour-a-day supervision for 2 weeks. All had serious behavioral problems. Six children were reported to have "responded favorably," and 2 children showed "suggestive responses."

   In late spring 1974 in Santa Cruz, Calif., 25 children went on the diet for 1 month. Four children were reported to have "responded dramatically," 12 children displayed "a favorable response," and 9 children did not respond; most of the non-responders had not adhered strictly to the diet.

   In the pediatrics department of the Santa Clara Kaiser-Permanente Medical Center, 10 children on the K-P diet showed a "very favorable response"; 4 of them were reportedly able to discontinue drug therapy.

   These studies are reported by Feingold in *Why Your Child Is Hyperactive*.

6. E. H. Wender, "The Food Additive–Free Diet in the Treatment of Behavior Disorders: A Review," *Developmental and Behavioral Pediatrics* 7 (1986): 35–42.

7. National Institutes of Health, "Defined Diets and Childhood Hyperactivity: Consensus Conference," *Journal of the American Medical Association* 248 (1982): 290–92.

8. In one study in England, 76 children were placed on a diagnostic elimination diet, called an *oligoantigenic* diet, which consists of only a few foods. Of these, 62 were reported to improve. When the offending foods were reintroduced, symptoms worsened. The magnitiude of these changes was statistically significant when compared with changes that occurred when the children got placebos. See J. Egger et al., "Controlled Trial of Oligoantigenic Treatment in the Hyperkinetic Syndrome," *The Lancet* (1985): 540–45.

   In another study, also in England, preschoolers with hyperactivity and known allergies were placed on a diet free of additives, caffeine, and other allergens. A double-blind method was used to collect data. Ten of the 24 children in the study improved by 25 percent. See B. J. Kaplan et al., "Dietary Replacement in Preschool-Aged Hyperactive Boys," *Pediatrics* 83 (1989): 7–17.

   Both these studies are described in B. Ingersoll and S. Goldstein, *Attention Deficit Disorder and Learning Disabilities* (New York: Doubleday, 1993).

9. D. J. Rapp, *Allergies and the Hyperactive Child* (New York: Simon & Schuster, 1979); *The Impossible Child* (Tacoma, Wash.: Life Sciences Press, 1986); *Is This Your Child? Discovering and Treating Unrecognized Allergies* (New York: William Morrow, 1991). *Is This Your Child's World?* (New York: Bantam, 1996); in the Notes section, there is a list of "Studies of Allergy Testing" including a section on "Hyperactivity" (pp. 549–50).

10. Thom Hartmann, *Attention Deficit Disorder: A Different Perception* (Novato, Calif.: Underwood-Miller, 1993), p. xx.

11. Feingold, *Why Your Child Is Hyperactive,* p. 140.

12. Ibid., p. 141.

13. L. Smith, *Feed Your Kids Right* (New York: McGraw-Hill, 1979), and *Improving Your Child's Behavior Chemistry* (New York: Prentice Hall, 1976).

14. For a brief discussion of herbal treatments including choline and homeopathic remedies for ADD, see Hartmann, *Attention Deficit Disorder,* pp. 83–84.

15. C. Keith Connors, *Feeding the Brain: How Foods Affect Children* (New York: Plenum Press, 1989). See also, S. Goldstein and B. Ingersoll, "Controversial Treatments for Children with ADD," CH.A.D.D. Fact Sheet No. 6, 1993; Ingersoll and Goldstein, *Attention Deficit Disorder and Learning Disabilities,* pp. 163–65.

16. Dana Ullman, *The Consumer's Guide to Homeopathy* (New York: Jeremy Tarcher, 1995).

17. Ibid. See also Judith R. Ullman and Robert Ullman, *Ritalin-Free Kids* (Rocklin, Calif.: Primary, 1996).

18. M. A. Tansey, "Brainwave Signatures: An Index Reflective of the Brain's Functional Neuroanatomy: Further Findings on the Effect of EEG Sensorimotor Rhythm Biofeedback Training on the Neurological Precursors of Learning Disabilities," *International Journal of Psychophysiology* 3 (1985): 85–99.

19. T. Janzen et al., "Differences in Baseline EEG Measures for ADD and Normally Achieving Preadolescent Males," *Biofeedback and Self-Regulation* 20 (1995): 65–82.

    C. Mann et al., "Quantitative Analysis of EEG in Boys with Attention Deficit-Hyperactivity Disorder (ADHD): A Controlled Study with Clinical Implications," *Pediatric Neurology* 8 (1992): 30–36.

20. E. Schnitzler, "ADD and the EEG," *Attention!,* Spring 1995, pp. 31–33.

21. Ibid.

22. M. Kinsbourne, "Minimal Brain Dysfunction as a Neurodevelopmental Lag," in F. de la Cruz et al., eds., *Minimal Brain Dysfunction: Annals of the New York Academy of Sciences* (1973), p. 205.

23. Most of the information in the sections "Neurofeedback Assessment," "A training session," and "A Course of Treatment" comes from direct observation and personal communications with the directors of two neurofeedback centers in San Diego, R. Alan Schuller, M.F.C.C., clinical director of the NeuroPsych Institute (interviews on March 22 and 23, 1996), and M. Robert Morrison, Ph.D., educational psychologist (March 25, 1996).

24. In working with children, neurofeedback trainers prefer to use the word *sensor* rather than *electrode.*

25. See Janzen et al., "Differences in Baseline EEG Measures for ADD and Normally Achieving Preadolescent Males": "The amount of descriptive EEG information for normal and ADD populations when performing cognitive tasks is virtually nonexistent. Logically, in order to set criteria for training, descriptive EEG information (i.e., the specification of normal ranges of theta and beta values for specific age groups) is necessary" (p. 66).

26. Ibid.: "Difference between groups for beta-all amplitudes were nonsignificant for all sites and for all tasks" (p. 71). Also: "Our data suggest that

theta may be the most important factor in establishing EEG differences between ADD and normal populations, while beta differences are negligible" (p. 80).

27. Most treatment facilities recommend 20 to 40 sessions conducted 2 or 3 times per week (see Note 23). In the outcome study conducted by Lubar, subjects trained once a day, Monday through Friday, for 8 to 10 weeks. In his 1995 study, Lubar explained his reason for this: "Based on our previous research . . . the goal was to provide as close to 40 sessions as possible." See Note 32.

28. J. F. Lubar and M. N. Shouse, "EEG and Behavioral Changes in a Hyperkinetic Child Concurrent with Training of the Sensorimotor Rhythm (SMR): A Preliminary Report," *Biofeedback and Self-Regulation* 3 (1976): 293–306.

29. The *Women's Day* article is cited in: Russell Barkley, "Is EEG Biofeedback Treatment Effective for ADHD Children? . . . Proceed with Much Caution," *HAAD Enough,* March–April 1992, p. 4.

30. Ibid., p. 8.

31. See Notes 25 and 32.

32. J. F. Lubar et al., "Evaluation of the Effectiveness of EEG Neurofeedback Training for ADHD in a Clinical Setting as Measured by Changes in T.O.V.A. Scores, Behavioral Ratings, and WISC-R Performance," *Biofeedback and Self-Regulation* 20 (1995): 83–99. This study is commendable in that it represents an effort to evaluate the effects of neurofeedback using both objective and subjective methods. Nonetheless, some serious methodological problems exist. The WISC-R (IQ) pretests were administered two years before treatment began. This makes it impossible to control for independent variables other than neurofeedback training; differences between pre- and posttests can be attributed to any number of factors that occurred during the intervening years, not just to neurofeedback. Also, the method of analyzing the TOVA results is unusual and the rationale for using it is flawed. The study used four measures: (1) errors of omission, (2) errors of commission, (3) mean correct response time, and (4) variability. Instead of analyzing test-retest data for each measure, one score was obtained per subject, namely, the total number of scales on which improvement occurred. According to the authors, analysis of test-retest data was not performed because some of the children could not receive standard scores. A raw score difference of 1 or several points can easily occur by chance; yet this result received exactly the same weight as a difference of substantial magnitude (one that would reach statistical significance if usual pre- and posttest analyses had been conducted). Also, there is no justification for clumping the four scales together as one measure. It homogenizes variables that were originally differentiated because presumably they measure separate functions.

33. Mann et al., "Quantitative Analysis of EEG in Boys with Attention Deficit–Hyperactivity Disorder (ADHD)," pp. 30–36.

34. See Note 32, regarding problematic timing of the WISC-R administration in the Lubar et al. 1995 study.

35. Alison Gendar, "Biofeedback: Experimental Program Offers Hope," *The Reporter Dispatch* (White Plains, N.Y.), April 11, 1996, pp. 1A & 2A.
36. M. M. Merzenich et al., "Temporal Processing Deficits of Language Learning–Impaired Children Ameliorated by Training," *Science,* January 5, 1996, pp. 77–81; and P. Tallal et al., "Language Comprehension in Language Learning–Impaired Children Improved with Acoustically Modified Speech," *Science,* January 5, 1996, pp. 81–84.
37. Tallal's early findings linking phonological and language difficulties with failure to identify fast elements embedded in ongoing speech that have durations in the range of a few tens of milliseconds were published in journals and books including *Neuropsychologia* 12 (1974), p. 84; *Brain and Language* 182 (1974), p. 9; *Annals of Dyslexia* 32 (1982), p. 163; *Brain and Language* 25 (1985), p. 314; and R. Stark and P. Tallal, *Language, Speech and Reading Disorders in Children: Neuropsychological Studies* (Boston: College-Hill Press, 1988).
38. M. Barinaga, "Giving Language Skills a Boost," *Science,* January 5, 1996, pp. 27–28 ("Research News").
39. " 'Flying Cows' Come to Aid of Language-Disabled Kids," Associated Press, January 5, 1996.
40. Tallal et al., "Language Comprehension in Language Learning–Impaired Children . . ." p. 83.
41. Ibid.
42. See Note 37.
43. Ingersoll and Goldstein, *Attention Deficit Disorder and Learning Disabilities,* p. 86.
44. C. Keith Connors, cited in ibid., p. 155.

PART IV—YOUR CHILD'S FUTURE
Chapter 17—Edisonian Leaders of the Information Age

1. R. J. Sternberg et al., "Testing Common Sense," *American Psychologist* 50 (Nov. 1995): 912–27.
2. Dr. Horvath is quoted by R. J. Sternberg; see Note 1.
3. "The End of the Job," *Fortune,* September 1994, cited in P. Latham and P. Latham, "Succeeding in the Workplace with ADD," *Attention!,* Spring 1995, p. 40.
4. Tom Peters, *Thriving on Chaos* (New York: Alfred A. Knopf, 1987), p. 3.
5. Alan Greenspan, quoted in *The Wall Street Journal,* April 22, 1996, p. A1 ("The Outlook" column).
6. Peters, *Thriving on Chaos,* p. 3.
7. Peter Drucker, *Innovation and Entrepreneurship* (New York: Harper & Row, 1985).
8. See Note 3.
9. Joseph Boyett and Henry Conn, *Workplace 2000* (New York: Dutton, 1991), p. 36.
10. Bill Gates was interviewed on *20/20,* June 25, 1993.

11. CNN facts and biographical information about Ted Turner are from Porter Bibb, *It Ain't as Easy as It Looks* (New York: Crown, 1993), and Alvin Toffler, *Power Shift* (New York: Bantam Books, 1990), pp. 333–34.

12. Biographical information about Maya Angelou is from Maya Angelou, *I Know Why the Caged Bird Sings* (New York: Random House, 1969), *Life Doesn't Frighten Me* (New York: Stewart, Tabori & Chang, 1978), and *Singin' and Swingin' and Gettin' Merry like Christmas* (New York: Random House, 1976); Dyan Machan, "The Last Article You Will Ever Have to Read on Executive Pay? No Way!" *Forbes*, May 20, 1996, pp. 176–77; Nancy Shuker, *Genius! The Artist and the Process* (New York: Simon & Schuster, 1990); Valerie Spain, *Meet Maya Angelou* (New York: Random House, 1994).

13. Robert Ornstein, *The Evolution of Consciousness* (New York: Prentice Hall, 1991), p. 264.

14. Toffler, *Power Shift*, p. 308.

15. Edward Lorenz, cited by Dr. Vandervert in *American Psychological Association Monitor*, January 1993.

16. Boyett and Conn, *Workplace 2000*, p. 300.

17. Ibid., pp. 300–301.

18. Toffler, *Power Shift*, p. 213.

19. Boyett and Conn, *Workplace 2000*, p. 4.

20. Ibid.

21. Ibid.

22. Peters, *Thriving on Chaos*, pp. xi–xii.

23. Boyett and Conn, *Workplace 2000*, pp. 27–40.

24. Patricia Minton, "This Web Now Snares Millions Around World," *San Diego Business Journal*, September 11, 1995, p. 16; Al Horne, "The Internet," *Personal Systems: The Journal of the San Diego Computer Society*, August–September 1995, p. 1.

25. Udayan Gupta, "Fortune Smiles on Some Entrepreneurs Who Held Large Stakes in Firms at IPO," *The Wall Street Journal*, February 9, 1996, p. A7A.

26. Boyett and Conn, *Workplace 2000*, pp. 39–40.

27. Peters, *Thriving on Chaos*, p. 394.

28. Toffler, *Power Shift*, pp. 81–82.

29. Boyett and Conn, *Workplace 2000*, p. 306.

30. John Gardner, quoted in Boyett and Conn, *Workplace 2000*, p. 154.

31. Warren Bennis and Burt Nanus, quoted in Peters, *Thriving on Chaos*, p. 399.

32. See, for example, Beth Azar, "Musical Studies Provide Clues to Brain Functions," for a description of the research that demonstrates that when people "hear" a song in their mind, the brain uses the same circuitry it uses when they hear a song with their ears. The brain does not need the sound waves to reproduce the sound. As researcher Robert Zatorre, Ph.D., concludes, "The same portion of the brain is being used when people imagine as when they hear." *American Psychological Association Monitor* 26 (April 1996): 1, 24.

INDEX

ABOUT THE AUTHOR

LUCY JO PALLADINO, PH.D., is a psychologist who has been in private practice for over twenty years. During this time, she has counseled hundreds of Edison-trait children and their families. As a consultant and lecturer, she has worked with parents, educators, and therapists.

Dr. Palladino grew up in New York City. She earned her bachelor of science degree from Fordham University, her master's and doctoral degrees from Arizona State University, and she completed an internship in clinical psychology at Southwestern Medical School in Dallas, Texas. She lives in Encinitas, California, with her husband and their two daughters.

Whether you're contemplating a second child, expecting one any day, or trying to cope with the changing dynamics of your newly expanded family, don't miss this indispensable guide:

FROM ONE CHILD TO TWO
What to Expect, How to Cope, and How to Enjoy Your Growing Family

In this commonsensical, down-to-earth, and eminently practical parenting book, Judy Dunn gives parents all the information, emotional support, and reassurance they need to handle the stress—and relish the joys—of raising two children. An internationally recognized expert in the field of sibling relations, Dunn draws on her own decade-long study of siblings at home, as well as from extensive interviews and observations of parents and children.

- How (and when) to break the news to the first child
- How to manage the days surrounding the birth, the hospital visit, and the crucial first month
- Being prepared for your firstborn's reaction to the new sibling by age group—toddlers, preschoolers, or children in early elementary school
- The major milestones that families face together—the changing role of fathers and grandparents, managing new schedules, and coping with parental burnout
- Sibling rivalry: what to do about fighting, when to intervene, and when it's supposed to get better!

Available in bookstores everywhere.
Published by Fawcett Books.
The Ballantine Publishing Group
www.randomhouse.com/BB